# A SYSTEM OF

# SYNTHETIC PHILOSOPHY

## VOL. I. i.

### FIRST PRINCIPLES. VOL. 4

# FIRST PRINCIPLES

BY

## HERBERT SPENCER

VOL. 1.

*THIRD IMPRESSION.    POPULAR EDITION*

## WILLIAMS & NORGATE

14 HENRIETTA ST., COVENT GARDEN, LONDON

1910

# PREFACE TO THE SIXTH EDITION

In ten days more, forty years will have passed since the first lines of this work were written. Nothing was done to it until 1867, when a further development of its leading conception necessitated re-organization of the second part. In 1875 some changes were made in the Chapters on "The Indestructibility of Matter," "The Continuity of Motion," and "The Persistence of Force," more fully harmonizing the views set forth in them with the conceptions at that time reached. Since then there have been introduced no alterations worth mentioning.

Of course the advances of knowledge in many directions during intervening years, have made needful sundry corrections in the illustrative passages. Criticisms, too, have prompted a few modifications of statement. Add to this that further developments of my own thoughts have suggested certain improvements in the exposition, among which may be included the explanatory "Postscript to Part I." Passing over changes of little moment, I may name as chief amendments those contained in §§71$a$–71$c$, §93, §150, §152, and §§182–3; and as noticeable ones those contained in §§46, 54, 65, 72, 79, 88, 111, 120, 123, 132, 139$a$, 157, 159, and 164; together with the appendices A and C.

Meanwhile neither the objections made by others nor further considerations of my own, have caused me to recede from the general principles set forth. Contrariwise, while writing the succeeding works on Biology, Psychology, Sociology, and Ethics, the multiplied illustrations of these principles furnished by the facts dealt with, and the guidance afforded by them in seeking interpretations, have tended continually to strengthen the belief that they rightly formulate the facts.

While the changes of substance in this edition constitute improvements of some significance, the changes of form constitute a greater general improvement. Between a too-curt presentation of ideas and a presentation too much amplified, it is difficult to find the judicious mean. Now that, after this long interval, I am able to criticize my exposition as though it had come from another, I discover a good deal of redundance—superfluous words, clauses, sentences, and occasionally paragraphs. The erasure of these, while it has, I believe, conduced to lucidity, has entailed considerable abridgment; so that, notwithstanding many additions, the work is now diminished by fifty pages.

It is a source of much satisfaction to me that the opportunity has arisen for making these final amendments, both of matter and of manner.

H. S.

Brighton, 27th *April*, 1900.

# PREFACE TO THE FOURTH EDITION

To the first edition of this work there should have been prefixed a definite indication of its origin; and the misapprehensions that have arisen in the absence of such indication, ought before now to have shown me the need for supplying it.

Though reference was made, in a note on the first page of the original preface, to certain Essays entitled "Progress: its Law and Cause," and "Transcendental Physiology," as containing generalizations which were to be elaborated in the "System of Philosophy," there set forth in programme, yet the dates of these Essays were not given; nor was there any indication of their cardinal importance as containing, in a brief form, the general Theory of Evolution. No clear evidence to the contrary standing in the way, there has been very generally uttered and accepted the belief that this work, and the works following it, originated after, and resulted from, the special doctrine contained in Mr. Darwin's *Origin of Species*.

The Essay on "Progress: its Law and Cause," co-extensive in the theory it contains with Chapters XV., XVI., XVII., and XX. in Part II. of this work, was first published in the *Westminster Review* for April, 1857; and the Essay in which was briefly set forth the general truth elaborated in Chapter XIX., originally appeared, under the title of "The Ultimate Laws of Physiology," in the *National Review* for October, 1857. Further, I may point out that in the first edition of *The Principles of Psychology*, published in July, 1855, mental phenomena were interpreted entirely from the evolution point of view; and the words used in the titles of sundry chapters, imply the presence, at that date, of ideas more widely applied in the Essays just named. As the first edition of *The Origin of Species* did not make its appearance till October, 1859, it is manifest that the theory set forth in this work and its successors, had an origin independent of, and prior to, that which is commonly assumed to have initiated it.

The distinctness of origin might, indeed, have been inferred from the work itself, which deals with Evolution at large—Inorganic, Organic, and Super-organic—in terms of Matter and Motion; and touches but briefly on those particular processes so luminously exhibited by Mr. Darwin. In § 159 only, when illustrating the law of " The Multiplication of Effects" as universally displayed, have I had occasion to refer to the doctrine set forth in the *Origin of Species:* pointing out, in a note, that the general cause I had previously assigned for the production of divergent varieties of organisms, would not suffice to account for all the facts without that special cause disclosed by Mr. Darwin. The absence of this note would, of course, leave a serious gap in the general argument; but the remainder of the work would stand exactly as it now does.

I do not make this explanation in the belief that the prevailing misapprehension will thereby soon be rectified; for I am conscious that, once having become current, misapprehensions of this kind long persist—all disproofs notwithstanding. Nevertheless, I yield to the suggestion that unless I state the facts as they stand, I shall continue to countenance the wrong conviction now entertained, and cannot expect it to cease.

With the exception of unimportant changes in one of the notes, and some typographical corrections, the text of this edition is identical with that of the last. I have, however, added an Appen-' dix dealing with certain criticisms that have been passed upon the general formula of Evolution, and upon the philosophical doctrine which precedes it.

*May,* 1880.

*[It is needless here to reproduce the prefaces to the second and third editions. That to the third edition simply notified certain alterations*

made in 1875, *which have already been referred to in the preface to this edition. And the preface to the second edition, which gave a detailed account of the re-organization made in 1867, drawn up in such way as to show at a glance the various ways in which it deviated from the first edition, has now ceased to be of any use. The original preface, however, it is proper to preserve for the reason named at its close.]*

# PREFACE

THIS volume is the first of a series described in a prospectus originally distributed in March, 1860. Of that prospectus, the annexed is a reprint.

## A SYSTEM OF PHILOSOPHY

MR. HERBERT SPENCER proposes to issue in periodical parts a connected series of works which he has for several years been preparing. Some conception of the general aim and scope of this series may be gathered from the following Programme.

## FIRST PRINCIPLES

PART I. THE UNKNOWABLE.—Carrying a step further the doctrine put into shape by Hamilton and Mansel; pointing out the various directions in which Science leads to the same conclusions; and showing that in this united belief in an Absolute that transcends not only human knowledge but human conception, lies the only possible reconciliation of Science and Religion.

PART II. LAWS OF THE KNOWABLE.—A statement of the ultimate principles discernible throughout all manifestations of the Absolute—those highest generalizations now being disclosed by Science which are severally true not of one class of phenomena but of *all* classes of phenomena; and which are thus the keys to all classes of phenomena.*

---

* One of these generalizations is that currently known as "the Conservation of Force"; a second may be gathered from a published essay on "Progress: its Law and Cause"; a third is indicated in a paper on "Transcendental Physiology"; and there are several others.

xi

[*In logical order should here come the application of these First Principles to Inorganic Nature. But this great division it is proposed to pass over: partly because, even without it, the scheme is too extensive ; and partly because the interpretation of Organic Nature after the proposed method, is of more immediate importance. The second work of the series will therefore be—*]

## THE PRINCIPLES OF BIOLOGY

### VOL. 1

PART 1. THE DATA OF BIOLOGY.—Including those general truths of Physics and Chemistry with which rational Biology must set out.

II. The INDUCTIONS OF BIOLOGY.—A statement of the leading generalizations which Naturalists, Physiologists, and Comparative Anatomists, have established.

III. THE EVOLUTION OF LIFE.—Concerning the speculation commonly known as "The Development Hypothesis"—its *à priori* and *à posteriori* evidences.

### VOL. II

IV. MORPHOLOGICAL DEVELOPMENT.—Pointing out the relations that are everywhere traceable between organic forms and the average of the various forces to which they are subject; and seeking in the cumulative effects of such forces a theory of the forms.

V. PHYSIOLOGICAL DEVELOPMENT.—The progressive differentiation of functions similarly traced; and similarly interpreted as consequent upon the exposure of different parts of organisms to different sets of conditions.

VI. THE LAWS OF MULTIPLICATION.—Generalizations respecting the rates of reproduction of the various classes of plants and animals; followed by an attempt to show the dependence of these variations upon certain necessary causes.*

* The ideas to be developed in the second volume of the *Principles of Biology* the writer has already briefly expressed in sundry Review-Articles. Part IV. will work out a doctrine suggested in a paper on "The Laws of Organic Form," published in the *Medico-Chirurgical Review* for January, 1859. The germ of Part V. is contained in the essay on "Transcendental Physiology." See *Essays*, pp. 280–90. And in Part VI. will be unfolded certain views crudely expressed in a "Theory of Population," published in the *Westminster Review* for April, 1852.

## THE PRINCIPLES OF PSYCHOLOGY

### Vol. I

PART I. THE DATA OF PSYCHOLOGY.—Treating of the general connexions of Mind and Life and their relations to other modes of the Unknowable.

II. THE INDUCTIONS OF PSYCHOLOGY.—A digest of such generalizations respecting mental phenomena as have already been empirically established.

III. GENERAL SYNTHESIS.—A republication, with additional chapters, of the same part in the already-published *Principles of Psychology*.

IV. SPECIAL SYNTHESIS.—A republication, with extensive revisions and additions, of the same part, &c., &c.

V. PHYSICAL SYNTHESIS.—An attempt to show the manner in which the succession of states of consciousness conforms to a certain fundamental law of nervous action that follows from the First Principles laid down at the outset.

### Vol. II

VI. SPECIAL ANALYSIS.—As at present published, but further elaborated by some additional chapters.

VII. GENERAL ANALYSIS.—As at present published, with several explanations and additions.

VIII. COROLLARIES.—Consisting in part of a number of derivative principles which form a necessary introduction to Sociology.*

## THE PRINCIPLES OF SOCIOLOGY

### Vol. I

PART I. THE DATA OF SOCIOLOGY.—A statement of the several sets of factors entering into social phenomena—human ideas and feelings

---

* Respecting the several additions to be made to the *Principles of Psychology*, it seems needful only to say that Part V. is the unwritten division named in the preface to that work—a division of which the germ is contained in a note on page 544, and of which the scope has since been more definitely stated in a paper in the *Medico-Chirurgical Review* for January, 1859.

considered in their necessary order of evolution; surrounding natural conditions; and those ever complicating conditions to which Society itself gives origin.

II. THE INDUCTIONS OF SOCIOLOGY.—General facts, structural and functional, as gathered from a survey of Societies and their changes: in other words, the empirical generalizations that are arrived at by comparing different societies, and successive phases of the same society.

III. POLITICAL ORGANIZATION.—The evolution of governments, general and local, as determined by natural causes; their several types and metamorphoses; their increasing complexity and specialization; and the progressive limitation of their functions.

## VOL. II

IV. ECCLESIASTICAL ORGANIZATION.—Tracing the differentiation of religious government from secular; its successive complications and the multiplication of sects; the growth and continued modification of religious ideas, as caused by advancing knowledge and changing moral character; and the gradual reconciliation of these ideas with the truths of abstract science.

V. CEREMONIAL ORGANIZATION.—The natural history of that third kind of government which, having a common root with the others, and slowly becoming separate from and supplementary to them, serves to regulate the minor actions of life.

VI. INDUSTRIAL ORGANIZATION.—The development of productive and distributive agencies, considered, like the foregoing, in its necessary causes: comprehending not only the progressive division of labour, and the increasing complexity of each industrial agency, but also the successive forms of industrial government as passing through like phases with political government.

## VOL. III

VII. LINGUAL PROGRESS.—The evolution of Languages regarded as a psychological process determined by social conditions.

VIII. INTELLECTUAL PROGRESS.—Treated from the same point of view: including the growth of classifications; the evolution of science out of common knowledge; the advance from qualitative to quantitative prevision, from the indefinite to the definite, and from the concrete to the abstract.

IX. Æsthetic Progress.—The Fine Arts similarly dealt with: tracing their gradual differentiation from primitive institutions and from each other; their increasing varieties of development; and their advance in reality of expression and superiority of aim.

X. Moral Progress.—Exhibiting the genesis of the slow emotional modifications which human nature undergoes in its adaptation to the social state.

XI. The Consensus.—Treating of the necessary interdependence of structures and of functions in each type of society, and in the successive phases of social development.*


## THE PRINCIPLES OF MORALITY

### Vol. I

Part I. The Data of Morality.—Generalizations furnished by Biology, Psychology, and Sociology, which underlie a true theory ot right living: in other words, the elements of that equilibrium between constitution and conditions of existence, which is at once the moral ideal and the limit towards which we are progressing.

II. The Inductions of Morality.—Those empirically-established rules of human action which are registered as essential laws by all civilized nations: that is to say—the generalizations of expediency.

III. Personal Morals.—The principles of private conduct—physical, intellectual, moral, and religious—that follow from the conditions to complete individual life: or, what is the same thing—those modes of private action which must result from the eventual equilibration of internal desires and external needs.

---

* Of this treatise on Sociology a few small fragments may be found in already-published essays. Some of the ideas to be developed in Part II. are indicated in an article on " The Social Organism," contained in the last number of the *Westminster Review*; those which Part V. will work out, may be gathered from the first half of a paper written some years since on "Manners and Fashion"; of Part VIII. the germs are contained in an article on the "Genesis of Science"; two papers on " The Origin and Function of Music" and "The Philosophy of Style," contain some ideas to be embodied in Part IX.; and from a criticism of Mr. Bain's work on " The Emotions and the Will," in the last number of the *Medico-Chirurgical Review*, the central idea to be developed in Part X. may be inferred.

Vol. II

IV. Justice.—The mutual limitations of men's actions necessitated by their co-existence as units of a society—limitations, the perfect observance of which constitutes that state of equilibrium forming the goal of political progress.

V. Negative Beneficence.—Those secondary limitations, similarly necessitated, which, though less important and not cognizable by law, are yet requisite to prevent mutual destruction of happiness in various indirect ways: in other words—those minor self-restraints dictated by what may be called passive sympathy.

VI. Positive Beneficence.—Comprehending all modes of conduct, dictated by active sympathy, which imply pleasure in giving pleasure— modes of conduct that social adaptation has induced and must render ever more general; and which, in becoming universal, must fill to the full the possible measure of human happiness.*

In anticipation of the obvious criticism that the scheme here sketched out is too extensive, it may be remarked that an exhaustive treatment of each topic is not intended; but simply the establishment of *principles*, with such illustrations as are needed to make their bearings fully understood. It may also be pointed out that, besides minor fragments, one large division (*The Principles of Psychology*) is already in great part, executed. And a further reply is, that impossible though it may prove to execute the whole, yet nothing can be said against an attempt to set forth the First Principles and to carry their applications as far as circumstances permit.

The price per Number to be half-a-crown; that is to say, the four Numbers yearly issued to be severally delivered, post free, to all annual subscribers of Ten Shillings.

---

This Programme I have thought well to reprint for two reasons :— the one being that readers may, from time to time, be able to ascertain what topics are next to be dealt with; the other being that an outline of the scheme may remain, in case it should never be completed.

* Part IV. of the *Principles of Morality* will be co-extensive (though not identical) with the first half of the writer's *Social Statics*.

# PREFACE

[*This volume, and many of the succeeding volumes, were at first issued to subscribers in instalments of 80 pages each, and at the end of the preface to each volume, it was stated at what dates the successive parts, included between certain pages named, first appeared.  In the original preface to this volume there was here given a statement of this kind.  Repetition of it would now be misleading, since the pagings have all been changed.*]

LONDON, *June 5th*, 1862.

# CONTENTS

## PART I.—THE UNKNOWABLE

## PART II.—THE KNOWABLE

# PART I

## THE UNKNOWABLE

# CHAPTER I

## RELIGION AND SCIENCE

§ 1. WE too often forget that not only is there "a soul of goodness in things evil," but very generally also, a soul of truth in things erroneous. While many admit the abstract probability that a falsity has usually a nucleus of verity, few bear this abstract probability in mind, when passing judgment on the opinions of others. A belief that is proved to be grossly at variance with fact is cast aside with indignation or contempt; and in the heat of antagonism scarcely any one inquires what there was in this belief which commended it to men's minds. Yet there must have been something. And there is reason to suspect that this something was its correspondence with certain of their experiences: an extremely limited or vague correspondence perhaps, but still, a correspondence. Even the absurdest report may in nearly every instance be traced to an actual occurrence; and had there been no such actual occurrence, this preposterous misrepresentation of it would never have existed. Though the distorted or magnified image transmitted to us through the refracting medium of rumour, is utterly unlike the reality; yet in the absence of the reality there would have been no distorted or magnified image. And thus it is with human beliefs in general. Entirely wrong as they may appear, the implication is that they originally contained, and perhaps still contain, some small amount of truth.

Definite views on this matter would be very useful to us. It is important that we should form something like a general theory of current opinions, so that we may neither over-estimate nor under-estimate their worth. Arriving at correct judgments on disputed questions, much depends on the mental attitude preserved while listening to, or taking part in, the controversies; and for the preservation of a right attitude, it is needful that we should learn how true, and yet how untrue, are average human beliefs. On the one hand, we must keep free from that bias in favour of received ideas which expresses itself in such dogmas as "What every one says must be true," or "The voice of the people is the voice of God." On the other hand, the fact disclosed by a survey of the past that majorities have usually been wrong, must not blind us to the complementary fact that majorities have usually not been *entirely* wrong. And the avoidance of these extremes being a pre-requisite to catholic thinking, we shall do well to provide ourselves with a safeguard against them, by making a valuation of opinions in the abstract. To this end we must contemplate the kind of relation that ordinarily subsists between opinions and facts. Let us do so with one of those beliefs which under various forms has prevailed among all nations in all times.

§ 2. Early traditions represent rulers as gods or demigods. By their subjects, primitive kings were regarded as superhuman in origin and superhuman in power. They possessed divine titles, received obeisances like those made before the altars of deities, and were in some cases actually worshipped. Of course along with the implied beliefs there existed a belief in the unlimited power of the ruler over his subjects, extending even to the taking of their lives at will; as until recently in Fiji, where a victim stood unbound to be killed at the word of his chief: himself declaring, "whatever the king says must be done."

In other times and among other races, we find these beliefs a little modified. The monarch, instead of being thought god or demigod, is conceived to be a man having divine authority, with perhaps more or less of divine nature. He retains, however, titles expressing his heavenly descent or relationships, and is still saluted in forms and words as humble as those addressed to the Deity. While in some places the lives and properties of his people, if not so completely at his mercy, are still in theory supposed to be his.

Later in the progress of civilization, as during the middle ages in Europe, the current opinions respecting the relationship of rulers and ruled are further changed. For the theory of divine origin there is substituted that of divine right. No longer god or demigod, or even god-descended, the king is now regarded simply as God's vicegerent. The obeisances made to him are not so extreme in their humility; and his sacred titles lose much of their meaning. Moreover, his authority ceases to be unlimited. Subjects deny his right to dispose at will of their lives and properties, and yield allegiance only in the shape of obedience to his commands.

With advancing political opinion has come still greater restriction of monarchical power. Belief in the supernatural character of the ruler, long ago repudiated by ourselves for example, has left behind it nothing more than the popular tendency to ascribe unusual goodness, wisdom, and beauty to the monarch. Loyalty, which originally meant implicit submission to the king's will, now means a merely nominal profession of subordination, and the fulfilment of certain forms of respect. By deposing some and putting others in their places, we have not only denied the divine rights of certain men to rule, but we have denied that they have any rights beyond those originating in the assent of the nation. Though our forms of speech and our State documents still assert the subjection of the citizens to the ruler, our actual beliefs and our daily proceedings implicitly assert the contrary. We have entirely divested the monarch of legislative power, and should immediately rebel against his or her dictation even in matters of small concern.

Nor has the rejection of primitive political beliefs resulted only in transferring the power of an autocrat to a representative body. The views held respecting governments in general, of whatever form, are now widely different from those once held. Whether popular or despotic, governments in ancient times were supposed to have unlimited authority over their subjects. Individuals existed for the benefit of the State; not the State for the benefit of individuals. In our days, however, not only has the national will been in many cases substituted for the will of the king, but the exercise of this national will has been restricted. In England, for instance, though there has been established no definite doctrine respecting the bounds to governmental action, yet, in practice, sundry bounds to it are tacitly recognized by all. There is no organic law declaring that a legislature may not freely dispose of citizens' lives, as kings did of old, but were it possible for our legislature to attempt such a thing, its own destruction would be the consequence, rather than the destruction of citizens. How fully we have established the personal liberties of the subject against the invasions of State power, would be quickly shown were it proposed by Act of Parliament to take possession of the nation, or of any class, and turn its services to public ends, as the services of the people were turned by Egyptian kings. Not only in our day have the claims of the citizen to life, liberty, and property been thus made good against the State, but sundry minor claims likewise. Ages ago laws regulating dress and mode of living fell into disuse, and any attempt to revive them would prove that such matters now lie beyond the sphere of legal control. For some centuries we asserted in practice, and have now established in theory, the right of every man to choose his own religious beliefs, instead of receiving State-authorized beliefs. Within the last few generations complete liberty of speech has been gained, in spite of all legislative attempts to suppress or limit it. And still more recently we have obtained, under a few exceptional restrictions, freedom to trade with whomsoever we please. Thus our political beliefs are widely different from ancient ones, not only as to the proper depositary of power to be exercised over a nation, but also as to the extent of that power.

Nor even here has the change ended. Besides the average opinions just described as current among ourselves, there exists a less widely-diffused opinion going still further in the same direction. There are to be found men who contend that the sphere of government should be narrowed even more than it is in England. They hold that the freedom of the individual, limited only by the like freedom of other individuals, is sacred. They assert that the sole function of the State is the protection of persons against one another, and against a foreign foe; and they believe that the ultimate political condition must be one in which personal freedom is the greatest possible and governmental power the least possible.

Thus in different times and places we find, concerning the origin, authority, and functions of government, a great variety of opinions. What now must be said about the truth or falsity of these opinions? Must we say that some one is wholly right and all the rest wholly wrong; or must we say that each of them contains truth more or less disguised by errors? The latter alternative is the one which analysis will force upon us. Every one of these doctrines has for its vital element the recognition of an unquestionable fact. Directly or by implication, each insists on a certain subordination of individual actions to social dictates. There are differences respecting the power to which this subordination is due; there are differences respecting the motive for this subordination; there are differences respecting its extent; but that there must be *some* subordination all are agreed. The most submissive and the most recalcitrant alike hold that there are limits which individual actions may not transgress—limits which the one regards as originating in a ruler's will, and which the other regards as deducible from the equal claims of fellow-citizens.

It may doubtless be said that we here reach a very unimportant conclusion. The question, however, is not the value or novelty of the particular truth in this case arrived at. My aim has been to exhibit the more general truth, that between the most diverse beliefs there is usually something in common,—something taken for granted in each; and that this something, if not to be set down as an unquestionable verity, may yet be considered to have the highest degree of probability. A postulate which, like the one above instanced, is not consciously asserted but unconsciously involved, and which is unconsciously involved not by one man or body of men, but by numerous bodies of men who diverge in countless ways and degrees in the rest of their beliefs, has a warrant far transcending any that can be usually shown.

Do we not thus arrive at a generalization which may habitually guide us when seeking for the soul of truth in things erroneous? While the foregoing illustration brings home the fact that in opinions seeming to be absolutely wrong something right is yet to be found, it also indicates a way of finding the something right.

This way is to compare all opinions of the same genus; to set aside as more or less discrediting one another those special and concrete elements in which such opinions disagree; to observe what remains after these have been eliminated; and to find for the remaining constituent that expression which holds true throughout its various disguises.

§ 3. A consistent adoption of the method indicated will greatly aid us in dealing with chronic antagonisms of belief. By applying it not only to ideas with which we are unconcerned, but also to our own ideas and those of our opponents, we shall be enabled to form more correct judgments. We shall be led to suspect that our convictions are not wholly right, and that the adverse convictions are not wholly wrong. On the one hand, we shall not, in common with the great mass of the unthinking, let our creed be determined by the mere accident of birth in a particular age on a particular part of the Earth's surface; while, on the other hand, we shall be saved from that error of entire and contemptuous negation, fallen into by most who take up an attitude of independent criticism.

Of all antagonisms of belief the oldest, the widest, the most profound, and the most important, is that between Religion and Science. It commenced when recognition of the commonest uniformities in surrounding things set a limit to all-pervading superstitions. It shows itself everywhere throughout the domain of human knowledge; affecting men's interpretations alike of the simplest mechanical accidents and the most complex events in the histories of nations. It has its roots deep down in the diverse habits of thought of different orders of minds. And the conflicting conceptions of Nature and Life, which these diverse habits of thought severally generate, influence for good or ill the tone of feeling and the daily conduct.

A battle of opinion like this, which has been carried on for ages under the banners of Religion and Science, has generated an animosity fatal to a just estimate of either party by the other. Happily the times display an increasing catholicity of feeling, which we shall do well to carry as far as our natures permit. In proportion as we love truth more and victory less, we shall become anxious to know what it is which leads our opponents to think as they do. We shall begin to suspect that the pertinacity of belief exhibited by them must result from a perception of something we have not perceived. And we shall aim to supplement the portion of truth we have found with the portion found by them. Making a rational estimate of human authority, we shall avoid alike the extremes of undue submission and undue rebellion—shall not regard some men's judgments as wholly good and others as wholly bad; but shall, contrariwise, lean to the more defensible position that none are completely right and none are completely wrong.

Preserving, as far as may be, this impartial attitude, let us then contemplate the two sides of this great controversy. Keeping guard against the bias of education and shutting out the whisperings of sectarian feeling, let us consider what are the *à priori* probabilities in favour of each party.

§ 4. The general principle above illustrated must lead us to anticipate that the diverse forms of religious belief, which have existed and which still exist, have all a basis in some ultimate fact. Judging by analogy the implication is, not that any one of them is altogether right, but that in each there is something right more or less disguised by other things wrong. It may be that the soul of truth contained in erroneous creeds is extremely unlike most, if not all, of its several embodiments; and indeed if, as we have good reason to assume, it is much more abstract than any of them, its unlikeness necessarily follows. But some essential verity must be looked for. To suppose that these multiform conceptions should be one and all *absolutely* groundless, discredits too profoundly that average human intelligence from which all our individual intelligences are inherited.

To the presumption that a number of diverse beliefs of the same class have some common foundation in fact, must in this case be added a further presumption derived from the omnipresence of the beliefs. Religious ideas of one kind or other are almost universal. Grant that among all men who have passed a certain stage of intellectual development, there are found vague notions concerning the origin and hidden nature of surrounding things, and there arises the inference that such notions are necessary products of progressing intelligence. Their endless variety serves but to strengthen this conclusion: showing as it does a more or less independent genesis—showing how, in different places and times, like conditions have led to similar trains of thought, ending in analogous results. A candid examination of the evidence quite negatives the supposition that creeds are priestly inventions. Even as a mere question of probabilities it cannot rationally be concluded that in every society, savage and civilized, certain men have combined to delude the rest in ways so analogous. Moreover, the hypothesis of artificial origin fails to account for the facts. It does not explain why, under all changes of form, certain elements of religious belief remain constant. It does not show how it happens that while adverse criticism has from age to age gone on destroying particular theological dogmas, it has not destroyed the fundamental conception underlying those dogmas. Thus the universality of religious ideas, their independent evolution among different primitive races, and their great vitality, unite in showing that their source must be deep-seated. In other words, we are obliged to admit that if not supernaturally derived as the majority contend, they must be derived out of human experiences, slowly accumulated and organized.

Should it be asserted that religious ideas are products of the religious sentiment which, to satisfy itself, prompts imaginations that it afterwards projects into the external world, and by-and-by mistakes for realities, the problem is not solved, but only removed farther back. Whence comes the sentiment? That it is a constituent in man's nature is implied by the hypothesis, and cannot indeed be denied by those who prefer other hypotheses. And if the religious sentiment, displayed constantly by the majority of mankind, and occasionally aroused even in those seemingly devoid of it, must be classed among human emotions, we cannot rationally ignore it. Here is an attribute which has played a conspicuous part throughout the entire past as far back as history records, and is at present the life of numerous institutions, the stimulus to perpetual controversies, and the prompter of countless daily actions. Evidently as a question in philosophy, we are called on to say what this attribute means; and we cannot decline the task without confessing our philosophy to be incompetent.

Two suppositions only are open to us; the one that the feeling which responds to religious ideas resulted, along with all other human faculties, from an act of special creation; the other that it, in common with the rest, arose by a process of evolution. If we adopt the first of these alternatives, universally accepted by our ancestors and by the immense majority of our contemporaries, the matter is at once settled: man is directly endowed with the religious feeling by a creator; and to that creator it designedly responds. If we adopt the second alternative, then we are met by the questions—What are the circumstances to which the genesis of the religious feeling is due? and—What is its office? Considering, as we must on this supposition, all faculties to be results of accumulated modifications caused by the intercourse of the organism with its environment, we are obliged to admit that there exist in the environment certain phenomena or conditions which have determined the growth of the religious feeling; and so are obliged to admit that it is as normal as any other faculty. Add to which that as, on the hypothesis of a development of lower forms into higher, the end towards which the progressive changes tend, must be adaptation to the requirements of life, we are also forced to infer that this feeling is in some way conducive to human welfare. Thus both alternatives contain the same ultimate implication. We must conclude that the religious sentiment is either directly created or is developed by the slow action of natural causes, and whichever conclusion we adopt requires us to treat the religious sentiment with respect.

One other consideration should not be overlooked—a consideration which students of Science more especially need to have pointed out. Occupied as such are with established truths, and accustomed to regard things not already known as things to be hereafter discovered, they are liable to forget that information, however extensive it may become, can never satisfy inquiry. Positive knowledge does not, and never can, fill the whole region of possible thought. At the uttermost reach of discovery there arises, and must ever arise, the question—What lies beyond? As it is impossible to think of a limit to space so as to exclude the idea of space lying outside that limit; so we cannot conceive of any explanation profound enough to exclude the question—What is the explanation of that explanation? Regarding Science as a gradually increasing sphere, we may say that every addition to its surface does but bring it into wider contact with surrounding nescience. There must ever remain therefore two antithetical modes of mental action. Throughout all future time, as now, the human mind may occupy itself, not only with ascertained phenomena and their relations, but also with that unascertained something which phenomena and their relations imply. Hence if knowledge cannot monopolize consciousness—if it must always continue possible for the mind to dwell upon that which transcends knowledge, then there can never cease to be a place for something of the nature of Religion; since Religion under all its forms is distinguished from everything else in this, that its subject matter passes the sphere of the intellect.

Thus, however untenable may be the existing religious creeds, however gross the absurdities associated with them, however irrational the arguments set forth in their defence, we must not ignore the verity which in all likelihood lies hidden within them. The general probability that widely-spread beliefs are not absolutely baseless, is in this case enforced by a further probability due to the omnipresence of the beliefs. In the existence of a religious sentiment, whatever be its origin, we have a second evidence of great significance. And as in that nescience which must ever remain the antithesis to science, there is a sphere for the exercise of this sentiment, we find a third general fact of like implication. We may be sure, therefore, that religions, even though no one of them be actually true, are yet all adumbrations of a truth.

§ 5. As, to the religious, it will seem absurd to set forth any justification for Religion, so, to the scientific, it will seem absurd to defend Science. Yet to do the last is certainly as needful as to do the first. If there exist some who, in contempt for its follies and disgust at its corruptions, have contracted towards Religion a repugnance which makes them overlook the fundamental truth contained in it; so, there are others offended to such a degree by the destructive criticisms men of science make on the religious tenets they hold essential, that they have acquired a strong prejudice against Science at large. They are not prepared with any reasons for their dislike. They have simply a remembrance of the rude shakes which Science has given to many of their cherished convictions, and a suspicion that it may eventually uproot all they regard as sacred; and hence it produces in them an inarticulate dread.

What is Science? To see the absurdity of the prejudice against it, we need only remark that Science is simply a higher development of common knowledge; and that if Science is repudiated, all knowledge must be repudiated along with it. The extremest bigot will not suspect any harm in the observation that the Sun rises earlier and sets later in summer than in winter; but will rather consider such an observation as a useful aid in fulfilling the duties of life. Well, Astronomy is an organized body of kindred observations, made with greater nicety, extended to a larger number of objects, and so analyzed as to disclose the real arrangements of the heavens and to dispel our false conceptions of them. That iron will rust in water, that wood will burn, that long kept viands become putrid, the most timid sectarian will teach without alarm, as things useful to be known. But these are chemical truths: Chemistry is a systematized collection of such facts, ascertained with precision, and so classified and generalized as to enable us to say with certainty, concerning each simple or compound substance, what change will occur in it under given conditions. And thus is it with all the sciences. They severally germinate out of the experiences of daily life; insensibly as they grow they draw in remoter, more numerous, and more complex experiences; and among these, they ascertain laws of dependence like those which make up our knowledge of the most familiar objects. Nowhere is it possible to draw a line and say —here Science begins. And as it is the function of common observation to serve for the guidance of conduct; so, too, is the guidance of conduct the office of the most recondite and abstract results of Science. Through the countless industrial processes and the various modes of locomotion it has given to us, Physics regulates more completely our social life than does his acquaintance with the properties of surrounding bodies regulate the life of the savage.    All Science is prevision; and all prevision ultimately helps us in greater or less degree to achieve the good and avoid the bad.    Thus being one in origin and function, the simplest forms of cognition and the most complex must be dealt with alike. We are bound in consistency to receive the widest knowledge our faculties can reach, or to reject along with it that narrow knowledge possessed by all.

To ask the question which more immediately concerns our argument—whether Science is substantially true—is much like asking whether the Sun gives light.    And it is because they are conscious how undeniably valid are most of its propositions, that the theological party regard Science with so much secret alarm. They know that during the five thousand years of its growth, some of its larger divisions—mathematics, physics, astronomy— have been subject to the rigorous criticism of successive generations, and have notwithstanding become ever more firmly established. . They know that, unlike many of their own doctrines, which were once universally received but have age by age been more widely doubted, the doctrines of Science, at first confined to a few scattered inquirers, have been slowly growing into general acceptance, and are now in great part admitted as beyond dispute. They know that scientific men throughout the world subject one another's results to searching examination, and that error is mercilessly exposed and rejected as soon as discovered.    And, finally, they know that still more conclusive evidence is furnished by the daily verification of scientific predictions, and by the never-ceasing triumphs of those arts which Science guides.

To regard with alienation that which has such high credentials is a folly.    Though in the tone which many of the scientific adopt towards them, the defenders of Religion may find some excuse for this alienation, yet the excuse is an insufficient one.    On the side of Science, as on their own side, they must admit that short-comings in the advocates do not tell essentially against that which is advocated.    Science must be judged by itself; and so judged, only the most perverted intellect can fail to see that it is worthy of all reverence.    Be there or be there not any other revelation, we have a veritable revelation in Science—a continuous disclosure of the established order of the Universe. This disclosure it is the duty of every one to verify as far as in him lies; and having verified, to receive with all humility.

§ 6. Thus there must be right on both sides of this great controversy. Religion, everywhere present as a warp running through the weft of human history, expresses some eternal fact; while Science is an organized body of truths, ever growing, and ever being purified from errors. And if both have bases in the reality of things, then between them there must be a fundamental harmony. It is impossible that there should be two orders of truth in absolute and everlasting opposition. Only in pursuance of some Manichean hypothesis, which among ourselves no one dares openly avow, is such a supposition even conceivable. That Religion is divine and Science diabolical, is a proposition which, though implied in many a clerical declamation, not the most vehement fanatic can bring himself distinctly to assert. And whoever does not assert this, must admit that under their seeming antagonism lies hidden an entire agreement.

Each side, therefore, has to recognize the claims of the other as representing truths which are not to be ignored. It behoves each to strive to understand the other, with the conviction that the other has something worthy to be understood; and with the conviction that when mutually recognized this something will be the basis of a reconciliation.

How to find this something thus becomes the problem we should perseveringly try to solve. Not to reconcile them in any makeshift way, but to establish a real and permanent peace. The thing we have to seek out is that ultimate truth which both will avow with absolute sincerity—with not the remotest mental reservation. There shall be no concession—no yielding on either side of something that will by-and-by be reasserted; but the common ground on which they meet shall be one which each will maintain for itself. We have to discover some fundamental verity which Religion will assert, with all possible emphasis, in the absence of Science; and which Science, with all possible emphasis, will assert in the absence of Religion. We must look for a conception which combines the conclusions of both—must see how Science and Religion express opposite sides of the same fact: the one its near or visible side, and the other its remote or invisible side.

Already in the foregoing pages the method of seeking such a reconciliation has been vaguely shadowed forth. Before proceeding, however, it will be well to treat the question of method more definitely. To find that truth in which Religion and Science coalesce, we must know in what direction to look for it, and what kind of truth it is likely to be.

§ 7. Only in some highly abstract proposition can Religion and Science find a common ground. Neither such dogmas as those of the trinitarian and unitarian, nor any such idea as that of propitiation, common though it may be to all religions, can serve as the desired basis of agreement; for Science cannot recognize beliefs like these: they lie beyond its sphere. Not only, as we have inferred, is the essential truth contained in Religion that most abstract element pervading all its forms, but, as we here see, this most abstract element is the only one in which Religion is likely to agree with Science.

Similarly if we begin at the other end, and inquire what scientific truth can unite Science with Religion. Religion can take no cognizance of special scientific doctrines, any more than Science can take cognizance of special religious doctrines. The truth which Science asserts and Religion indorses cannot be one furnished by mathematics; nor can it be a physical truth; nor can it be a truth in chemistry. No generalization of the phenomena of space, of time, of matter, or of force, can become a Religious conception. Such a conception, if it anywhere exists in Science, must be more general than any of these—must be one underlying all of them.

Assuming, then, that since these two great realities are constituents of the same mind, and respond to different aspects of the same Universe, there must be a fundamental harmony between them, we see good reason to conclude that the most abstract truth contained in Religion and the most abstract truth contained in Science must be the one in which the two coalesce. The largest fact to be found within our mental range must be the one of which we are in search. Uniting these positive and negative poles of human thought, it must be the ultimate fact in our intelligence.

§ 8. Before proceeding let me bespeak a little patience. The next three chapters, setting out from different points and converging to the same conclusion, will be unattractive. Students of philosophy will find in them much that is familiar; and to most of those who are unacquainted with modern metaphysics, their reasonings may prove difficult to follow.

Our argument, however, cannot dispense with these chapters, and the greatness of the question at issue justifies even a heavier tax on the reader's attention. Though it affects us little in a direct way, the view we arrive at must indirectly affect us in all our relations—must determine our conceptions of the Universe, of Life, of Human Nature—must influence our ideas of right and wrong, and therefore modify our conduct. To reach that point of view from which the seeming discordance of Religion and Science disappears, and the two merge into one, must surely be worth an effort.

Here ending preliminaries let us now address ourselves to this all-important inquiry.

# CHAPTER II

## ULTIMATE RELIGIOUS IDEAS

§ 9. WHEN, on the sea-shore, we note how the hulls of distant vessels are hidden below the horizon, and how, of still remoter vessels, only the uppermost sails are visible, we may conceive with tolerable clearness the slight curvature of that portion of the sea's surface which lies before us. But when we try to follow out in imagination this curved surface as it actually exists, slowly bending round until all its meridians meet in a point eight thousand miles below our feet, we find ourselves utterly baffled. We cannot conceive in its real form and magnitude even that small segment of our globe which extends a hundred miles on every side of us, much less the globe as a whole. The piece of rock on which we stand can be mentally represented with something like completeness: we are able to think of its top, its sides, and its under surface at the same time, or so nearly at the same time that they seem present in consciousness together; and so we can form what we call a conception of the rock. But to do the like with the Earth is impossible. If even to imagine the antipodes as at that distant place in space which it actually occupies is beyond our power; much more beyond our power must it be at the same time to imagine all other remote points on the Earth's surface as in their actual places. Yet we commonly speak as though we had an idea of the Earth—as though we could think of it in the same way that we think of minor objects.

What conception, then, do we form of it? the reader may ask. That its name calls up in us some state of consciousness is unquestionable; and if this state of consciousness is not a conception, properly so called, what is it? The answer seems to be this:—We have learnt by indirect methods that the Earth is a sphere; we have formed models approximately representing its shape and the distribution of its parts; usually when the Earth is referred to, we either think of an indefinitely extended mass beneath our feet, or else, leaving out the actual Earth, we think of a body like a terrestrial globe; but when we seek to imagine the Earth as it really is, we join these two ideas as well as we can—such perception as our eyes give us of the Earth's surface we couple with the conception of a sphere. And thus we form of the Earth not a conception properly so called, but only a symbolic conception.*

A large proportion of our conceptions, including all those of much generality, are of this order. Great magnitudes, great durations, great numbers, are none of them actually conceived, but are all of them conceived more cr less symbolically; and so, too, are all those classes of objects of which we predicate some common fact. When mention is made of any individual man, a tolerably complete idea of him is formed. If the family he belongs to be spoken of, probably but a part of it will be represented in thought: under the necessity of attending to that which is said about the family, we realize in imagination only its most important or familiar members, and pass over the rest with a nascent consciousness which we know could, if requisite, be made complete. Should something be remarked of the class, say farmers, to which this family belongs, we neither enumerate in thought all the individuals contained in the class, nor believe that we could do so if required; but we are content with taking some few samples of it, and remembering that these could be indefinitely multiplied. Supposing the subject of which something is predicated be Englishmen, the answering state of consciousness is a still more inadequate representative. Yet more remote is the likeness of the thought to the thing, if reference be made to Europeans or to human beings. And when we come to propositions concerning the mammalia, or concerning the whole of the vertebrata, or concerning animals in general, or concerning all organic beings, the unlikenesses of our conceptions to the realities become extreme. Throughout which series of instances we see that as the number of objects grouped together in

* Those who may have before met with this term will perceive that it is here used in quite a different sense.

thought increases, the concept, formed of a few typical samples joined with the notion of multiplicity, becomes more and more a mere symbol; not only because it gradually ceases to represent the size of the group, but also because, as the group grows more heterogeneous, the typical samples thought of are less like the average objects which the group contains.

This formation of symbolic conceptions, which inevitably arises as we pass from small and concrete objects to large and to discrete ones, is mostly a useful, and indeed necessary, process. When, instead of things whose attributes can be tolerably well united in a single state of consciousness, we have to deal with things whose attributes are too vast or numerous to be so united, we must either drop in thought part of their attributes, or else not think of them at all—either form a more or less symbolic conception, or no conception. We must predicate nothing of objects too great or too multitudinous to be mentally represented, or we must make our predications by the help of extremely inadequate representations of them.

But while by doing this we are enabled to form general propositions, and so to reach general conclusions, we are perpetually led into danger, and very often into error. We mistake our symbolic conceptions for real ones; and so are betrayed into countless false inferences. Not only is it that in proportion as the concept we form of any thing, or class of things, misrepresents the reality, we are apt to be wrong in any assertion we make respecting the reality; but it is that we are led to suppose we have truly conceived many things which we have conceived only in this fictitious way; and then to confound with these some things which cannot be conceived in any way. How we fall into this error almost unavoidably it will be needful here to observe.

From objects fully representable, to those of which we cannot form even approximate representations, there is an insensible transition. Between a pebble and the entire Earth a series of magnitudes might be introduced, severally differing from adjacent ones so slightly that it would be impossible to say at what point in the series our conceptions of them became inadequate. Similarly, there is a gradual progression from those groups of a few individuals which we can think of as groups with tolerable completeness, to those larger and larger groups of which we can form nothing like true ideas. Thus we pass from actual conceptions to symbolic ones by infinitesimal steps. Note next that we are led to deal with our symbolic conceptions as though they were actual ones, not only because we cannot clearly separate the two, but also because, in most cases, the first serve our purposes nearly or quite as well as the last—are simply the abbreviated signs we substitute for those more elaborate signs which are our equivalents for real objects. Those imperfect representations of ordinary things which we make in thinking, we know can be developed into adequate ones if needful. Those concepts of larger magnitudes and more extensive classes which we cannot make adequate, we still find can be verified by some indirect process of measurement or enumeration. And even in the case of such an utterly inconceivable object as the Solar System, we yet, through the fulfilment of predictions founded on our symbolic conception of it, gain the conviction that this stands for an actual existence, and, in a sense, truly expresses certain of its constituent relations. So that having learnt by long experience that our symbolic conceptions can, if needful, be verified, we are led to accept them without verification. Thus we open the door to some which profess to stand for known things, but which really stand for things that cannot be known in any way.

The implication is clear. When our symbolic conceptions are such that no cumulative or indirect processes of thought can enable us to ascertain that there are corresponding actualities, nor any fulfilled predictions be assigned in justification of them, then they are altogether vicious and illusive, and in no way distinguishable from pure fictions.

§ 10. And now to consider the bearings of this general truth on our immediate topic—Ultimate Religious Ideas.

To the primitive man sometimes happen things which are out of the ordinary course—diseases, storms, earthquakes, echoes, eclipses. From dreams arises the idea of a wandering double ; whence follows the belief that the double, departing permanently at death, is then a ghost. Ghosts thus become assignable causes for strange occurrences. The greater ghosts are presently supposed to have extended spheres of action. As men grow intelligent the conceptions of these minor invisible agencies merge into the conception of a universal invisible agency; and there result hypotheses concerning the origin, not of special incidents only, but of things in general.

A critical examination, however, will prove not only that no current hypothesis is tenable, but also that no tenable hypothesis can be framed.

§ 11. Respecting the origin of the Universe three verbally intelligible suppositions may be made. We may assert that it is self-existent; or that it is self-created; or that it is created by an external agency. Which of these suppositions is most credible it is not needful here to inquire. The deeper question, into which this finally merges, is, whether any one of them is even conceivable in the true sense of the word. Let us successively test them.

When we speak of a man as self-supporting, of an apparatus as self-acting, or of a tree as self-developed, our expressions, however inexact, stand for things that can be figured in thought with tolerable completeness. Our conception of the self-development of a tree is doubtless symbolic. But though we cannot really represent in consciousness the entire series of complex changes through which the tree passes, yet we can thus represent the leading traits of the series ; and general experience teaches us that by long continued observation we could gain the power of more fully representing it. That is, we know that our symbolic conception of self-development can be expanded into something like a real conception; and that it expresses, however rudely, an actual process. But when we speak of self-existence and, helped by the above analogies, form some vague symbolic conception of it, we delude ourselves in supposing that this symbolic conception is of the same order as the others. On joining the word *self* to the word *existence*, the force of association makes us believe we have a thought like that suggested by the compound word self-acting. An endeavour to expand this symbolic conception, however, will undeceive us. In the first place, it is clear that by self-existence we especially mean an existence independent of any other —not produced by any other: the assertion of self-existence is an indirect denial of creation. In thus excluding the idea of any antecedent cause, we necessarily exclude the idea of a beginning;

for to admit that there was a time when the existence had not commenced, is to admit that its commencement was determined by something, or was caused, which is a contradiction. . Self-existence, therefore, necessarily means existence without a beginning; and to form a conception of self-existence is to form a conception of existence without a beginning. Now by no mental effort can we do this. To conceive existence through infinite past-time, implies the conception of infinite past-time, which is an impossibility. To this let us add that even were self-existence conceivable, it would not be an explanation of the Universe. No one will say that the existence of an object at the present moment is made easier to understand by the discovery that it existed an hour ago, or a day ago, or a year ago; and if its existence now is not made more comprehensible by knowledge of its existence during some previous finite period, then no knowledge of it during many such finite periods, even could we extend them to an infinite period, would make it more comprehensible. Thus the Atheistic theory is not only absolutely unthinkable, but, even were it thinkable, would not be a solution. The assertion that the Universe is self-existent does not really carry us a step beyond the cognition of its present existence; and so leaves us with a mere re-statement of the mystery.

The hypothesis of self-creation, which practically amounts to what is called Pantheism, is similarly incapable of being represented in thought. Certain phenomena, such as the precipitation of invisible vapour into cloud, aid us in forming a symbolic conception of a self-evolved Universe; and there are not wanting indications in the Heavens, and on the Earth, which help us in giving to this conception some distinctness. But while the succession of phases through which the visible Universe has passed in reaching its present form may perhaps be comprehended as in a sense self-determined; yet the impossibility of expanding our symbolic conception of self-creation into a real conception, remains as complete as ever. Really to conceive self-creation, is to conceive potential existence passing into actual existence by some inherent necessity, which we cannot. We cannot form any idea of a potential existence of the Universe, as distinguished from its actual existence. If represented in thought at all, potential existence must be represented as *something*, that is, as an actual existence : to suppose that it can be represented as nothing involves two absurdities—that nothing is more than a negation, and can be positively represented in thought, and that one nothing is distinguished from all other nothings by its power to develop into something. Nor is this all. We have no state of consciousness answering to the words—an inherent necessity by which potential existence became actual existence. To render them into thought, existence, having for an indefinite period remained in one form, must be conceived as passing without any external impulse into another form; and this involves the idea of a change without a cause—a thing of which no idea is possible. Thus the terms of this hypothesis do not stand for real thoughts, but merely suggest the vaguest symbols not admitting of any interpretation. Moreover, even were potential existence conceivable as a different thing from actual existence, and could the transition from the one to the other be mentally realized as self-determined, we should still be no forwarder: the problem would simply be removed a step back. For whence the potential existence? This would just as much require accounting for as actual existence, and just the same difficulties would meet us. The self-existence of a potential Universe is no more conceivable than the self-existence of the actual Universe. The self-creation of a potential Universe would involve over again the difficulties just stated—would imply behind this potential universe a more remote potentiality, and so on in an infinite series, leaving us at last no forwarder than at first. While to assign an external agency as its origin, would be to introduce the notion of a potential Universe for no purpose whatever.

There remains the commonly-received or theistic hypothesis— creation by external agency. Alike in the rudest creeds and in the cosmogony long current among ourselves, it is assumed that the Heavens and the Earth were made somewhat after the manner in which a workman makes a piece of furniture. And this is the assumption not only of theologians but of most philosophers. Equally in the writings of Plato and in those of not a few living men of science, we find it assumed that there is an analogy between the process of creation and the process of manufacture. Now not only is this conception one which cannot by any cumulative process of thought, or the fulfilment of predictions based on it, be shown to answer to anything actual; but it cannot be mentally realized, even when all its assumptions are granted. Though the proceedings of a human artificer may vaguely symbolize a method after which the Universe might be shaped, yet imagination of this method does not help us to solve the ultimate problem ; namely, the origin of the materials of which the Universe consists. The artizan does not make the iron, wood, or stone, he uses, but merely fashions and combines them. If we suppose suns, and planets, and satellites, and all they contain to have been similarly formed by a "Great Artificer," we suppose merely that certain pre-existing elements were thus put into their present arrangement. But whence the pre-existing elements ? The production of matter out of nothing is the real mystery, which neither this simile nor any other enables us to conceive ; and a simile which does not enable us to conceive this may as well be dispensed with. Still more manifest becomes the insufficiency of this theory of things, when we turn from material objects to that which contains them— when instead of matter we contemplate space. Did there exist nothing but an immeasurable void, explanation would be needed as much as it is now. There would still arise the question—how came it so ? If the theory of creation by external agency were an adequate one, it would supply an answer; and its answer would be —space was made in the same mannner that matter was made. But the impossibility of conceiving this is so manifest that no one dares to assert it. For if space was created it must have been previously non-existent. The non-existence of space cannot, how-ever, by any mental effort be imagined. And if the non-existence of space is absolutely inconceivable, then, necessarily, its creation is absolutely inconceivable. Lastly, even supposing that the genesis of the Universe could really be represented in thought as due to an external agency, the mystery would be as great as ever ; for there would still arise the question—how came there to be an external agency ? To account for this only the same three hypotheses are possible—self-existence, self-creation, and creation by external agency. Of these the last is useless : it commits us to an infinite series of such agencies, and even then leaves us where we were. By the second we are led into the same predicament ;

since, as already shown, self-creation implies an infinite series of potential existences. We are obliged, therefore, to fall back on the first, which is the one commonly accepted and commonly supposed to be satisfactory. Those who cannot conceive a self-existent Universe, and therefore assume a creator as the source of the Universe, take for granted that they can conceive a self-existent Creator. The mystery which they recognize in this great fact surrounding them on every side, they transfer to an alleged source of this great fact, and then suppose that they have solved the mystery. But they delude themselves. As was proved at the outset of the argument, self-existence is inconceivable; and this holds true whatever be the nature of the object of which it is predicated. Whoever agrees that the atheistic hypothesis is untenable because it involves the impossible idea of self-existence, must perforce admit that the theistic hypothesis is untenable if it contains the same impossible idea.

Thus these three different suppositions, verbally intelligible though they are, and severally seeming to their respective adherents quite rational, turn out, when critically examined, to be literally unthinkable. It is not a question of probability, or credibility, but of conceivability. Experiment proves that the elements of these hypotheses cannot even be put together in consciousness; and we can entertain them only as we entertain such pseud-ideas as a square fluid and a moral substance—only by abstaining from the endeavour to render them into actual thoughts. Or, reverting to our original mode of statement, we may say that they severally involve symbolic conceptions of the illegitimate and illusive kind. Differing so widely as they seem to do, the atheistic, the pantheistic, and the theistic hypotheses contain the same ultimate element. It is impossible to avoid making the assumption of self-existence somewhere; and whether that assumption be made nakedly or under complicated disguises, it is equally vicious, equally unthinkable. Be it a fragment of matter, or some fancied potential form of matter, or some more remote and still less imaginable mode of being, our conception of its self-existence can be framed only by joining with it the notion of unlimited duration through past time. And as unlimited duration is inconceivable, all those formal ideas into which it enters are inconceivable:

and indeed, if such an expression is allowable, are the more inconceivable in proportion as the other elements of the ideas are indefinite. So that in fact, impossible as it is to think of the actual Universe as self-existing, we do but multiply impossibilities of thought by every attempt we make to explain its existence.

§ 12. If from the origin of the Universe we turn to its nature, the like insurmountable difficulties rise up before us on all sides —or rather, the same difficulties under new aspects. We find ourselves obliged to make certain assumptions; and yet we find these assumptions cannot be represented in thought.

When we inquire what is the meaning of the effects produced on our senses—when we ask how there come to be in our consciousness impressions of sounds, of colours, of tastes, and of those various attributes we ascribe to bodies, we are compelled to regard them as the effects of some cause. We may stop short in the belief that this cause is what we call matter. Or we may conclude, as some do, that matter is only a certain mode of manifestation of spirit, which is therefore the true cause. Or, regarding matter and spirit as proximate agencies, we may ascribe the changes wrought in our consciousness to immediate divine power. But be the cause we assign what it may, we are obliged to suppose *some* cause. And we are obliged not only to suppose some cause, but also a first cause. The matter, or spirit, or other agent producing these impressions on us, must either be the first cause of them or not. If it is the first cause the conclusion is reached. If it is not the first cause, then by implication there must be a cause behind it, which thus becomes the real cause of the effect. Manifestly, however complicated the assumptions, the same conclusion must be reached. We cannot ask how the changes in our consciousness are caused, without inevitably committing ourselves to the hypothesis of a First Cause.

But now if we ask what is the nature of this First Cause, we are driven by an inexorable logic to certain further conclusions. Is the First Cause finite or infinite? If we say finite we involve ourselves in a dilemma. To think of the First Cause as finite, is to think of it as limited. To think of it as limited implies a consciousness of something beyond its limits: it is impossible to conceive a thing as bounded without assuming a region surrounding its boundaries. What now must we say of this region? If the First Cause is limited, and there consequently lies something outside of it, this something must have no First Cause—must be uncaused. But if we admit that there can be something uncaused, there is no reason to assume a cause for anything. If beyond that finite region over which the First Cause extends, there lies a region, which we are compelled to regard as infinite, over which it does not extend— if we admit that there is an infinite uncaused surrounding the finite caused ; we tacitly abandon the hypothesis of causation altogether. Thus it is impossible to consider the First Cause as finite. But if it cannot be finite it must be infinite.

Another inference concerning the First Cause is equally necessary. It must be independent. If it is dependent it cannot be the First Cause ; for that must be the First Cause on which it depends. It is not enough to say that it is partially independent ; since this implies some necessity which determines its partial dependence, and this necessity, be it what it may, must be a higher cause, or the true First Cause, which is a contradiction. But to think of the First Cause as totally independent, is to think of it as that which exists in the absence of all other existence ; seeing that if the presence of any other existence is necessary, it must be partially dependent on that other existence, and so cannot be the First Cause. Not only however must the First Cause be a form of being which has no necessary relation to any other form of being, but it .can have no necessary relation within itself. There can be nothing in it which determines change, and yet nothing which prevents change. For if it contains something which imposes such necessities or restraints, this something must be a cause higher than the First Cause, which is absurd. Thus the First Cause must be in every sense perfect, complete, total: including within itself all power and transcending all law. Or to use the established word, it must be Absolute. ..

Certain conclusions respecting the nature of the Universe, thus seem unavoidable. In our search after causes, we discover no resting place until we arrive at a First Cause ; and we have no alternative but to regard this First Cause as Infinite and Absolute. These are inferences forced on us by arguments from which there

appears no escape.   Nevertheless neither arguments nor inferences
have more than nominal values.   It might easily be shown that
the materials of which the arguments are built, equally with the
conclusions based on them, are merely symbolic conceptions of the
illegitimate order.   Instead, however, of repeating the disproof
used above, it will be well to pursue another method ; showing the
fallacy of these conclusions by disclosing their mutual contradictions.

Here I cannot do better than avail myself of the demonstration
which Mr. Mansel, carrying out in detail the doctrine of Sir
William Hamilton, has given in his *Limits of Religious Thought*.
And I gladly do this, not only because his mode of presentation
cannot be improved, but also because, writing as he does in defence
of the current Theology, his reasonings will be the more acceptable
to the majority of readers.

§ 13.  Having given preliminary definitions of the First Cause,
of the Infinite, and of the Absolute, Mr. Mansel says :—

"But these three conceptions, the Cause, the Absolute, the
Infinite, all equally indispensable, do they not imply contradiction
to each other, when viewed in conjunction, as attributes of one
and the same Being ?   A Cause cannot, as such, be absolute : the
Absolute cannot, as such, be a cause.   The cause, as such, exists
only in relation to its effect : the cause is a cause of the effect ; the
effect is an effect of the cause.   On the other hand, the conception
of the Absolute implies a possible existence out of all relation.
We attempt to escape from this apparent contradiction, by introducing the idea of succession in time.   The Absolute exists first by
itself, and afterwards becomes a Cause.   But here we are checked
by the third conception, that of the Infinite.   How can the Infinite
become that which it was not from the first ?   If Causation is a
possible mode of existence, that which exists without causing is
not infinite; that which becomes a cause has passed beyond its
former limits.   *  *  *

"Supposing the Absolute to become a cause, it will follow that
it operates by means of freewill and consciousness.   For a necessary
cause cannot be conceived as absolute and infinite.   If necessitated
by something beyond itself, it is thereby limited by a superior
power ; and if necessitated by itself, it has in its own nature a

necessary relation to its effect. The act of causation must therefore be voluntary; and volition is only possible in a conscious
being. But consciousness again is only conceivable as a relation.
There must be a conscious subject, and an object of which he is
conscious. The subject is a subject to the object; the object is an
object to the subject; and neither can exist by itself as the absolute.
This difficulty, again, may be for the moment evaded, by distinguishing between the absolute as related to another and the
absolute as related to itself. The Absolute, it may be said, may
possibly be conscious, provided it is only conscious of itself. But
this alternative is, in ultimate analysis, no less self-destructive than
the other. For the object of consciousness, whether a mode of the
subject's existence or not, is either created in and by the act of
consciousness, or has an existence independent of it. In the
former case, the object depends upon the subject, and the subject
alone is the true absolute. In the latter case, the subject depends
upon the object, and the object alone is the true absolute. Or if
we attempt a third hypothesis, and maintain that each exists
independently of the other, we have no absolute at all, but only a
pair of relatives; for coexistence, whether in consciousness or not,
is itself a relation.

" The corollary from this reasoning is obvious. Not only is the
Absolute, as conceived, incapable of a necessary relation to anything else; but it is also incapable of containing, by the constitution of its own nature, an essential relation within itself; as a
whole, for instance, composed of parts, or as a substance consisting
of attributes, or as a conscious subject in antithesis to an object.
For if there is in the absolute any principle of unity, distinct from
the mere accumulation of parts or attributes, this principle alone is
the true absolute. If, on the other hand, there is no such principle,
then there is no absolute at all, but only a plurality of relatives.
The almost unanimous voice of philosophy, in pronouncing that
the absolute is both one and simple, must be accepted as the voice
of reason also, so far as reason has any voice in the matter. But
this absolute unity, as indifferent and containing no attributes, can
neither be distinguished from the multiplicity of finite beings by
any characteristic feature, nor be identified with them in their
multiplicity. Thus we are landed in an inextricable dilemma.

The Absolute cannot be conceived as conscious, neither can it be conceived as unconscious: it cannot be conceived as complex, neither can it be conceived as simple: it cannot be conceived by difference, neither can it be conceived by the absence of difference: it cannot be identified with the universe, neither can it be distinguished from it.   The One and the Many, regarded as the beginning of existence, are thus alike incomprehensible.

"The fundamental conceptions of Rational Theology being thus self-destructive, we may naturally expect to find the same antagonism manifested in their special applications. * * * How, for example, can Infinite Power be able to do all things, and yet Infinite Goodness be unable to do evil?   How can Infinite Justice exact the utmost penalty for every sin, and yet Infinite Mercy pardon the sinner?   How can Infinite Wisdom know all that is to come, and yet Infinite Freedom be at liberty to do or to forbear?   How is the existence of Evil compatible with that of an infinitely perfect Being; for if he wills it, he is not infinitely good; and if he wills it not, his will is thwarted and his sphere of action limited? * * *

"Let us, however, suppose for an instant that these difficulties are surmounted, and the existence of the Absolute securely established on the testimony of reason.   Still we have not succeeded in reconciling this idea with that of a Cause: we have done nothing towards explaining how the absolute can give rise to the relative, the infinite to the finite.   If the condition of causal activity is a higher state than that of quiescence, the Absolute, whether acting voluntarily or involuntarily, has passed from a condition of comparative imperfection to one of comparative perfection; and therefore was not originally perfect.   If the state of activity is an inferior state to that of quiescence, the Absolute, in becoming a cause, has lost its original perfection.   There remains only the supposition that the two states are equal, and the act of creation one of complete indifference.   But this supposition annihilates the unity of the absolute, or it annihilates itself.   If the act of creation is real, and yet indifferent, we must admit the possibility of two conceptions of the absolute, the one as productive, the other as non-productive.   If the act is not real, the supposition itself vanishes. * * *

"Again, how can the relative be conceived as coming into being? If it is a distinct reality from the absolute, it must be conceived as passing from non-existence into existence. But to conceive an object as non-existent, is again a self-contradiction; for that which is conceived exists, as an object of thought, in and by that conception. We may abstain from thinking of an object at all; but, if we think of it, we cannot but think of it as existing. It is possible at one time not to think of an object at all, and at another to think of it as already in being; but to think of it in the act of becoming, in the progress from not being into being, is to think that which, in the very thought, annihilates itself.  *  *  *

"To sum up briefly this portion of my argument. The conception of the Absolute and Infinite, from whatever side we view it, appears encompassed with contradictions. There is a contradiction in supposing such an object to exist, whether alone or in conjunction with others; and there is a contradiction in supposing it not to exist. There is a contradiction in conceiving it as one; and there is a contradiction in conceiving it as many. There is a contradiction in conceiving it as personal; and there is a contradiction in conceiving it as impersonal. It cannot, without contradiction, be represented as active; nor, without equal contradiction, be represented as inactive. It cannot be conceived as the sum of all existence; nor yet can it be conceived as a part only of that sum."

§ 14. And now what is the bearing of these results on the question before us? Our examination of Ultimate Religious Ideas has been carried on with the view of making manifest some fundamental verity contained in them. Thus far, however, we have arrived at negative conclusions only. Passing over the consideration of credibility, and confining ourselves to that of conceivability, we have seen that Atheism, Pantheism, and Theism, when rigorously analysed, severally prove to be wholly unthinkable. Instead of disclosing a fundamental verity existing in each, our inquiry seems rather to have shown that there is no fundamental verity contained in any. To carry away this conclusion, however, would be a fatal error, as we shall shortly see.

Leaving out the accompanying code of conduct, which is a

supplementary growth, a religious creed is definable as a theory of original causation. By the lowest savages the genesis of things is not inquired about: only strange appearances and actions raise the question of agency. But be it in the primitive Ghost theory, which assumes a human personality behind each unusual phenomenon; be it in Polytheism, in which such personalities are partially generalized; be it in Monotheism, in which they are wholly generalized; or be it in Pantheism, in which the generalized personality becomes one with the phenomena; we equally find an hypothesis which is supposed to render the Universe comprehensible. Nay, even that which is regarded as the negation of all Religion— even positive Atheism—comes within the definition; for it, too, in asserting the self-existence of Space, Matter, and Motion, propounds a theory from which it holds the facts to be deducible. Now every theory tacitly asserts two things: first, that there is something to be explained; second, that such and such is the explanation. Hence, however widely different speculators disagree in the solutions they give of the same problem, yet by implication they agree that there is a problem to be solved. Here then is an element which all creeds have in common. Religions diametrically opposed in their overt dogmas, are perfectly at one in the tacit conviction that the existence of the world with all it contains and all which surrounds it, is a mystery calling for interpretation.

Thus we come within sight of that which we seek. In the last chapter, reasons were given for inferring that human beliefs in general, and especially the perennial ones, contain, under whatever disguises of error, some soul of truth; and here we have arrived at a truth underlying even the rudest beliefs. We saw, further, that this soul of truth is most likely some constituent common to conflicting opinions of the same order; and here we have a constituent contained by all religions. It was pointed out that this soul of truth would almost certainly be more abstract than any of the creeds involving it; and the truth above reached is one exceeding in abstractness the most abstract religious doctrines. In every respect, therefore, our conclusion answers to the requirements.

That this is the vital element in all religions is further shown by the fact that it is the element which not only survives every change, but grows more distinct the more highly the religion is developed.

Aboriginal creeds, pervaded by thoughts of personal agencies which are usually unseen, conceive these agencies under perfectly concrete and ordinary forms—class them with the visible agencies of men and animals; and so hide a vague perception of mystery in disguises as unmysterious as possible. Polytheistic conceptions in their advanced phases, represent the presiding personalities in idealized shapes, working in subtle ways, and communicating with men by omens or through inspired persons; that is, the ultimate causes of things are regarded as less familiar and comprehensible. The growth of a Monotheistic faith, accompanied as it is by lapse of those beliefs in which the divine nature is assimilated to the human in all its lower propensities, shows us a further step in the same direction; and however imperfectly this higher faith is at first held, we yet see in altars "to the unknown and unknowable God," and in the worship of a God who cannot by any searching be found out, that there is a clearer recognition of the inscrutableness of creation. Further developments of theology, ending in such assertions as that "a God understood would be no God at all," and "to think that God is, as we can think him to be, is blasphemy," exhibit this recognition still more distinctly. It pervades all the cultivated theology of the present day. So that while other elements of religious creeds one by one drop away, this remains and grows ever more manifest, and thus is shown to be the essential element.

Here, then, is a truth in which religions in general agree with one another, and with a philosophy antagonistic to their special dogmas. If Religion and Science are to be reconciled, the basis of reconciliation must be this deepest, widest, and most certain of all facts—that the Power which the Universe manifests to us is inscrutable.

# CHAPTER III

## ULTIMATE SCIENTIFIC IDEAS

§ 15. What are Space and Time? Two hypotheses are current respecting them : the one that they are objective, the other that they are subjective. Let us see what becomes of these hypotheses under analysis.

To say that Space and Time exist objectively, is to say that they are entities. The assertion that they are non-entities is self-destructive: non-entities are non-existences; and to allege that non-existences exist objectively, is a contradiction in terms. Moreover, to deny that Space and Time are things, and so by implication to call them nothings, involves the absurdity that there are two kinds of nothing. Neither can they be regarded as attributes of some entity. Not only is it impossible to conceive any entity of which they are attributes, but we cannot think of them as disappearing, even if everything else disappeared; whereas attributes necessarily disappear along with the entities they belong to. Thus as Space and Time can be neither non-entities nor the attributes of entities, we are compelled to consider them as entities. But while, on the hypothesis of their objectivity, Space and Time must be classed as things, we find that to represent them in thought as things is impossible. To be conceived at all, a thing must be conceived as having attributes. We can distinguish something from nothing, only by the power which the something has to act on our consciousness. The effects it mediately or immediately produces on our consciousness we attribute to it, and call its attributes; and the absence of these attributes is the absence of the terms in which the something is conceived, and involves the absence of a conception. What, now, are the attributes of Space? The only one which it is possible to think of as belonging to it is that of extension, and to credit it with this is to identify object and attribute. For extension and Space are convertible terms: by extension, as we ascribe it to surrounding objects, we mean occupancy of Space; and thus to say that Space is extended, is to say that Space occupies Space. How we are similarly unable to assign any attribute to Time, scarcely needs pointing out. Nor are Time and Space unthinkable as entities only from the absence of attributes. There is another peculiarity, familiar to most people, which equally excludes them from the category. All entities actually known as such, are limited; and even if we suppose ourselves either to know or to be able to conceive some unlimited entity, we necessarily in so classing it separate it from the class of limited entities. But of Space and Time we cannot assert either limitation or the absence of limitation. We find ourselves unable to form any mental image of unbounded Space; and yet are unable to imagine bounds beyond which there is no Space. Similarly at the other extreme: it is impossible to think of a limit to the divisibility of Space; yet equally impossible to think of its infinite divisibility. And, without stating them, it will be seen that we labour under like impotences in respect to Time. Thus we cannot conceive Space and Time as entities, and are equally disabled from conceiving them as either the attributes of entities or as non-entities. We are compelled to think of them as existing, and yet cannot bring them within those conditions under which existences are represented in thought.

Shall we then take refuge in the Kantian doctrine? shall we say that Space and Time are forms of the intellect,—"à priori laws or conditions of the conscious mind"? To do this is to escape from great difficulties by rushing into greater. The proposition with which Kant's philosophy sets out, verbally intelligible though it is, cannot by any effort be rendered into thought—cannot be interpreted into an idea properly so called, but stands merely for a pseud-idea. In the first place, to assert that Space and Time are subjective conditions is, by implication, to assert that they are not objective realities: if the Space and Time present to our minds belong to the *ego*, then of necessity they do not belong to the *non-ego*. Now it is impossible to think this. The very fact on which Kant bases his hypothesis—namely that our consciousness of Space and Time cannot be suppressed—testifies as much; for that consciousness of Space and Time which we cannot rid ourselves of, is the consciousness of them as existing objectively. It is useless to reply that such an inability must inevitably result if they are subjective forms. The question here is—What does consciousness directly testify? And the direct testimony of consciousness is, that Time and Space are not within the mind but without the mind; and so absolutely independent that we cannot conceive them to become non-existent even supposing the mind to become non-existent. Besides being positively unthinkable in what it tacitly denies, the theory of Kant is equally unthinkable in what it openly affirms. It is not simply that we cannot combine the thought of Space with the thought of our own personality, and contemplate the one as a property of the other—though our inability to do this would prove the inconceivableness of the hypothesis—but it is that the hypothesis carries in itself the proof of its own inconceivableness. For if Space and Time are forms of intuition, they can never be intuited; since it is impossible for anything to be at once the *form* of intuition and the *matter* of intuition. That Space and Time are objects of consciousness, Kant emphatically asserts by saying that it is impossible to suppress the consciousness of them. How then, if they are *objects* of consciousness, can they at the same time be *conditions* of consciousness? If Space and Time are the conditions under which we think, then when we think of Space and Time themselves, our thoughts must be unconditioned; and if there can thus be unconditioned thoughts, what becomes of the theory?

It results, therefore, that Space and Time are wholly incomprehensible. The immediate knowledge which we seem to have of them proves, when examined, to be total ignorance. While our belief in their objective reality is insurmountable, we are unable to give any rational account of it. And to posit the alternative belief (possible to state but impossible to realize) is merely to multiply irrationalities.

§ 16. Were it not for the necessities of the argument, it would be inexcusable to occupy the reader's attention with the threadbare, and yet unended, controversy respecting the divisibility of matter. Matter is either infinitely divisible or it is not: no third possibility can be named. Which of the alternatives shall we accept? If we say that Matter is infinitely divisible, we commit ourselves to a supposition not realizable in thought. We can bisect and re-bisect a body, and continually repeating the act until we reduce its parts to a size no longer physically divisible, may then mentally continue the process. To do this, however, is not really to conceive the infinite divisibility of matter, but to form a symbolic conception not admitting of expansion into a real one, and not admitting of other verification. Really to conceive the infinite divisibility of matter, is mentally to follow out the divisions to infinity; and to do this would require infinite time. On the other hand, to assert that matter is not infinitely divisible, is to assert that it is reducible to parts which no power can divide; and this verbal supposition can no more be represented in thought than the other. For each of such ultimate parts, did they exist, must have an under and an upper surface, a right and a left side, like any larger fragment. Now it is impossible to imagine its sides so near that no plane of section can be conceived between them; and however great be the assumed force of cohesion, it is impossible to shut out the idea of a greater force capable of overcoming it. So that to human intelligence the one hypothesis is no more acceptable than the other; and yet the conclusion that one or other must agree with the fact, seems to human intelligence unavoidable.

Again, let us ask whether substance has anything like that extended solidity which it presents to our consciousness. The portion of space occupied by a piece of metal, seems to eyes and fingers perfectly filled: we perceive a homogeneous, resisting mass, without any breach of continuity. Shall we then say that Matter is actually as solid as it appears? Shall we say that, whether it consists of an infinitely divisible element or of units which cannot be further divided, its parts are everywhere in actual contact? To assert as much entangles us in insuperable difficulties. Were Matter thus absolutely solid it would be—what it is not—absolutely incompressible; since compressibility, implying the nearer approach of constituent parts, is not thinkable unless there is unoccupied space among the parts.

The supposition that Matter is absolutely solid being untenable, there presents itself the Newtonian supposition, that it consists of solid atoms not in contact but acting on one another by attractive and repulsive forces, varying with the distances. To assume this, however, merely shifts the difficulty. For granting that Matter as we perceive it, is made up of dense extended units attracting and repelling, the question still arises—What is the constitution of these units? We must regard each of them as a small piece of matter. Looked at through a mental microscope, each becomes a mass such as we have just been contemplating. Just the same inquiries may be made respecting the parts of which each atom consists; while just the same difficulties stand in the way of every answer. Even were the hypothetical atom assumed to consist of still minuter ones, the difficulty would reappear at the next step; and so on perpetually.

Boscovich's conception yet remains to us. Seeing that Matter could not, as Leibnitz suggested, be composed of unextended monads (since the juxtaposition of an infinity of points having no extension could not produce that extension which matter possesses), and perceiving objections to the view entertained by Newton, Boscovich proposed an intermediate theory. This theory is that the constituents of Matter are centres of force—points without dimensions—which attract and repel one another in such wise as to be kept at specific distances apart. And he argues, mathematically, that the forces possessed by such centres might so vary with the distances that, under given conditions, the centres would remain in stable equilibrium with definite interspaces; and yet, under other conditions, would maintain larger or smaller interspaces. This speculation, however, escapes all the inconceivabilities above indicated by merging them in the one inconceivability with which it sets out. A centre of force absolutely without extension is unthinkable. The idea of resistance cannot be separated in thought from the idea of something which offers resistance, and this something must be thought of as occupying space. To suppose that central forces can reside in points having positions only, with nothing to mark their positions—points in no respect distinguishable from surrounding points which are not centres of force—is beyond human power.

But though the conception of Matter as consisting of dense indivisible units is symbolic, and cannot by any effort be thought out, it may yet be supposed to find indirect verification in the truths of chemistry. These, it is argued, necessitate the belief that Matter consists of particles of specific weights, and therefore of specific sizes. The law of definite proportions seems impossible on any other condition than the existence of ultimate atoms; and though the combining weights of the respective elements are termed by chemists their "equivalents," for the purpose of avoiding a questionable assumption, we are unable to think of the combination of such definite weights, without supposing it to take place between definite molecules. Thus it would appear that the Newtonian view is at any rate preferable to that of Boscovich. A disciple of Boscovich, however, may reply that his master's theory is involved in that of Newton, and cannot indeed be escaped. "What holds together the parts of these ultimate atoms?" he may ask. "A cohesive force," his opponent must answer. "And what," he may continue, "holds together the parts of any fragments into which, by sufficient force, an ultimate atom might be broken?" Again the answer must be—a cohesive force. "And what," he may still ask, "if the ultimate atom were reduced to parts as small in proportion to it, as it is in proportion to a tangible mass of matter—what must give each part the ability to sustain itself?" Still there is no answer but—a cohesive force. Carry on the mental process and we can find no limit until we arrive at the symbolic conception of centres of force without any extension.

Matter then, in its ultimate nature, is as absolutely incomprehensible as Space and Time. Whatever supposition we frame leaves us nothing but a choice between opposite absurdities.*

* To discuss Lord Kelvin's hypothesis of vortex-atoms, from the scientific point of view, is beyond my ability. From the philosophical point of view, however, I may say that since it postulates a homogeneous medium which is strictly continuous (non-molecular), which is incompressible, which is a perfect fluid in the sense of having no viscosity, and which has inertia, it sets out with what appears to me an inconceivability. A fluid which has inertia, implying mass, and which is yet absolutely frictionless, so that its

§ 17. A body impelled by the hand is perceived to move, and to move in a definite direction: doubt about its motion seems impossible. Yet we not only may be, but usually are, quite wrong in both these judgments. Here, for instance, is a ship which we will suppose to be anchored at the equator with her head to the West. When the captain walks from stem to stern, in what direction does he move? East is the obvious answer—an answer which for the moment may pass without criticism. But now the anchor is heaved, and the vessel sails to the West with a velocity equal to that at which the captain walks. In what direction does he now move when he goes from stem to stern? You cannot say East, for the vessel is carrying him as fast towards the West as he walks to the East; and you cannot say West for the converse reason. In respect to things outside the vessel he is stationary, though to all on board he seems to be moving. But now are we quite sure of this conclusion?—Is he really stationary? On taking into account the Earth's motion round its axis, we find that he is travelling at the rate of 1000 miles per hour to the East; so that neither the perception of one who looks at him, nor the inference of one who allows for the ship's motion, is anything like right. Nor indeed, on further consideration, do we find this revised conclusion to be much better. For we have not allowed for the Earth's motion in its orbit. This being some 68,000 miles per hour, it follows that, assuming the time to be midday, he is moving, not at the rate of 1000 miles per hour to the East, but at the rate of 67,000 miles per hour to the East. Nay, not even now have we discovered the true rate and the true direction of his movement. With the Earth's progress in its orbit, we have to join that of the whole Solar system towards the constellation Hercules. When we do this, we perceive that he is moving neither East nor West, but in a line inclined to the plane of the Ecliptic, and at a velocity greater or less (according to the time of the year) than that above named. And were the constitution of our Sidereal System fully known, we should probably discover the direction and rate of his actual movement to differ

parts move among one another without any loss of motion, cannot be truly represented in consciousness. Even were it otherwise, the hypothesis is held by Prof. Clerk Maxwell to be untenable (see art. "Atom," *Ency. Brit.*).

considerably even from these.    Thus we are taught that what we are conscious of is not the real motion of any object, either in its rate or direction, but merely its motion as measured from an assigned position—either our own or some other.  Yet in this very process of concluding that the motions we perceive are not the real motions, we tacitly assume that there are real motions. We take for granted that there is an absolute course and an absolute velocity, and we find it impossible to rid ourselves of this idea.  Nevertheless, absolute motion cannot even be imagined, much less known.  Apart from those marks in space which we habitually associate with it, motion is unthinkable.  For motion is change of place ; but in space without marks, change of place is inconceivable, because place itself is inconceivable.  Place can be conceived only by reference to other places ; and in the absence of objects dispersed through space, a place could be conceived only in relation to the limits of space ; whence it follows that in unlimited space, place cannot be conceived—all places must be equidistant from boundaries which do not exist.  Thus while obliged to think that there is an absolute motion, we find absolute motion cannot be represented in thought.

Another insuperable difficulty presents itself when we contemplate the transfer of Motion.    Habit blinds us to the marvellousness of this phenomenon.  Familiar with the fact from childhood, we see nothing remarkable in the ability of a moving thing to generate movement in a thing that is stationary.  It is, however, impossible to understand it.  In what respect does a body after impact differ from itself before impact ?  What is this added to it which does not sensibly affect any of its properties and yet enables it to traverse space ?  Here is an object at rest and here is the same object moving.  In the one state it has no tendency to change its place, but in the other it is obliged at each instant to assume a new position.  What is it which will for ever go on producing this effect without being exhausted ? and how does it dwell in the object ?  The motion you say has been communicated. But how ?—What has been communicated ?  The striking body has not transferred a *thing* to the body struck ; and it is equally out of the question to say that it has transferred an *attribute*. What then has it transferred ?

Once more there is the old puzzle concerning the connexion between Motion and Rest. A body travelling at a given velocity cannot be brought to a state of rest, or no velocity, without passing through all intermediate velocities. It is quite possible to think of its motion as diminishing insensibly until it becomes infinitesimal; and many will think equally possible to pass in thought from infinitesimal motion to no motion. But this is an error. Mentally follow out the decreasing velocity as long as you please, and there still remains *some* velocity; and the smallest movement is separated by an impassable gap from no movement. As something, however minute, is infinitely great in comparison with nothing; so is even the least conceivable motion infinite as compared with rest.

Thus neither when considered in connexion with Space, nor when considered in connexion with Matter, nor when considered in connexion with Rest, do we find that Motion is truly cognizable. All efforts to understand its essential nature do but bring us to alternative impossibilities of thought.

§ 18. On lifting a chair the force exerted we regard as equal to that antagonistic force called the weight of the chair, and we cannot think of these as equal without thinking of them as like in kind; since equality is conceivable only between things that are connatural. Yet, contrariwise, it is incredible that the force existing in the chair resembles the force present to our minds. It scarcely needs to point out that since the force as known to us is an affection of consciousness, we cannot conceive the force to exist in the chair under the same form without endowing the chair with consciousness. So that it is absurd to think of Force as in itself like our sensation of it, and yet necessary so to think of it if we represent it in consciousness at all.

How, again, can we understand the connexion between Force and Matter? Matter is known to us only through its manifestations of Force: abstract its resistance mediately or immediately offered and there remains nothing but empty extension. Yet, on the other hand, resistance is equally unthinkable apart from Matter—apart from something extended. Not only are centres of force devoid of extension unimaginable, but we cannot imagine either extended or unextended centres of force to attract and repel other such centres at a distance, without the intermediation of some kind of matter. The hypothesis of Newton, equally with that of Boscovich, is open to the charge that it supposes one thing to act on another through empty space—a supposition which cannot be represented in thought. This charge is indeed met by introducing a hypothetical fluid existing among the atoms or centres. But the problem is not thus solved: it is simply shifted, and reappears when the constitution of this fluid is inquired into.        How impossible it is to elude the difficulty is best seen in the case of astronomical forces. The Sun gives us sensations of light and heat; and we have ascertained that between the cause as existing in the Sun, and the effect as experienced on the Earth, a lapse of eight minutes occurs: whence unavoidably result in us the conceptions of both a force and a motion. So that for assuming a luminiferous ether, there is the defence, not only that the exercise of force through 92,000,000 of miles of absolute vacuum is inconceivable, but also that it is impossible to conceive motion in the absence of something moved. Similarly in the case of gravitation. Newton described himself as unable to think that the attraction of one body for another at a distance, could be exerted in the absence of an intervening medium. But now let us ask how much the forwarder we are if an intervening medium be assumed. This ether whose undulations according to the received hypothesis constitute heat and light, and which is the vehicle of gravitation —how is it constituted? We must regard it in the way that physicists usually regard it, as composed of atoms or molecules which attract and repel one another: infinitesimal it may be in comparison with those of ordinary matter, but still atoms or molecules. And remembering that this ether is imponderable, we are obliged to conclude that the ratio between the interspaces of these atoms and the atoms themselves is immense. Hence we have to conceive these infinitesimal molecules acting on one another through relatively vast distances. How is this conception easier than the other? We still have mentally to represent a body as acting where it is not, and in the absence of anything by which its action may be transferred; and what matters it whether this takes place on a large or a small scale? Thus we are obliged to conclude that matter, whether ponderable or imponderable, and whether aggregated or in its hypothetical units, acts on matter through absolutely vacant space; and yet this conclusion is unthinkable.

Another difficulty of conception, converse in nature but equally insurmountable, must be added. If, on the one hand, we cannot in thought see matter acting upon matter through vacant space; on the other hand, it is incomprehensible that the gravitation of one particle of matter towards another, and towards all others, should be the same whether the intervening space is filled with matter or not. I lift from the ground, and continue to hold, a pound weight. Now, into the vacancy between it and the ground, is introduced a mass of matter of any kind whatever, in any state whatever; and the gravitation of the weight is entirely unaffected. Each individual of the infinity of particles composing the Earth acts on the pound in absolutely the same way, whatever intervenes, or if nothing intervenes. Through eight thousand miles of the Earth's substance, each molecule at the antipodes affects each molecule of the weight, in utter indifference to the fulness or emptiness of the space between them. So that each portion of matter in its dealings with remote portions, treats all intervening portions as though they did not exist; and yet, at the same time, it recognizes their existence with scrupulous exactness in its direct dealings with them.

While then it is impossible to form any idea of Force in itself, it is equally impossible to comprehend its mode of exercise.

§ 19. Turning now from the outer to the inner world, let us contemplate, not the agencies to which we ascribe our subjective modifications, but the subjective modifications themselves. These constitute a series. Difficult as we find it distinctly to individualize them, it is nevertheless beyond question that our states of consciousness occur in succession.

Is this chain of states of consciousness infinite or finite? We cannot say infinite; not only because we have indirectly reached the conclusion that there was a period when it commenced, but also because all infinity is inconceivable—an infinite series included. If we say finite we say it inferentially; for we have no direct knowledge of either of its ends. Go back in memory as far as we may, we are wholly unable to identify our first states of consciousness. Similarly at the other extreme. We infer a termination to the series at a future time, but cannot directly know it; and we cannot really lay hold of that temporary termination reached at the present moment. For the state of consciousness recognized by us as our last, is not truly our last. That any mental affection may be known as one of the series, it must be remembered—*represented* in thought, not *presented*. The truly last state of consciousness is that which is passing in the very act of contemplating a state just past—that in which we are thinking of the one before as the last. So that the proximate end of the change eludes us, as well as the remote end.

" But," it may be said, " though we cannot directly *know* consciousness to be finite in duration, because neither of its limits can be actually reached, yet we can very well *conceive* it to be so." No : not even this is true. We cannot *conceive* the terminations of that consciousness which alone we really know—our own—any more than we can *per*ceive its terminations. For in truth the two acts are here one. In either case such terminations must be, as above said, not presented in thought, but represented; and they must be represented as in the act of occurring. Now to represent the termination of consciousness as occurring in ourselves, is to think of ourselves as contemplating the cessation of the last state of consciousness; and this implies a supposed continuance of consciousness after its last state, which is absurd.

Hence, while we are unable either to believe or to conceive that the duration of consciousness is infinite, we are equally unable either to know it as finite, or to conceive it as finite : we can only infer from indirect evidence that it is finite.

§ 20. Nor do we meet with any greater success when, instead of the extent of consciousness, we consider its substance. The question—What is this that thinks? admits of no better solution than the question to which we have just found none but inconceivable answers.

The existence of each individual as known to himself, has always been held the most incontrovertible of truths. To say—" I am as sure of it as I am sure that I exist," is, in common speech, the most emphatic expression of certainty.   And this fact of personal existence, testified to by the universal consciousness of men, has been made the basis of more philosophies than one.

Belief in the reality of self cannot, indeed, be escaped while normal consciousness continues.   What shall we say of these successive impressions and ideas which constitute consciousness? Are they affections of something called mind, which, as being the subject of them, is the real *ego*?  If we say this we imply that the *ego* is an entity.   Shall we assert that these impressions and ideas are not the mere superficial changes wrought on some thinking substance, but are themselves the very body of this substance— are severally the modified forms which it from moment to moment assumes?   This hypothesis, equally with the foregoing, implies that the conscious self exists as a permanent continuous being; since modifications necessarily involve something modified.   Shall we then betake ourselves to the sceptic's position, and argue that our impressions and ideas themselves are to us the only existences, and that the personality said to underlie them is a fiction?  We do not even thus escape; since this proposition, verbally intelligible but really unthinkable, itself makes the assumption which it professes to repudiate.   For how can consciousness be wholly resolved into impressions and ideas, when an impression of necessity implies something impressed?   Or again, how can the sceptic, who has decomposed his consciousness into impressions and ideas, explain the fact that he considers them as *his* impressions and ideas?   Or once more, if, as he must, he admits that he has an impression of his personal existence, what warrant can he show for rejecting this impression as unreal while he accepts all his other impressions as real?

But now, unavoidable as is this belief, it is yet a belief admitting of no justification by reason: nay, indeed, it is a belief which reason, when pressed for a distinct answer, rejects.   One of the most recent writers who has touched on this question— Mr. Mansel—does, indeed, contend that in the consciousness of self we have a piece of real knowledge.   His position is that " let system-makers say what they will, the unsophisticated sense of mankind refuses to acknowledge that mind is but a bundle of states of consciousness, as matter is (possibly) a bundle of sensible qualities." But this position does not seem a consistent one for a Kantist, who pays but small respect to "the unsophisticated sense of mankind" when it testifies to the objectivity of space. Moreover, it may readily be shown that a cognition of self, properly so called, is negatived by those laws of thought which he emphasizes. The fundamental condition to all consciousness, insisted upon by Mr. Mansel in common with Sir William Hamilton and others, is the antithesis of subject and object. On this "primitive dualism of consciousness," "from which the explanations of philosophy must take their start," Mr. Mansel founds his refutation of the German absolutists. But now what is the corollary, as bearing on the consciousness of self? The mental act in which self is known implies, like every other mental act, a perceiving subject and a perceived object. If, then, the object perceived is self, what is the subject that perceives? or if it is the true self which thinks, what other self can it be that is thought of? Clearly, a true cognition of self implies a state in which the knowing and the known are one—in which subject and object are identified; and this Mr. Mansel rightly holds to be the annihilation of both.

So that the personality of which each is conscious, and the existence of which is to each a fact beyond all others the most certain, is yet a thing which cannot be known at all, in the strict sense of the word.

§ 21. Ultimate Scientific Ideas, then, are all representative of realities that cannot be comprehended. After no matter how great a progress in the colligation of facts and the establishment of generalizations ever wider and wider, the fundamental truth remains as much beyond reach as ever. The explanation of that which is explicable, does but bring into greater clearness the inexplicableness of that which remains behind. Alike in the external and the internal worlds, the man of science sees himself in the midst of perpetual changes of which he can discover neither the beginning nor the end. If he allows himself to entertain the hypothesis that the Universe originally existed in a diffused form, he finds it impossible to conceive how this came to be so; and equally, if he speculates on the future, he can assign no limit to the grand succession of phenomena ever unfolding themselves before him. In like manner if he looks inward he perceives that both ends of the thread of consciousness are beyond his grasp. Neither end can be represented in thought. When, again, he turns from the succession of phenomena, external or internal, to their intrinsic nature, he is just as much at fault. Supposing him in every case able to resolve the appearances, properties, and movements of things, into manifestations of Force in Space and Time; he still finds that Force, Space, and Time pass all understanding. Similarly, though analysis of mental actions may finally bring him down to sensations, as the original materials out of which all thought is woven, yet he is little forwarder; for he can give no account either of sensations themselves or of that which is conscious of sensations. Objective and subjective things he thus ascertains to be alike inscrutable in their substance and genesis. In all directions his investigations eventually bring him face to face with an insoluble enigma; and he ever more clearly perceives it to be an insoluble enigma. He learns at once the greatness and the littleness of the human intellect—its power in dealing with all that comes within the range of experience, its impotence in dealing with all that transcends experience. He, more than any other, truly *knows* that in its ultimate nature nothing can be known.

# CHAPTER IV

## THE RELATIVITY OF ALL KNOWLEDGE

§ 22. THE same conclusion is thus arrived at from whichever point we set out. Ultimate religious ideas and ultimate scientific ideas, alike turn out to be merely symbols of the actual, not cognitions of it.

The conviction, so reached, that human intelligence is incapable of absolute knowledge, is one that has been slowly gaining ground. Each new ontological theory, propounded in lieu of previous ones shown to be untenable, has been followed by a new criticism leading to a new scepticism. All possible conceptions have been one by one tried and found wanting; and so the entire field of speculation has been gradually exhausted without positive result: the only result reached being the negative one above stated—that the reality existing behind all appearances is, and must ever be, unknown. To this conclusion almost every thinker of note has subscribed. "With the exception," says Sir William Hamilton, "of a few late Absolutist theorisers in Germany, this is, perhaps, the truth of all others most harmoniously re-echoed by every philosopher of every school." And among these he names—Protagoras, Aristotle, St. Augustin, Boethius, Averroes, Albertus Magnus, Gerson, Leo Hebræus, Melancthon, Scaliger, Francis Piccolomini, Giordano Bruno, Campanella, Bacon, Spinoza, Newton, Kant.

It remains to point out how this belief may be established rationally, as well as empirically. Not only is it that, as in the earlier thinkers above named, a vague perception of the inscrutableness of things in themselves results from discovering the illusiveness of sense-impressions; and not only is it that, as shown in the foregoing chapters, experiments evolve alternative impossibilities of thought out of every fundamental conception; but it is that the relativity of our knowledge may be proved analytically. The induction drawn from general and special experiences, may be confirmed by a deduction from the nature of our intelligence. Two ways of reaching such a deduction exist. Proof that our cognitions are not, and never can be, absolute, is obtainable by analyzing either the *product* of thought, or the *process* of thought. Let us analyze each.

§ 23. If, when walking through the fields some day in September, you hear a rustle a few yards in advance, and on observing the ditch-side where it occurs, see the herbage agitated, you will probably turn towards the spot to learn by what this sound and motion are produced. As you approach there flutters into the ditch a partridge; on seeing which your curiosity is satisfied—you have what you call an *explanation* of the appearances. The explanation, mark, amounts to this; that whereas throughout life you have had countless experiences of disturbance among small stationary bodies, accompanying the movement of other bodies among them, and have generalised the relation between such disturbances and such movements, you consider this particular disturbance explained, on finding it to present an instance of the like relation.    Suppose you catch the partridge; and, wishing to ascertain why it did not escape, examine it, and find at one spot a trace of blood on its feathers. You now *understand*, as you say, what has disabled the partridge. It has been wounded by a sportsman—adds another case to the cases already seen by you, of birds being killed or injured by the shot discharged at them from fowling-pieces. And in assimilating this case to other such cases, consists your understanding of it.    But now, on consideration, a difficulty suggests itself. Only a single shot has struck the partridge, and that not in a vital place: the wings are uninjured, as are also those muscles which move them; and the creature proves by its struggles that it has abundant strength. Why then, you inquire of yourself, does it not fly? Occasion favouring, you put the question to an anatomist, who furnishes you with *a solution*. He points out that this solitary shot has passed close to the place at which the nerve supplying the wing-muscles of one side, diverges from the spine; and explains that a slight injury to this nerve, extending even to the rupture of a few fibres, may, by preventing a perfect co-ordination in the actions of the two wings, destroy the power of flight. You are no longer puzzled. But what has happened? —what has changed your state from one of perplexity to one of *comprehension?* Simply the disclosure of a class of previously known cases, along with which you can include this case. The connexion between lesions of the nervous system and paralysis of limbs has been already many times brought under your notice; and you here find a relation of cause and effect that is essentially similar.

Let us suppose you are led to ask the anatomist questions about some organic actions which, remarkable though they are, you had not before cared to understand. How is respiration effected? you ask—why does air periodically rush into the lungs? The answer is that influx of air is caused by an enlargement of the thoracic cavity, due, partly to depression of the diaphragm, partly to motion of the ribs. But how can these bony hoops move, and how does motion of them enlarge the cavity? In reply the anatomist explains that though attached by their ends the ribs can move a little round their points of attachment; he then shows you that the plane of each pair of ribs makes an acute angle with the spine; that this angle widens when the sternal ends of the ribs are raised; and he makes you realize the consequent dilatation of the cavity, by pointing out how the area of a parallelogram increases as its angles approach to right angles: you understand this special fact when you see it to be an instance of a general geometrical fact. There still arises, however, the question—why does the air rush into this enlarged cavity? To which comes the answer that, when the thoracic cavity is enlarged, the contained air, partially relieved from pressure, expands, and so loses some of its resisting power; that hence it opposes to the pressure of the external air a less pressure; and that as air, like every other fluid, presses equally in all directions, motion must result along any line in which the resistance is less than elsewhere; whence follows an inward current. And this *interpretation* you recognize as one, when a few facts of like kind, exhibited more plainly in a visible fluid such as water, are cited in illustration. Again, after being shown that the limbs are compound levers acting in essentially the same way as levers of iron, you would consider yourself as having obtained a partial *rationale* of animal movements. The contraction of a muscle, seeming before quite unaccountable, would seem less unaccountable were you shown how, by a galvanic current, a series of soft iron magnets could be made to shorten itself through the attraction of each magnet for its neighbours :—an alleged analogy which especially answers the purpose of our argument, since, whether real or fancied, it equally illustrates the mental illumination that results on finding a class of cases within which a particular case may perhaps be included. Similarly when you learn that animal heat arises from chemical combination, and so may be classed with heat evolved in other chemical combinations—when you learn that the absorption of nutrient liquids through the coats of the intestines is an instance of osmotic action—when you learn that the changes undergone by food during digestion, are like changes artificially producible in the laboratory ; you regard yourself as *knowing* something about the natures of these phenomena.

Observe now what we have been doing. We began with special and concrete facts. In explaining each, and afterwards explaining the general facts of which they are instances, we have got down to certain highly general facts :—to a geometrical principle, to a simple law of mechanical action, to a law of fluid equilibrium—to truths in physics, in chemistry, in thermology. The particular phenomena with which we set out have been merged in larger and larger groups of phenomena ; and as they have been so merged, we have arrived at solutions we consider profound in proportion as this process has been carried far. Still deeper explanations are simply further steps in the same direction. When, for instance, it is asked why the law of action of the lever is what it is, or why fluid equilibrium and fluid motion exhibit the relations they do, the answer furnished by mathematicians consists in the disclosure of the principle of virtual velocities—a principle holding true alike in fluids and solids—a principle under which the others are comprehended.

Is this process limited or unlimited? Can we go on for ever

explaining classes of facts by including them in larger classes; or must we eventually come to a largest class? The supposition that the process is unlimited, were any one absurd enough to espouse it, would still imply that an ultimate explanation could not be reached, since infinite time would be required to reach it. While the unavoidable conclusion that it is limited, equally implies that the deepest fact cannot be understood. For if the successively deeper interpretations of Nature which constitute advancing knowledge are merely successive inclusions of special truths in general truths, and of general truths in truths still more general; it follows that the most general truth, not admitting of inclusion in any other, does not admit of interpretation. Of necessity, therefore, explanation must eventually bring us down to the inexplicable. Comprehension must become something other than comprehension, before the ultimate fact can be comprehended.

§ 24. The inference which is thus forced on us when we analyze the product of thought, as exhibited objectively in scientific generalizations, is equally forced on us by an analysis of the process of thought, as exhibited subjectively in consciousness. The demonstration of the relative character of our knowledge, as deduced from the nature of intelligence, has been brought to its most definite shape by Sir William Hamilton. I cannot here do better than extract from his essay on the "Philosophy of the Unconditioned," the passage containing the substance of his doctrine.

"The unconditionally unlimited, or the *Infinite*, the unconditionally limited, or the *Absolute*, cannot positively be construed to the mind; they can be conceived, only by a thinking away from, or abstraction of, those very conditions under which thought itself is realized; consequently, the notion of the Unconditioned is only negative,—negative of the conceivable itself. For example, on the one hand we can positively conceive, neither an absolute whole, that is, a whole so great, that we cannot also conceive it as a relative part of a still greater whole; nor an absolute part, that is, a part so small, that we cannot also conceive it as a relative whole, divisible into smaller parts. On the other hand, we cannot positively represent, or realize, or construe to the mind (as here understanding and imagination coincide), an infinite whole, for this could only be done by the infinite synthesis in thought of finite wholes, which would itself require an infinite time for its accomplishment; nor, for the same reason, can we follow out in thought an infinite divisibility of parts. The result is the same, whether we apply the process to limitation in *space*, in *time*, or in *degree*. * * *

" As the conditionally limited (which we may briefly call the *conditioned*) is thus the only possible object of knowledge and of positive thought—thought necessarily supposes conditions. To *think* is *to condition*; and conditional limitation is the fundamental law of the possibility of thought. For, as the greyhound cannot outstrip his shadow, nor (by a more appropriate simile) the eagle outsoar the atmosphere in which he floats, and by which alone he may be supported; so the mind cannot transcend that sphere of limitation, within and through which exclusively the possibility of thought is realized. * * * How, indeed, it could ever be doubted that thought is only of the conditioned, may well be deemed a matter of the profoundest admiration. Thought cannot transcend consciousness; consciousness is only possible under the antithesis of a subject and object of thought, known only in correlation, and mutually limiting each other; while, independently of this, all that we know either of subject or object, either of mind or matter, is only a knowledge in each of the particular, of the plural, of the different, of the modified, of the phænomenal. We admit that the consequence of this doctrine is,—that philosophy, if viewed as more than a science of the conditioned, is impossible. Departing from the particular, we admit, that we can never, in our highest generalizations, rise above the finite; that our knowledge, whether of mind or matter, can be nothing more than a knowledge of the relative manifestations of an existence, which in itself it is our highest wisdom to recognize as beyond the reach of philosophy. * * *

" We are thus taught the salutary lesson, that the capacity of thought is not to be constituted into the measure of existence; and are warned from recognizing the domain of our knowledge as necessarily co-extensive with the horizon of our faith. And by a wonderful revelation, we are thus, in the very consciousness of our inability to conceive aught above the relative and finite, inspired with a belief in the existence of something unconditioned beyond the sphere of all comprehensible reality."

Clear and conclusive as this statement of the case appears when carefully studied, it is expressed in so abstract a manner as to be not very intelligible to the general reader. A more popular presentation of it, with illustrative applications, as given by Mr. Mansel in his *Limits of Religious Thought*, will make it more fully understood. The following extracts, which I take the liberty of making from his pages, will suffice.

" The very conception of consciousness, in whatever mode it may be manifested, necessarily implies *distinction between one object and another*. To be conscious, we must be conscious of something ; and that something can only be known, as that which it is, by being distinguished from that which it is not. But distinction is necessarily limitation; for, if one object is to be distinguished from another, it must possess some form of existence which the other has not, or it must not possess some form which the other has. * * * If all thought is limitation ;—if whatever we conceive is, by the very act of conception, regarded as finite,— *the infinite*, from a human point of view, is merely a name for the absence of those conditions under which thought is possible. To speak of a *Conception of the Infinite* is, therefore, at once to affirm those conditions and to deny them. The contradiction, which we discover in such a conception, is only that which we have ourselves placed there, by tacitly assuming the conceivability of the inconceivable. The condition of consciousness is distinction ; and condition of distinction is limitation. We can have no consciousness of Being in general which is not some Being in particular : a *thing*, in consciousness, is one thing out of many. In assuming the possibility of an infinite object of consciousness, I assume, therefore, that it is at the same time limited and unlimited ;—actually something, without which it could not be an object of consciousness, and actually nothing, without which it could not be infinite. * * *

" A second characteristic of Consciousness is, that it is only possible in the form of a *relation*. There must be a Subject, or person conscious, and an Object, or thing of which he is conscious. There can be no consciousness without the union of these two factors ; and, in that union, each exists only as it is related to the other. The subject is a subject, only in so far as it is conscious of an object: the object is an object, only in so far as it is apprehended by a subject: and the destruction of either is the destruction of consciousness itself. It is thus manifest that a consciousness of the Absolute is equally self-contradictory with that of the Infinite. To be conscious of the Absolute as such, we must know that an object, which is given in relation to our consciousness, is identical with one which exists in its own nature, out of all relation to consciousness. But to know this identity, we must be able to compare the two together; and such a comparison is itself a contradiction. We are in fact required to compare that of which we are conscious with that of which we are not conscious; the comparison itself being an act of consciousness, and only possible through the consciousness of both its objects. It is thus manifest that, even if we could be conscious of the absolute, we could not possibly know that it *is* the absolute: and, as we can be conscious of an object as such, only by knowing it to be what it is, this is equivalent to an admission that we cannot be conscious of the absolute at all. As an object of consciousness, every thing is necessarily relative; and what a thing may be out of consciousness no mode of consciousness can tell us. * * *

" This contradiction, again, admits of the same explanation as the former. * * * *Existence*, as we conceive it, is but a name for the several ways in which objects are presented to our consciousness, —a general term, embracing a variety of relations. *The Absolute*, on the other hand, is a term expressing no object of thought, but only a denial of the relation by which thought is constituted."

Here let me point out how the same general inference may be evolved from another fundamental condition to thought, omitted by Sir W. Hamilton and not supplied by Mr. Mansel ;—a condition which, under its obverse aspect, we have already contemplated in the last section. Every complete act of consciousness, besides distinction and relation, also implies likeness. Before it can constitute a piece of knowledge, or even become an idea, a mental state must be known not only as separate in kind or quality from certain foregoing states to which it is known as related by succession, but it must further be known as of the same kind or quality with certain other foregoing states. That organization of changes which constitutes thinking, involves continuous integration as well as continuous differentiation. Were each new affection of the mind perceived simply as an affection in some way contrasted with preceding ones—were there but a chain of impressions, each of which as it arose was merely distinguished from its predecessors; consciousness would be a chaos. To produce that orderly consciousness which we call intelligence, there requires the assimilation of each impression to others that occurred earlier in the series. Both the successive mental states, and the successive relations which they bear to one another, must be classified; and classification involves not only a parting of the unlike, but also a binding together of the like. In brief, a true cognition is possible only through an accompanying recognition. Should it be objected that if so there cannot be a first cognition, and hence there can be no cognition, the reply is that cognition proper arises gradually —that during the first stage of incipient intelligence, before the feelings produced by intercourse with the outer world have been put into order, there *are* no cognitions ; and that, as every infant shows us, these slowly emerge out of the confusion of unfolding consciousness as fast as the experiences are arranged into groups— as fast as the most frequently repeated sensations, and their relations to one another, become familiar enough to admit of their recognition as such or such, whenever they recur. Should it be further objected that if cognition presupposes recognition, there can be no cognition, even by an adult, of an object never before seen ; there is still the sufficient answer that in so far as it is not assimilated to previously-seen objects, it is *not* known, and that it *is* known only in so far as it is assimilated to them. Of this paradox the interpretation is, that an object is classifiable in various ways with various degrees of completeness. An animal hitherto *unknown* (mark the word), though not referable to any established species or genus, is yet *recognized* as belonging to one of the larger divisions—mammals, birds, reptiles, or fishes ; or should it be so anomalous that its alliance with any of these is not determinable, it may yet be classed as vertebrate or invertebrate ; or if it be one of those organisms in which it is doubtful whether the animal or vegetal traits predominate, it is still known as a living body.

Even should it be questioned whether it is organic, it remains beyond question that it is a material object, and it is cognized by being recognized as such. Whence it is clear that a thing is perfectly known only when it is in all respects like certain things previously observed; that in proportion to the number of respects in which it is unlike them, is the extent to which it is unknown; and that hence when it has absolutely no attribute in common with anything else, it must be absolutely beyond the bound of knowledge.

Observe the corollary which here concerns us. A cognition of the Real, as distinguished from the Phenomenal, must, if it exists, conform to this law of cognition in general. The First Cause, the Infinite, the Absolute, to be known at all, must be classed. To be positively thought of, it must be thought of as such or such—as of this or that kind. Can it be like in kind to anything of which we have experience? Obviously not. Between the creating and the created, there must be a distinction transcending any of the distinctions between different divisions of the created. That which is uncaused cannot be assimilated to that which is caused: the two being, in the very naming, antithetically opposed. The Infinite cannot be grouped along with something finite; since, in being so grouped, it must be regarded as not-infinite. It is impossible to put the Absolute in the same category with anything relative, so long as the Absolute is defined as that of which no necessary relation can be predicated. Is it then that the Actual, though unthinkable by classification with the Apparent, is thinkable by classification with itself? This supposition is equally absurd with the other. It implies the plurality of the First Cause, the Infinite, the Absolute; and this implication is self-contradictory. There cannot be more than one First Cause; seeing that the existence of more than one would involve the existence of something necessitating more than one, which something would be the true First Cause. How self-destructive is the assumption of two or more Infinites, is manifest on remembering that such Infinites, by limiting each other, would become finite. And similarly, an Absolute which existed not alone but along with other Absolutes, would no longer be an absolute but a relative. The Unconditioned therefore, as classable neither with any form of the conditioned nor with any other Unconditioned, cannot be classed at all. And to admit that it cannot be known as of such or such kind, is to admit that it is unknowable.

Thus, from the very nature of thought, the relativity of our knowledge is inferable in three ways. As we find by analyzing it, and as we see it objectively displayed in every proposition, a thought involves *relation, difference, likeness.* Whatever does not present each of these does not admit of cognition. And hence we may say that the Unconditioned, as presenting none of them, is trebly unthinkable.

§ 25. From yet another point of view we may discern the same great truth. If, instead of examining our intellectual powers directly as displayed in the act of thought, or indirectly as displayed in thought when expressed by words, we look at the connexion between the mind and the world, a like conclusion is forced on us. The very definition of Life, phenomenally considered, when reduced to its most abstract shape, discloses this ultimate implication.

All vital actions, considered not separately but in their *ensemble,* have for their final purpose the balancing of certain outer processes by certain inner processes. There are external forces having a tendency to bring the matter of which living bodies consist into that stable equilibrium shown by inorganic bodies; there are internal forces by which this tendency is constantly antagonized; and the unceasing changes which constitute Life, may be regarded as incidental to the maintenance of the antagonism. For instance, to preserve the erect posture certain weights have to be neutralized by certain strains: each limb or other organ, gravitating to the Earth and pulling down the parts to which it is attached, has to be preserved in position by the tension of sundry muscles; or, in other words, the forces which would, if allowed, bring the body to the ground have to be counterbalanced by other forces. Again, to keep up the temperature at a particular point, the external process of radiation and absorption of heat by the surrounding medium, must be met by a corresponding internal process of chemical combination, whereby more heat may be evolved; to which add that if from atmospheric changes the loss becomes greater or less, the production must become greater or less. Similarly throughout the organic actions at large.

In the lower kinds of life the adjustments thus maintained are direct and simple; as in a plant, the vitality of which mainly consists in osmotic and chemical actions responding to the co-existence of light, heat, water, and carbon-dioxide around it. But in animals, and especially in the higher orders of them, the adjustments become extremely complex. Materials for growth and repair not being, like those which plants require, everywhere present, but being widely dispersed and under special forms, have to be found, to be secured, and to be reduced to a fit state for assimilation. Hence the need for locomotion; hence the need for the senses; hence the need for prehensile and destructive appliances; hence the need for an elaborate digestive apparatus. Observe, however, that these complications are nothing but aids to the maintenance of the organic balance, in opposition to those physical, chemical, and other agencies which tend to overturn it. And observe, further, that while these complications aid this fundamental adaptation of inner to outer actions, they are themselves nothing but additional adaptations of inner to outer actions. For what are those movements by which a predatory creature pursues its prey, or by which its prey seeks to escape, but certain changes in the organism fitted to meet certain changes in its environment? What is that operation which constitutes the perception of a piece of food, but a particular correlation of nervous modifications, answering to a particular correlation of physical properties? What is that process by which food when swallowed is made fit for assimilation, but a set of mechanical and chemical actions responding to the mechanical and chemical characters of the food? Hence, while Life in its simplest form is the correspondence of certain inner physico-chemical actions with certain outer physico-chemical actions, each advance to a higher form of Life consists in a better preservation of this primary correspondence by the establishment of other correspondences.

So that, passing over its noumenal nature of which we know nothing, Life is definable as the continuous adjustment of internal relations to external relations. And when we so define it, we discover that the physical and the psychical life are equally comprehended by the definition. This, which we call Intelligence, arises when the external relations to which the internal ones are adjusted become numerous, complex, and remote in time or space. Every advance in Intelligence essentially consists in the establishment of more varied, more complete, or more involved adjustments. And even the highest generalizations of science consist of mental relations of co-existence and sequence, so co-ordinated as exactly to tally with certain relations of co-existence and sequence that occur externally. A caterpillar, finding its way on to a plant having a certain odour, begins to eat—has inside of it an organic relation between a particular impression and a particular set of actions, answering to the relation outside of it between scent and nutriment. The sparrow, guided by the more complex correlation of impressions which the colour, form, and movements of the caterpillar gave it, and guided by other correlations which measure the position and distance of the caterpillar, adjusts certain correlated muscular movements so as to seize the caterpillar. Through a much greater distance is the hawk, hovering above, affected by the relations of shape and motion which the sparrow presents; and the much more complicated and prolonged series of related nervous and muscular changes, gone through in correspondence with the sparrow's changing relations of position, finally succeed when they are precisely adjusted to these changing relations. In the fowler, experience has established a relation between the appearance and flight of a hawk and the destruction of other birds, including game. There is also in him an established relation between those visual impressions answering to a certain distance in space, and the range of his gun. And he has learned, too, what relations of position the sights must bear to a point somewhat in advance of the flying bird, before he can fire with success. Similarly if we go back to the manufacture of the gun. By relations of co-existence between colour, density, and place in the earth, a particular mineral is known as one which yields iron; and the obtainment of iron from it, results when certain correlated acts of ours are adjusted to certain correlated affinities displayed by ironstone, coal, and lime, at a high temperature. If we descend yet a step further, and ask a chemist to explain the explosion of gunpowder, or apply to a mathematician for a theory of projectiles, we still find that special or general relations of co-existence and sequence among properties, motions, spaces, &c., are all they can teach us. And lastly, let it be noted that what we call *truth*, guiding us to successful action and consequent maintenance of life, is simply the accurate correspondence of subjective to objective relations; while *error*, leading to failure and therefore towards death, is the absence of such accurate correspondence.

If, then, Life, as knowable by us, inclusive of Intelligence in its highest forms, consists in the continuous adjustment of internal relations to external relations, the relative character of our knowledge is necessarily implied. The simplest cognition being the establishment of some connexion between subjective states, answering to some connexion between objective agencies; and each successively more complex cognition being the establishment of some more involved connexion of such states, answering to some more involved connexion of such agencies; it is clear that the process, no matter how far it be carried, can never bring within the reach of Intelligence, either the states themselves or the agencies themselves. Ascertaining which things occur along with which, and what things follow what, supposing it to be pursued exhaustively, must still leave us with co-existences and sequences only. If every act of knowing is the formation of a relation in consciousness answering to a relation in the environment, then the relativity of knowledge is self-evident—becomes indeed a truism. Thinking being relationing, no thought can ever express more than relations.

And here let us note how that to which our intelligence is confined is that with which alone our intelligence is concerned. The knowledge within our reach is the only knowledge that can be of service to us. This maintenance of a correspondence between internal actions and external actions, merely requires that the agencies acting upon us shall be known in their co-existences and sequences, and not that they shall be known in themselves. If $x$ and $y$ are two uniformly connected properties in some outer object, while $a$ and $b$ are the effects they produce in our consciousness, then the sole need is that $a$ and $b$ and the relation between them, shall always answer to $x$ and $y$ and the relation between them. It matters nothing to us if $a$ and $b$ are like $x$ and $y$ or not. Could they be identical with them, we should not be one whit the better off; and their total dissimilarity is no disadvantage.

Deep down then in the very nature of Life, the relativity of our knowledge is discernible. The analysis of vital actions in general, leads not only to the conclusion that things in themselves cannot be known to us, but also to the conclusion that knowledge of them, were it possible, would be useless.

§ 26. There remains the final question—What must we say concerning that which transcends knowledge? Are we to rest wholly in the consciousness of phenomena? Is the result of inquiry to exclude utterly from our minds everything but the relative? or must we also believe in something beyond the relative?

The answer of pure logic is held to be that by the limits of our intelligence we are rigorously confined within the relative, and that anything transcending the relative can be thought of only as a pure negation, or as a non-existence. "The *absolute* is conceived merely by a negation of conceivability," writes Sir William Hamilton. "The *Absolute* and the *Infinite*," says Mr. Mansel, "are thus, like the *Inconceivable* and the *Imperceptible*, names indicating, not an object of thought or of consciousness at all, but the mere absence of the conditions under which consciousness is possible." So that since reason cannot warrant us in affirming the positive existence of that which is cognizable only as a negation, we cannot rationally affirm the positive existence of anything beyond phenomena.

Unavoidable as this conclusion seems, it involves, I think, a grave error. If the premiss be granted the inference must be admitted; but the premiss, in the form presented by Sir William Hamilton and Mr. Mansel, is not strictly true. Though, in the foregoing pages, the arguments used by these writers to show that the Absolute is unknowable, have been approvingly quoted; and though these arguments have been enforced by others equally thoroughgoing; yet there remains to be stated a qualification which saves us from the scepticism otherwise necessitated. It is not to be denied that so long as we confine ourselves to the purely logical aspect of the question, the propositions quoted above must be accepted in their entirety; but when we contemplate its more general, or psychological, aspect, we find that these propositions are imperfect statements of the truth : omitting, or rather excluding, as they do, an all-important fact. To speak specifically :—Besides that *definite* consciousness of which Logic formulates the laws, there is also an *indefinite* consciousness which cannot be formulated. Besides complete thoughts, and besides the thoughts which though incomplete admit of completion, there are thoughts which it is impossible to complete, and yet which are still real, in the sense that they are normal affections of the intellect.

Observe, in the first place, that every one of the arguments by which the relativity of our knowledge is demonstrated, distinctly postulates the positive existence of something beyond the relative. To say that we cannot know the Absolute, is, by implication, to affirm that there *is* an Absolute. In the very denial of our power to learn *what* the Absolute is, there lies hidden the assumption *that* it is; and the making of this assumption proves that the Absolute has been present to the mind, not as a nothing but as a something. Similarly with every step in the reasoning by which this doctrine is upheld. The Noumenon, everywhere named as the antithesis to the Phenomenon, is necessarily thought of as an actuality. It is impossible to conceive that our knowledge is a knowledge of Appearances only, without at the same time assuming a Reality of which they are appearances ; for appearance without reality is unthinkable. Strike out from the argument the terms Unconditioned, Infinite, Absolute, and in place of them write, " negation of conceivability," or " absence of the conditions under which consciousness is possible," and the argument becomes nonsense. To realize in thought any one of the propositions of which the argument consists, the Unconditioned must be represented as positive and not negative. How then can it be a legitimate conclusion from the argument, that our consciousness of it is negative ? An argument the very construction of which assigns to a certain term a certain meaning, but which ends in showing that this term has no such meaning, is simply an elaborate suicide. Clearly, then, the very demonstration that a *definite* consciousness of the Absolute is impossible to us, unavoidably presupposes an *indefinite* consciousness of it.

Perhaps the best way of showing that we are obliged to form

5

a positive though vague consciousness of this which transcends distinct consciousness, is to analyze our conception of the antithesis between Relative and Absolute. It is a doctrine called in question by none, that such antinomies of thought as Whole and Part, Equal and Unequal, Singular and Plural, are necessarily conceived as correlatives: the conception of a part is impossible without the conception of a whole; there can be no idea of equality without one of inequality. And it is undeniable that in the same manner, the Relative is itself conceivable as such, only by opposition to the Irrelative or Absolute.          Sir William Hamilton, however, in his trenchant (and in most parts unanswerable) criticism on Cousin, contends, in conformity with his position above stated, that one of these correlatives is nothing more than the negation of the other. "Correlatives," he says, "certainly suggest each other, but correlatives may, or may not, be equally real and positive. In thought contradictories necessarily imply each other, for the knowledge of contradictories is one. But the reality of one contradictory, so far from guaranteeing the reality of the other, is nothing else than its negation. Thus every positive notion (the concept of a thing by what it is) suggests a negative notion (the concept of a thing by what it is not); and the highest positive notion, the notion of the conceivable, is not without its corresponding negative in the notion of the inconceivable. But though these mutually suggest each other, the positive alone is real; the negative is only an abstraction of the other, and in the highest generality, even an abstraction of thought itself."          Now the assertion that of such contradictories "the negative is *only* an abstraction of the other"—"is *nothing else* than its negation,"—is not true. In such correlatives as Equal and Unequal, it is obvious enough that the negative concept contains something besides the negation of the positive one; for the things of which equality is denied are not abolished from consciousness by the denial. And the fact overlooked by Sir William Hamilton is, that the like holds even with those correlatives of which the negative is inconceivable, in the strict sense of the word. Take for example the Limited and the Unlimited. Our notion of the Limited is composed, firstly of a consciousness of some kind of being, and secondly of a consciousness of the limits under which it is known. In the antithetical notion of the Unlimited, the consciousness of limits is abolished, but not .the consciousness of some kind of being. It is quite true that in the absence of conceived limits, this consciousness ceases to be a concept properly so called; but it is none the less true that it remains as a mode of consciousness. If, in such cases, the negative contradictory were, as alleged, "*nothing else*" than the negation of the other, and therefore a mere non-entity, then it would follow that negative contradictories could be used interchangeably: the Unlimited might be thought of as antithetical to the Divisible; and the Indivisible as antithetical to the Limited. While the fact that they cannot be so used, proves that in consciousness the Unlimited and the Indivisible are qualitatively distinct, and therefore positive or real; since distinction cannot exist between nothings. The error, (naturally fallen into by philosophers intent on demonstrating the limits and conditions of consciousness,) consists in assuming that consciousness contains *nothing but* limits and conditions; to the entire neglect of that which is limited and conditioned. It is forgotten that there is something which alike forms the raw material of definite thought and remains after the definiteness which thinking gave it has been destroyed.  Now all this applies by change of terms to the last and highest of these antinomies—that between the Relative and the Non-relative. We are conscious of the Relative as existence under conditions and limits. It is impossible that these conditions and limits can be thought of apart from something to which they give the form. The abstraction of these conditions and limits is, by the hypothesis, the abstraction of them *only*. Consequently there must be a residuary consciousness of something which filled up their outlines. And this indefinite something constitutes our consciousness of the Non-relative or Absolute. Impossible though it is to give to this consciousness any qualitative or quantitative expression whatever, it is not the less certain that it remains with us as a positive and indestructible element of thought.

More manifest still will this truth become when it is observed that our conception of the Relative itself disappears, if our consciousness of the Absolute is a pure negation. It is admitted, or rather it is contended, by the writers I have quoted above, that contradictories can be known only in relation to each other— that Equality, for instance, is unthinkable apart from Inequality; and that thus the Relative can itself be conceived only by opposition to the Non-relative. It is also admitted, or rather contended, that the consciousness of a relation implies a consciousness of both the related terms. If we are required to conceive the relation between the Relative and Non-relative without being conscious of both, " we are in fact" (to quote the words of Mr. Mansel differently applied) " required to compare that of which we are conscious with that of which we are not conscious; the comparison itself being an act of consciousness, and only possible through the consciousness of both its objects." What then becomes of the assertion that " the Absolute is conceived merely by a negation of conceivability," or as " the mere absence of the conditions under which consciousness is possible?" If the Non-relative or Absolute is present in thought only as a mere negation, then the relation between it and the Relative becomes unthinkable, because one of the terms of the relation is absent from consciousness. And if this relation is unthinkable, then is the Relative itself unthinkable, for want of its antithesis: whence results the disappearance of all thought whatever.

Both Sir William Hamilton and Mr. Mansel do, in other places, distinctly imply that our consciousness of the Absolute, indefinite though it is, is positive. The very passage in which Sir William Hamilton asserts that " the *absolute* is conceived merely by a negation of conceivability," itself ends with the remark that, " by a wonderful revelation we are thus, in the very consciousness of our inability to conceive aught above the relative and finite, inspired with a belief in the existence of something unconditioned beyond the sphere of all comprehensible reality." The last of these assertions practically admits that which the first denies. By the laws of thought as Sir William Hamilton interprets them, he finds himself forced to the conclusion that our consciousness of the Absolute is a pure negation. He nevertheless finds that there does exist in consciousness an irresistible conviction of the real " existence of something unconditioned." And he gets over the inconsistency by speaking of this conviction as " a wonderful revelation,"—" a belief" with which we are " inspired": thus apparently hinting that it is supernaturally at variance with the laws of thought.  Mr. Mansel is betrayed into a like inconsistency. When he says that " we are compelled, by the constitution of our minds, to believe in the existence of an Absolute and Infinite Being, —a belief which appears forced upon us, as the complement of our consciousness of the relative and the finite "; he clearly says by implication that this consciousness is positive, and not negative. He tacitly admits that we are obliged to regard the Absolute as something more than a negation—that our consciousness of it is *not* " the mere absence of the conditions under which consciousness is possible."

The supreme importance of this question must be my apology for taxing the reader's attention a little further, in the hope of clearing up the remaining difficulties.  The necessarily positive character of our consciousness of the Unconditioned, which, as we have seen, follows from an ultimate law of thought, will be better understood on contemplating the process of thought.

One of the arguments used to prove the relativity of our knowledge, is, that we cannot conceive Space or Time as either limited or unlimited.  It is pointed out that when we imagine a limit, there simultaneously arises the consciousness of a space or time beyond the limit.  This remoter space or time, though not contemplated as definite, is yet contemplated as real.  Though we do not form of it a conception proper, since we do not bring it within bounds, there is yet in our minds the unshaped material of a conception.  Similarly with our consciousness of Cause.  We are no more able to form a circumscribed idea of Cause, than of Space or Time; and we are consequently obliged to think of the Cause which transcends the limits of our thought as positive though indefinite.  As on conceiving any bounded space, there arises a nascent consciousness of space outside the bounds; so, when we think of any definite cause, there arises a nascent consciousness of a cause behind it; and in the one case as in the other, this nascent consciousness is in substance like that which suggests it, though without form.  The momentum of thought carries us beyond conditioned existence to unconditioned existence; and this ever persists in us as the body of a thought to which we can give no shape.

Hence our firm belief in objective reality.  When we are taught that a piece of matter, regarded by us as existing externally, cannot be really known, but that we can know only certain impressions produced on us, we are yet, by the relativity of thought, compelled to think of these in relation to a cause—the notion of a real existence which generated these impressions becomes nascent. If it be proved that every notion of a real existence which we can frame, is inconsistent with itself—that matter, however conceived by us, cannot be matter as it actually is, our conception, though transfigured, is not destroyed: there remains the sense of reality, dissociated as far as possible from those special forms under which it was before represented in thought. Though Philosophy condemns successively each attempted conception of the Absolute—though in obedience to it we negative, one after another, each idea as it arises; yet, as we cannot expel the entire contents of consciousness, there ever remains behind an element which passes into new shapes. The continual negation of each particular form and limit, simply results in the more or less complete abstraction of all forms and limits; and so ends in an indefinite consciousness of the unformed and unlimited.

And here we come face to face with the ultimate difficulty—How can there be constituted a consciousness of the unformed and unlimited, when, by its very nature, consciousness is possible only under forms and limits? Though not directly withdrawn by the withdrawal of its conditions, must not the raw material of consciousness be withdrawn by implication? Must it not vanish when the conditions of its existence vanish? That there must be a solution of this difficulty is manifest; since even those who would put it do, as already shown, admit that we have some such consciousness; and the solution appears to be that above shadowed forth. Such consciousness is not, and cannot be, constituted by any single mental act, but is the product of many mental acts. In each concept there is an element which persists. It is impossible for this element to be absent from consciousness, or for it to be present in consciousness alone. Either alternative involves unconsciousness—the one from want of the substance; the other from want of the form. But the persistence of this element under successive conditions, *necessitates* a sense of it as distinguished from the conditions, and independent of them. The sense of a something that is conditioned in every thought cannot be got rid of, because the something cannot be got rid of. How then must the sense of this something be constituted? Evidently by combining successive concepts deprived of their limits and conditions. We form this indefinite thought, as we form many of our definite thoughts, by the coalescence of a series of thoughts. Let me illustrate this. A large complex object, having attributes too numerous to be represented at once, is yet tolerably well conceived by the union of several representations, each standing for part of its attributes. On thinking of a piano, there first rises in imagination its outer appearance, to which are instantly added (though by separate mental acts) the ideas of its remote side and of its solid substance. A complete conception, however, involves the strings, the hammers, the dampers, the pedals; and while successively adding these, the attributes first thought of lapse partially or wholly out of consciousness. Nevertheless, the whole group constitutes a representation of the piano. Now as in this case we form a definite concept of a special existence, by imposing limits and conditions in successive acts; so, in the converse case, by taking away limits and conditions in successive acts, we form an indefinite notion of general existence. By fusing a series of states of consciousness, from each of which, as it arises, the limitations and conditions are abolished, there is produced a consciousness of something unconditioned. To speak more rigorously:—this consciousness is not the abstract of any one group of thoughts, ideas, or conceptions; but it is the abstract of *all* thoughts, ideas, or conceptions. That which is common to them all we predicate by the word existence. Dissociated as this becomes from each of its modes by the perpetual change of those modes, it remains as an indefinite consciousness of something constant under all modes—of being apart from its appearances. The distinction we feel between specialized existences and general existence, is the distinction between that which is changeable in us and that which is unchangeable. The contrast between the Absolute and the Relative in our minds, is really the contrast between that mental element which exists absolutely, and those which exist relatively.

So that this ultimate mental element is at once necessarily

indefinite and necessarily indestructible. Our consciousness of the unconditioned being literally the unconditioned consciousness, or raw material of thought to which in thinking we give definite forms, it follows that an ever-present sense of real existence is the basis of our intelligence. As we can in successive mental acts get rid of all particular conditions and replace them by others, but cannot get rid of that undifferentiated substance of consciousness which is conditioned anew in every thought, there ever remains with us a sense of that which exists persistently and independently of conditions. While by the laws of thought we are prevented from forming a conception of absolute existence; we are by the laws of thought prevented from excluding the consciousness of absolute existence: this consciousness being, as we here see, the obverse of self-consciousness. And since the measure of relative validity among our beliefs, is the degree of their persistence in opposition to the efforts made to change them, it follows that this which persists at all times, under all circumstances, has the highest validity of any.

The points in this somewhat too elaborate argument are these:— In the very assertion that all knowledge, properly so called, is Relative, there is involved the assertion that there exists a Non-relative. In each step of the argument by which this doctrine is established, the same assumption is made. From the necessity of thinking in relations, it follows that the Relative is itself inconceivable, except as related to a real Non-relative. Unless a real Non-relative or Absolute be postulated, the Relative itself becomes absolute, and so brings the argument to a contradiction. And on watching our thoughts we have seen how impossible it is to get rid of the consciousness of an Actuality lying behind Appearances; and how, from this impossibility, results our indestructible belief in that Actuality.

# CHAPTER V

## THE RECONCILIATION

§ 27. THUS do all lines of argument converge to the same conclusion. Those imbecilities of the understanding which disclose themselves when we try to answer the highest questions of objective science, subjective science proves to be necessitated by the laws of that understanding. Finally, we discover that this conclusion which, in its unqualified form, seems opposed to the instinctive convictions of mankind, falls into harmony with them when the missing qualification is supplied.

Here, then, is that basis of agreement we set out to seek. This conclusion which objective science illustrates and subjective science shows to be unavoidable,—this conclusion which brings the results of speculation into harmony with those of common sense; is also the conclusion which reconciles Religion with Science. Common Sense asserts the existence of a reality; Objective Science proves that this reality cannot be what we think it; Subjective Science shows why we cannot think of it as it is, and yet are compelled to think of it as existing; and in this assertion of a Reality utterly inscrutable in nature, Religion finds an assertion essentially coinciding with her own. We are obliged to regard every phenomenon as a manifestation of some Power by which we are acted upon; though Omnipresence is unthinkable, yet, as experience discloses no bounds to the diffusion of phenomena, we are unable to think of limits to the presence of this Power; while the criticisms of Science teach us that this Power is Incomprehensible. And this consciousness of an Incomprehensible Power, called Omnipresent from inability to assign its limits, is just that consciousness on which Religion dwells.

To understand fully how real is the reconciliation thus reached, it will be needful to look at the respective attitudes that Religion and Science have all along maintained towards this conclusion.

§ 28. In its earliest and crudest forms Religion manifested, however vaguely and inconsistently, an intuition forming the germ of this highest belief in which philosophies finally unite. The consciousness of a mystery is traceable in the rudest ghost theory. Each higher creed, rejecting those definite and simple interpreta- tions of Nature previously given, has become more religious by doing this. As the concrete and conceivable agencies assigned as the causes of things, have been replaced by agencies less concrete and conceivable, the element of mystery has necessarily become more predominant. Through all its phases the disappearance of those dogmas by which the mystery was made unmysterious, has formed the essential change delineated in religious history. And so Religion has been approaching towards that complete recog- nition of this mystery which is its goal.

For its essentially valid belief Religion has constantly done battle. Gross as were the disguises under which it first espoused this belief, and cherishing this belief, even still, under disfiguring vestments, it has never ceased to maintain and defend it. Though from age to age Science has continually defeated it wherever they have come in collision, and has obliged it to relinquish one or more of its positions, it has held the remaining ones with undiminished tenacity. After criticism has abolished its arguments, there has still remained with it the indestructible consciousness of a truth which, however faulty the mode in which it had been expressed, is yet a truth beyond cavil.

But while from the beginning, Religion has had the all-essential office of preventing men from being wholly absorbed in the relative or immediate, and of awakening them to a consciousness of some- thing beyond it, this office has been but very imperfectly discharged. In its early stages the consciousness of supernature being simply the consciousness of numerous supernatural persons essentially man- like, was not far removed from the ordinary consciousness. As thus constituted, Religion was and has ever been more or less irreligious; and indeed continues to be largely irreligious even now.        In the first place (restricting ourselves to Religion in its more developed form), it has all along professed to have some knowledge of that which transcends knowledge, and has so contradicted its own teachings.  While with one breath it has asserted that the Cause of all things passes understanding, it has, with the next breath, asserted that the Cause of all things possesses such or such attributes—can be in so far understood.        In the second place, while in great part sincere in its fealty to the great truth it has had to uphold, it has often been insincere, and consequently irreligious, in maintaining the untenable doctrines by which it has obscured this great truth.  Each assertion respecting the nature, acts, or motives of that Power which the Universe manifests to us, has been repeatedly called in question, and proved to be inconsistent with itself, or with accompanying assertions. Yet each of them has been age after age insisted on.  Just as though unaware that its central position was impregnable, Religion has obstinately held every outpost long after it was obviously indefensible.        And this introduces us to the third and most serious form of irreligion which Religion has displayed ; namely, an imperfect belief in that which it especially professes to believe. How truly its central position *is* impregnable, Religion has never adequately realized.  In the devoutest faith as we commonly see it, there lies hidden a core of scepticism ; and it is this scepticism which causes that dread of inquiry shown by Religion when face to face with Science.  Obliged to abandon one by one the superstitions it once tenaciously held, and daily finding other cherished beliefs .more and more shaken, Religion secretly fears that all things may some day be explained ; and thus itself betrays a lurking doubt whether that Incomprehensible Cause of which it is conscious, is really incomprehensible.

Of Religion then, we must always remember, that amid its many errors and corruptions it has asserted and diffused a supreme verity.  From the first, the recognition of this supreme verity, in however imperfect a manner, has been its vital element ; and its chief defects, once extreme but gradually diminishing, have been its failures to recognize in full that which it recognized in part.  The truly religious element of Religion has always been good ; that which has proved untenable in doctrine and vicious in practice, has been its irreligious element; and from this it has been undergoing purification.

§ 29. And now observe that the agent which has effected the purification has been Science. On both sides this fact is overlooked. Religion ignores its immense debt to Science; and Science is scarcely at all conscious how much Religion owes it. Yet it is demonstrable that every step by which Religion has progressed from its first low conception to the comparatively high one now reached, Science has helped it, or rather forced it, to take; and that even now, Science is urging further steps in the same direction.

When we include under the name Science all definite knowledge of the order existing among phenomena, it becomes manifest that from the outset, the discovery of an established order has modified that conception of disorder, or undetermined order, which underlies every superstition. As fast as experience proves that certain familiar changes always present the same sequences, there begins to fade from the mind the conception of special personalities to whose variable wills they were before ascribed. And when, step by step, accumulating observations do the like with the less familiar changes, a similar modification of belief takes place respecting them.

While this process seems to those who effect it, and those who undergo it, an anti-religious one, it is really the reverse. Instead of the specific comprehensible agency before assigned, there is substituted a less specific and less comprehensible agency; and though this, standing in opposition to the previous one, cannot at first call forth the same feeling, yet, as being less comprehensible, it must eventually call forth this feeling more fully. Take an instance. Of old the Sun was regarded as the chariot of a god, drawn by horses. How far the idea thus grossly expressed was idealized, we need not inquire. It suffices to remark that this accounting for the apparent motion of the Sun by an agency like certain visible terrestrial agencies, reduced a daily wonder to the level of the commonest intellect. When, many centuries after, Copernicus having enunciated the heliocentric theory of the solar system, Kepler discovered that the orbits of the planets are ellipses,

and that the planets describe equal areas in equal times, he concluded
that in each of them there must exist a spirit to guide its movements.  Here we see that with the progress of Science, there had
disappeared the idea of a gross mechanical traction, such as was
first assigned in the case of the Sun ; but that while for the celestial
motions there was substituted a less-easily conceivable force, it
was still thought needful to assume personal agents as causes of
the regular irregularity of the motions.  When, finally, it was
proved that these planetary revolutions with all their variations
and disturbances, conform to one universal law—when the presiding spirits which Kepler conceived were set aside, and the force of
gravitation put in their places ; the change was really the abolition
of an imaginable agency, and the substitution of an unimaginable
one.  For though the *law* of gravitation is within our mental
grasp, it is impossible to realize in thought the *force* of gravitation.
Newton himself confessed the force of gravitation to be incomprehensible without the intermediation of an ether ; and, as we have
already seen, (§ 18,) the assumption of an ether does not help
us.          Thus it is with Science in general.  Its progress in
grouping particular relations of phenomena under laws, and these
special laws under laws more and more general, is of necessity a
progress to causes more and more abstract.  And causes more and
more abstract, are of necessity causes less and less conceivable;
since the formation of an abstract conception involves the dropping of certain concrete elements of thought.  Hence the most
abstract conception, to which Science is slowly approaching, is
one that merges into the inconceivable or unthinkable, by the
dropping of all concrete elements of thought.  And so is justified
the assertion that the beliefs which Science has forced upon
Religion, have been intrinsically more religious than those which
they supplanted.
     Science, however, like Religion, has but very incompletely
fulfilled its office.  As Religion has fallen short of its function in
so far as it has been irreligious ; so has Science fallen short of its
function in so far as it has been unscientific.  Let us note the
several parallelisms.          In its earlier stages Science, while it
began to teach the constant relations of phenomena, and thus
discredited the belief in separate personalities as the causes of

them, itself substituted the belief in causal agencies which, if not personal, were yet concrete. When certain facts were said to show "Nature's abhorrence of a vacuum," when the properties of gold were explained as due to some entity called "aureity," and when the phenomena of life were attributed to "a vital principle"; there was set up a mode of interpreting the facts which, while antagonistic to the religious mode, because assigning other agencies, was also unscientific, because it assumed a knowledge of that about which nothing was known. Having abandoned these metaphysical agencies—having seen that they are not independent existences, but merely special combinations of general causes, Science has more recently ascribed extensive groups of phenomena to electricity, chemical affinity, and other like general powers. But in speaking of these as ultimate and independent entities, Science has preserved substantially the same attitude as before. Accounting thus for all phenomena, it has not only maintained its seeming antagonism to Religion, by alleging agencies of a radically unlike kind; but, in so far as it has tacitly implied its comprehension of these agencies, it has continued unscientific. At the present time, however, the most advanced men of science are abandoning these later conceptions, as their predecessors abandoned the earlier ones. Magnetism, heat, light, &c., which were early in the century spoken of as so many distinct imponderables, physicists now regard as different modes of manifestation of some one universal force; and in so regarding them are ceasing to think of this force as comprehensible. In each phase of its progress, Science has thus stopped short with superficial solutions—has unscientifically neglected to ask what were the natures of the agents it familiarly invoked. Though in each succeeding phase it has gone a little deeper, and merged its supposed agents in more general and abstract ones, it has still, as before, rested content with these as if they were ascertained realities. And this, which has all along been an unscientific characteristic of Science, has all along been a part-cause of its conflict with Religion.

§ 30. Thus from the outset the faults of both Religion and Science have been the faults of imperfect development. Originally a mere rudiment, each has been growing more complete; the vice of each has in all times been its incompleteness; the disagreements between them have been consequences of their incompleteness; and as they reach their final forms they come into harmony.

The progress of intelligence has throughout been dual. Though it has not seemed so to those who made it, every step in advance has been a step towards both the natural and the supernatural. The better interpretation of each phenomenon has been, on the one hand, the rejection of a cause that was relatively conceivable in its nature but unknown in the order of its actions, and, on the other hand, the adoption of a cause that was known in the order of its actions but relatively inconceivable in its nature. The first advance involved the conception of agencies less assimilable to the familiar agencies of men and animals, and therefore less understood; while, at the same time, such newly-conceived agencies, in so far as they were distinguished by their uniform effects, were better understood than those they replaced. All subsequent advances display the same double result; and thus the progress has been as much towards the establishment of a positively unknown as towards the establishment of a positively known. Though as knowledge advances, unaccountable and seemingly supernatural facts are brought into the category of facts that are accountable or natural; yet, at the same time, all accountable or natural facts are proved to be in their ultimate genesis unaccountable and supernatural. And so there arise two antithetical states of mind, answering to the opposite sides of that existence about which we think. While our consciousness of Nature under the one aspect constitutes Science, our consciousness of it under the other aspect constitutes Religion.

In other words, Religion and Science have been undergoing a slow differentiation, and their conflicts have been due to the imperfect separation of their spheres and functions. Religion has, from the first, struggled to unite more or less science with its nescience; Science has, from the first, kept hold of more or less nescience as though it were a part of science. So long as the process of differentiation is incomplete, more or less of antagonism must continue. Gradually as the limits of possible cognition are established, the causes of conflict will diminish. And a permanent peace will be reached when Science becomes fully convinced that its explanations are proximate and relative, while Religion becomes fully convinced that the mystery it contemplates is ultimate and absolute.

Religion and Science are therefore necessary correlatives. To carry further a metaphor before used,—they are the positive and negative poles of thought ; of which neither can gain in intensity without increasing the intensity of the other.

§ 31. Some do indeed allege that though the Ultimate Cause of things cannot really be conceived by us as having specified attributes, it is yet incumbent upon us to assert those attributes. Though the forms of our consciousness are such that the Absolute cannot in any manner or degree be brought within them, we are nevertheless told that we must represent the Absolute to ourselves as having certain characters. As writes Mr. Mansel, in the work from which I have already quoted largely—" It is our duty, then, to think of God as personal ; and it is our duty to believe that He is infinite."

Now if there be any meaning in the foregoing arguments, duty requires us neither to affirm nor deny personality. Our duty is to submit ourselves to the established limits of our intelligence, and not perversely to rebel against them. Let those who can, believe that there is eternal war set between our intellectual faculties and our moral obligations. I, for one, admit no such radical vice in the constitution of things.

This which to most will seem an essentially irreligious position, is an essentially religious one—nay is *the* religious one, to which, as already shown, all others are but approximations. In the estimate it implies of the Ultimate Cause, it does not fall short of the alternative position, but exceeds it. Those who espouse this alternative position, assume that the choice is between personality and something lower than personality ; whereas the choice is rather between personality and something that may be higher. Is it not possible that there is a mode of being as much transcending Intelligence and Will, as these transcend mechanical motion? Doubtless we are totally unable to imagine any such higher mode of being. But this is not a reason for questioning its existence; it is rather the reverse. Have we not seen how utterly unable our minds are to form even an approach to a conception of that which

underlies all phenomena? Is it not proved that we fail because of
the incompetency of the Conditioned to grasp the Unconditioned?
Does it not follow that the Ultimate Cause cannot in any respect
be conceived because it is in every respect greater than can be
conceived? And may we not therefore rightly refrain from assigning to it any attributes whatever, on the ground that such
attributes, derived as they must be from our own natures, are not
elevations but degradations? Indeed it seems strange that men
should suppose the highest worship to lie in assimilating the object
of their worship to themselves. Not in asserting a transcendent
difference, but in asserting a certain likeness, consists the element
of their creed which they think essential. It is true that from the
time when the rudest savages imagined the causes of things to be
persons like themselves but invisible, down to our own time, the
degree of assumed likeness has been diminishing. But though a
bodily form and substance similar to that of man, has long since
ceased, among cultivated races, to be a literally-conceived attribute
of the Ultimate Cause—though the grosser human desires have
been also rejected as unfit elements of the conception—though
there is some hesitation in ascribing even the higher human feelings,
save in idealized shapes; yet it is still thought not only proper,
but imperative, to ascribe the most abstract qualities of our nature.
To think of the Creative Power as in all respects anthropomorphous,
is now considered impious by men who yet hold themselves bound
to think of the Creative Power as in some respects anthropomorphous; and who do not see that the one proceeding is but an
evanescent form of the other. And then, most marvellous of all,
this course is persisted in even by those who contend that we are
wholly unable to frame any conception whatever of the Creative
Power. After it has been shown that every supposition respecting
the genesis of the Universe commits us to alternative impossibilities
of thought—after it has been shown why, by the very constitution
of our minds, we are debarred from thinking of the Absolute; it
is still asserted that we ought to think of the Absolute thus and
thus. In all ways we find thrust on us the truth, that we are not
permitted to know—nay are not even permitted to conceive—that
Reality which is behind the veil of Appearance; and yet it is said
to be our duty to believe (and in so far to conceive) that this

6

Reality exists in a certain defined manner. Shall we call this reverence? or shall we call it the reverse?

Volumes might be written upon the impiety of the pious. Through the printed and spoken thoughts of religious teachers, may everywhere be traced a professed familiarity with the ultimate mystery of things, which, to say the least of it, is anything but congruous with the accompanying expressions of humility. The attitude thus assumed can be fitly represented only by further developing a simile long current in theological controversies—the simile of the watch. If for a moment we made the grotesque supposition that the tickings and other movements of a watch constituted a kind of consciousness; and that a watch possessed of such a consciousness, insisted on regarding the watchmaker's actions as determined like its own by springs and escapements; we should simply complete a parallel of which religious teachers think much. And were we to suppose that a watch not only formulated the cause of its existence in these mechanical terms, but held that watches were bound out of reverence so to formulate this cause, and even vituperated, as atheistic watches, any that did not venture so to formulate it; we should merely illustrate the presumption of theologians by carrying their own argument a step further.　　　A few extracts will bring home to the reader the justice of this comparison. We are told, for example, by one of high repute among religious thinkers, that the Universe is "the manifestation and abode of a Free Mind, like our own; embodying His personal thought in its adjustments, realizing His own ideal in its phenomena, just as we express our inner faculty and character through the natural language of an external life. In this view, we interpret Nature by Humanity; we find the key to her aspects in such purposes and affections as our own consciousness enables us to conceive; we look everywhere for physical signals of an ever-living Will; and decipher the universe as the autobiography of an Infinite Spirit, repeating itself in miniature within our Finite Spirit." The same writer goes still further. He not only thus parallels the assimilation of the watchmaker to the watch,—he not only thinks the created can "decipher" "the autobiography" of the Creating; but he asserts that the necessary limits to the one are necessary limits to the other. The primary qualities of bodies, he says, "belong eternally to the material datum objective to God" and control his acts; while the secondary ones are "products of pure Inventive Reason and Determining Will"—constitute "the realm of Divine originality." * * * "While on this Secondary field His Mind and ours are thus contrasted, they meet in resemblance again upon the Primary; for the evolutions of deductive Reason there is but one track possible to all intelligences; no *merum arbitrium* can interchange the false and true, or make more than one geometry, one scheme of pure Physics, for all worlds; and the Omnipotent Architect Himself, in realizing the Kosmical conception, in shaping the orbits out of immensity and determining seasons out of eternity, could but follow the laws of curvature, measure and proportion." That is to say, the Ultimate Cause is like a human mechanic, not only as "shaping" the "material datum objective to" Him, but also as being obliged to conform to the necessary properties of that datum. Nor is this all. There follows some account of "the Divine psychology," to the extent of saying that "we learn" "the character of God—the order of affections in Him" from "the distribution of authority in the hierarchy of our impulses." In other words, it is alleged that the Ultimate Cause has desires that are to be classed as higher and lower like our own.* Every one has heard of the king who wished he had been present at the creation of the world, that he might have given good advice. He was humble, however, compared with those who profess to understand not only the relation of the Creating to the created, but also how the Creating is constituted. And yet this transcendent audacity, which thinks to penetrate the secrets of the Power manifested through all existence—nay, even to stand behind that Power and note the conditions to its action—this it is which passes current as piety! May we not affirm that a sincere recognition of the truth that our own and all other existence is a mystery absolutely beyond our comprehension, contains more of true religion than all the dogmatic theology ever written?

Meanwhile let us recognize whatever of permanent good there is in these persistent attempts to frame conceptions of that which

* These extracts are from an article entitled "Nature and God," published in the *National Review* for October, 1860, by Dr. Martineau.

cannot be conceived. From the beginning it has been only through the successive failures of such conceptions to satisfy the mind, that higher and higher ones have been gradually reached; and doubtless, the conceptions now current are indispensable as transitional modes of thought. Even more than this may be willingly conceded. It is possible, nay probable, that under their most abstract forms, ideas of this order will always continue to occupy the background of our consciousness. Very likely there will ever remain a need to give shape to that indefinite sense of an Ultimate Existence, which forms the basis of our intelligence. We shall always be under the necessity of contemplating it as *some* mode of being; that is—of representing it to ourselves in *some* form of thought, however vague. And we shall not err in doing this so long as we treat every notion we thus frame as merely a symbol. Perhaps the constant formation of such symbols and constant rejection of them as inadequate, may be hereafter, as it has hitherto been, a means of discipline. Perpetually to construct ideas requiring the utmost stretch of our faculties, and perpetually to find that such ideas must be abandoned as futile imaginations, may realize to us more fully than any other course, the greatness of that which we vainly strive to grasp. By continually seeking to know and being continually thrown back with a deepened conviction of the impossibility of knowing, we may keep alive the consciousness that it is alike our highest wisdom and our highest duty to regard that through which all things exist as The Unknowable.

§ 32. An immense majority will refuse, with more or less of indignation, a belief seeming to them so shadowy and indefinite. "You offer us," they will say, "an unthinkable abstraction in place of a Being towards whom we may entertain definite feelings. Though we are told that the Absolute is the only reality, yet since we are not allowed to conceive it, it might as well be a pure negation. Instead of a Power which we can regard as having some sympathy with us, you would have us contemplate a Power to which no emotion whatever can be ascribed. And so we are to be deprived of the very substance of our faith."

This kind of protest of necessity accompanies every change from a lower creed to a higher. The belief in a community of nature between himself and the object of his worship, has always been to Man a satisfactory one; and he has always accepted with reluctance those successively less concrete conceptions which have been forced upon him. Doubtless, in all times and places, it has consoled the barbarian to think of his deities as so like himself in nature, that they might be bribed by offerings of food; and the assurance that deities could not be so propitiated must have been repugnant, because it deprived him of an easy method of gaining supernatural protection. To the Greeks it was manifestly a source of comfort that on occasions of difficulty they could obtain, through oracles, the advice of their gods,—nay, might even get the personal aid of their gods in battle; and it was probably a very genuine anger which they visited upon philosophers who called in question these gross ideas of their mythology. A religion which teaches the Hindoo that it is impossible to purchase eternal happiness by placing himself under the wheel of Juggernaut, can scarcely fail to seem a cruel one to him; since it deprives him of the pleasurable consciousness that he can at will exchange miseries for joys. Nor is it less clear that to our Catholic ancestors, the beliefs that crimes could be compounded for by the building of churches, that their own punishments and those of their relatives could be abridged by the saying of masses, and that divine aid or forgiveness might be gained through the intercession of saints, were highly solacing ones; and that Protestantism, in substituting the conception of a God so comparatively unlike themselves as not to be influenced by such methods, must have appeared hard and cold. Naturally, therefore, we must expect a further step in the same direction to meet with a similar resistance from outraged sentiments. No mental revolution can be accomplished without more or less laceration. Be it a change of habit or a change of conviction, it must, if the habit or conviction be strong, do violence to some of the feelings; and these must of course oppose it. For long-experienced, and therefore definite, sources of satisfaction, have to be substituted sources of satisfaction that have not been experienced, and are therefore indefinite. That which is relatively well known and real, has to be given up for that which is relatively unknown and ideal. And of course such an exchange cannot be made without a conflict involving pain. Especially, then, must there arise a strong antagonism to any alteration in so deep and vital a conception as that with which we are here dealing. Underlying, as this conception does, all ideas concerning the established order of things, a modification of it threatens to reduce the superstructure to ruins. Or to change the metaphor—being the root with which are connected our ideas of goodness, rectitude, or duty, it appears impossible that it should be transformed without causing these to wither away and die. The whole higher part of the nature takes up arms against a change which seems to eradicate morality.

This is by no means all that has to be said for such protests. There is a deeper meaning in them. They do not simply express the natural repugnance to a revolution of belief, here made specially intense by the vital importance of the belief to be revolutionized; but they also express an instinctive adhesion to a belief that is in one sense the best—the best for those who thus cling to it, though not abstractedly the best. For here it is to be remarked that what were above spoken of as the imperfections of Religion, at first great but gradually diminishing, have been imperfections as measured by an absolute standard, and not as measured by a relative one. Speaking generally, the religion current in each age and among each people, has been as near an approximation to the truth as it was then and there possible for men to receive. The concrete forms in which it has embodied the truth, have been the means of making thinkable what would otherwise have been unthinkable; and so have for the time being served to increase its impressiveness.       If we consider the conditions of the case, we shall find this to be an unavoidable conclusion. During each stage of progress men must think in such terms of thought as they possess. While all the conspicuous changes of which they can observe the origins, have men and animals as antecedents, they are unable to think of antecedents in general under any other shapes; and hence creative agencies are almost of necessity conceived by them in these shapes. If, during this phase, these concrete conceptions were taken from them and the attempt made to give them comparatively abstract conceptions, the result would be to leave their minds with none at all; since the substituted ones could not be mentally represented. Similarly with every successive stage of religious belief, down to the last. Though, as accumulating experiences slowly modify the earliest ideas of causal personalities, there grow up more general and vague ideas of them; yet these cannot be at once replaced by others still more general and vague. Further experiences must supply the needful further abstractions, before the mental void left by the destruction of such inferior ideas can be filled by ideas of a superior order. And at the present time, the refusal to abandon a relatively concrete consciousness for a relatively abstract one, implies the inability to frame the relatively abstract one; and so implies that the change would be premature and injurious. Still more clearly shall we see the injuriousness of any such premature change, on observing that the effects of a belief upon conduct must be diminished in proportion as the vividness with which it is realized becomes less. Evils and benefits akin to those which the savage has personally felt, or learned from those who have felt them, are the only evils and benefits he can understand; and these must be looked for as coming in ways like those of which he has had experience. His deities must be imagined to have like motives and passions and methods with the beings around him; for motives and passions and methods of a higher character, being unknown to him, and in great measure unthinkable by him, cannot be so represented in thought as to influence his deeds. During every phase of civilization, the actions of the Unseen Reality, as well as the resulting rewards and punishments, being conceivable only in such forms as experience furnishes, to supplant them by higher ones before wider experiences have made higher ones conceivable, is to set up vague and uninfluential motives for definite and influential ones. Even now, for the great mass of men, unable to trace out with clearness those good and bad consequences which conduct brings round through the established order of things, it is well that there should be depicted future punishments and future joys—pains and pleasures of definite kinds, produced in ways direct and simple enough to be clearly imagined. Nay still more must be conceded. Few are as yet wholly fitted to dispense with such conceptions as are current. The highest abstractions take so great a mental power to realize with any vividness, and are so inoperative on conduct unless they are vividly realized, that their regulative effects must for a long period to come be appreciable on but a small minority. To see clearly how a right or wrong act generates consequences, internal and external, that go on branching out more widely as years progress, requires a rare power of analysis. And to estimate these consequences in their totality requires a grasp of thought possessed by none. Were it not that throughout the progress of the race, men's experiences of the effects of conduct have been slowly generalized into principles—were it not that these principles have been from generation to generation insisted on by parents, upheld by public opinion, sanctified by religion, and enforced by threats of eternal damnation for disobedience—were it not that under these potent influences habits have been modified, and the feelings proper to them made innate ; disastrous results would follow the removal of those strong and distinct motives which the current belief supplies. Even as it is, those who relinquish the faith in which they have been brought up, for this most abstract · faith in which Science and Religion unite, may not uncommonly fail to act up to their convictions. Left to their organic morality, enforced only by general reasonings difficult to keep before the mind, their defects of nature will often come out more strongly than they would have done under their previous creed. The substituted creed can become adequately operative only when it becomes, like the present one, an element in early education, and has the support of a strong social sanction. Nor will men be quite ready for it until, through the continuance of a discipline which has partially moulded them to the conditions of social existence, they are completely moulded to those conditions.

We must therefore recognize the resistance to a change of theological opinion, as in great measure salutary. Forms of religion, like forms of government, must be fit for those who live under them ; and in the one case as in the other, the form which is fittest is that for which there is an instinctive preference. As a barbarous race needs a harsh terrestrial rule, and shows attachment to a despotism capable of the necessary rigour ; so does such a race need a belief in a celestial rule that is similarly harsh, and shows attachment to such a belief. And as the sudden substitution of free institutions for despotic ones, is sure to be followed by a re-

action; so, if a creed full of dreadful ideal penalties is all at once
replaced by one presenting ideal penalties that are comparatively
gentle, there will inevitably be a return to some modification of the
old belief.          The parallelism holds yet further. During those
early stages in which there is extreme incongruity between the relatively best and the absolutely best, both political and religious
changes, when at rare intervals they occur, are violent; and they
entail violent retrogressions.    But as the incongruity between that
which is and that which should be, diminishes, the changes become
more moderate, and are succeeded by more moderate counter-movements; until, as these movements and counter-movements decrease
in amount and increase in frequency, they merge into an almost
continuous growth.   This holds true of religious creeds and forms,
as of civil ones.   And so we learn that theological conservatism,
like political conservatism, has an important function.

§ 33. That spirit of toleration which is so marked a trait of
modern times, has thus a deeper meaning than is supposed.   What
we commonly regard simply as a due respect for the right of
private judgment, is really a necessary condition to the balancing
of the progressive and conservative tendencies—is a means of
maintaining the adaptation between men's beliefs and their natures.
It is therefore a spirit to be fostered; and especially by the
catholic thinker, who perceives the functions of these conflicting
creeds.          Doubtless whoever feels the greatness of the
error his fellows cling to and the greatness of the truth they reject,
will find it hard to show a due patience.   It is hard to listen
calmly to the futile arguments used in support of irrational
doctrines, and to the misrepresentations of antagonist doctrines.
It is hard to bear the display of that pride of ignorance which
so far exceeds the pride of science.   Naturally such a one will
be indignant when charged with irreligion because he declines
to accept the carpenter theory of creation as the most worthy
one.   He may think it needless, as it is difficult, to conceal
his repugnance to a creed which tacitly ascribes to The Unknowable a love of adulation such as would be despised in a human
being.   Convinced as he is that pain, as we see it in the order
of nature, is an aid to the average welfare, there will perhaps escape

from him an angry condemnation of the belief that punishment is a divine vengeance, and that divine vengeance is eternal. He may be tempted to show his contempt when he is told that actions instigated by an unselfish sympathy or by a pure love of rectitude, are intrinsically sinful; and that conduct is truly good only when it is due to a faith whose openly-professed motive is other-worldliness. But he must restrain such feelings. Though he may be unable to do this during the excitement of controversy, he must yet qualify his antagonism in calmer moments; so that his mature judgment and resulting conduct may be without bias.

To this end let him bear in mind three cardinal facts—two of them already dwelt on, and one still to be pointed out. The first is that with which we commenced; namely, the existence of a fundamental verity under all forms of religion, however degraded. In each of them there is a soul of truth. The second, set forth at length in the foregoing section, is that while those concrete elements in which each creed embodies this soul of truth are bad as measured by an absolute standard, they are good as measured by a relative standard. The remaining one is that these various beliefs are parts of the constituted order of things, and, if not in their special forms yet in their general forms, necessary parts. Seeing how one or other of them is everywhere present, is of perennial growth, and when cut down redevelops in a form but slightly modified, we cannot avoid the inference that they are needful accompaniments of human life, severally fitted to the societies in which they are indigenous. We must recognize them as elements in that great evolution of which the beginning and end are beyond our knowledge or conception—as modes of manifestation of The Unknowable, and as having this for their warrant.

Our toleration therefore should be the widest possible. In dealing with alien beliefs our endeavour must be, not simply to refrain from injustice of word or deed, but also to do justice by an open recognition of positive worth. We must qualify our disagreement with as much as may be of sympathy.

§ 34. These admissions will perhaps be held to imply that the current theology should be passively accepted, or, at any rate, should not be actively opposed. " Why," it may be asked, "if creeds are severally fit for their times and places, should we not rest content with that to which we are born ? If the established belief contains an essential truth—if the forms under which it presents this truth, though intrinsically bad, are extrinsically good— if the abolition of these forms would be at present detrimental to the great majority—nay, if there are scarcely any to whom the ultimate and most abstract belief can furnish an adequate rule of life; surely it is wrong, for the present at least, to propagate this ultimate and most abstract belief."

The reply is that though existing religious ideas and institutions have an average adaptation to the characters of the people who live under them, yet, as these characters are ever changing, the adaptation is ever becoming imperfect; and the ideas and institutions need remodelling with a frequency proportionate to the rapidity of the change. Hence, while it is requisite that free play should be given to conservative thought and action, progressive thought and action must also have free play. Without the agency of both there cannot be those continual re-adaptations which orderly progress demands.

Whoever hesitates to utter that which he thinks the highest truth, lest it should be too much in advance of the time, may reassure himself by looking at his acts from an impersonal point of view. Let him remember that opinion is the agency through which character adapts external arrangements to itself, and that his opinion rightly forms part of this agency—is a unit of force constituting, with other such units, the general power which works out social changes; and he will perceive that he may properly give utterance to his innermost conviction: leaving it to produce what effect it may. It is not for nothing that he has in him these sympathies with some principles and repugnance to others. He, with all his capacities, and aspirations, and beliefs, is not an accident but a product of the time. While he is a descendant of the past he is a parent of the future; and his thoughts are as children born to him, which he may not carelessly let die. Like every other man he may properly consider himself as one of the myriad agencies through whom works the Unknown Cause; and when the Unknown Cause produces in him a certain belief, he is thereby authorized to profess and act out that belief. For, to render in their highest sense the words of the poet—

> ———— Nature is made better by no mean,
> But nature makes that mean : over that art
> Which you say adds to nature, is an art
> That nature makes.

Not as adventitious therefore will the wise man regard the faith which is in him. The highest truth he sees he will fearlessly utter; knowing that, let what may come of it, he is thus playing his right part in the world—knowing that if he can effect the change he aims at—well ; if not—well also ; though not *so* well.

# POSTSCRIPT TO PART I

Of multitudinous criticisms made on the preceding five chapters since the publication of *First Principles* in 1862, it is practicable to notice only those of chief importance. Even to do this would be impracticable were it not that most of them are essentially the same and may be met by the same answers.

Several opponents have contended that it is illegitimate to assert of the Ultimate Reality lying behind Appearance, that it is unknown and *unknowable*. The statement that it is *unknowable* is said to assume knowledge greater than we can have: alike as putting an arbitrary limit to possible human faculty, and as asserting something concerning that of which we are said to know nothing : a contradiction.

To the first of these objections, that an arbitrary limit is put to possible human faculty, an answer has already been given in § 24, where it has been shown that knowledge involves the three elements, *Relation, Difference, Likeness;* and that unconditioned existence, of which no one of these can be affirmed without contradiction, consequently does not present a subject-matter for knowledge. Further, in the next section it was pointed out that in the process of knowing there is the same implication. Thinking being relationing, no thought can express more than relations. From which truth it is inferable that human faculty must become fundamentally unlike what it is, and knowledge must become something other than what we call knowledge, before anything can be known about the Unconditioned.

The second objection is not thus easily met. It is doubtless true that saying what a thing is not, is, in some measure, saying what it is; since if, of all possible assertions respecting it, one is cancelled, the cancelling, by diminishing the number of possible asser-

tions, implies an incipient definition. A series of statements of what
it is not, excluding one possibility after another, becomes eventually
a line of exclusions drawn round it—a definition of it. The game
of Twenty Questions illustrates this. Hence it cannot be denied
that to affirm of the Ultimate Reality that it is unknowable is, in
a remote way, to assert some knowledge of it, and therefore involves
a contradiction.

This extreme case, however, does but serve to bring out the truth
that, limited as our intelligence is to the relative, and obliged as
we are to use words which have been moulded to it, we cannot say
anything concerning the non-relative without carrying into our
propositions meanings connoted by those words—meanings foreign
to a subject-matter which transcends relations. Intellect being
framed simply by and for converse with phenomena, involves us in
nonsense when we try to use it for anything beyond phenomena.
This inability of the thinking faculty in presence of the Unconditioned, is shown not only by the self-contradictory nature of its
*product*, but also by the arrest of its *process* before completion.
In attempting to pass the limit it breaks down before it has
finished its first step. For since every thought expresses a relation
—since thinking is relationing—thinking ceases when one of the
two terms of a relation remains blank. As the relation is incomplete there is no thought properly so called: thought fails. So
that we cannot rightly conceive even a connexion between noumenon
and phenomenon. We are unable in any consistent way to assert
a Reality standing in some relation to the Apparent. Such a
relation is not truly imaginable.

And yet by the very nature of our intelligence we are compelled
continually to ascribe the effects we know to some cause we do not
know—to regard the manifestations we are conscious of as implying something manifested. We find it impossible to think of the
world as constituted of appearances, and to exclude all thought
of a reality of which they are appearances. The inconsistencies
in the views set forth are in fact organic. Intellectual action
being a perpetual forming of relations between the states from
moment to moment passing, and being incapable of arresting
itself, tends irresistibly to form them when it reaches the limit
of intelligence. The inevitable effect of our mental constitution

is that on reaching the limit thought rushes out to form a new relation and cannot form it. A conflict hence arises between an effort to pass into the Unknowable and an inability to pass—a conflict which involves the inconsistency of feeling obliged to think something and being unable to think it.

And here we come as before to the conclusion that while it is impossible for us to have a conception, there yet ever remains a consciousness—a consciousness of which no logical account can be given, but which is the necessary result of our mental action since the perpetually-foiled endeavour to think the relation between Appearance and Reality, ever leaves behind a feeling that though a second term cannot be framed in thought yet there *is* a second term. This distinction, here emphasized as it was emphasized in § 26, my critics have ignored. Their arguments are directed against one or other elements in a *conception* which they ascribe to me. forgetting that, equally with them, I deny the possibility of any conception, and affirm only that after all our futile attempts to conceive, there remains the undefinable substance of a conception —a consciousness which cannot be put into any shape.

But now let it be understood that the reader is not called on to judge respecting any of the arguments or conclusions contained in the foregoing five chapters and in the above paragraphs. The subjects on which we are about to enter are independent of the subjects thus far discussed; and he may reject any or all of that which has gone before, while leaving himself free to accept any or all of that which is now to come.

When drawing up the programme of the Synthetic Philosophy, it appeared to me that, in the absence of any statement of theologico-metaphysical beliefs, the general doctrine set forth might be misconstrued; and Part I, "The Unknowable," was written for the purpose of excluding the possible misconstructions. Unfortunately I did not foresee that Part I would be regarded as a basis for Part II; with the result that the acceptance or rejection of the conclusions in Part I, would be supposed to determine acceptance or rejection of those in Part II. Very many have in consequence been prevented from reading beyond this point.

But an account of the Transformation of Things, given in the pages which follow, is simply an orderly presentation of facts ; and the interpretation of the facts is nothing more than a statement of the ultimate uniformities they present—the laws to which they conform. Is the reader an atheist ? the exposition of these facts and these laws will neither yield support to his belief nor destroy it. Is he a pantheist ? The phenomena and the inferences as now to be set forth will not force on him any incongruous implication. Does he think that God is immanent throughout all things, from concentrating nebulæ to the thoughts of poets ? Then the theory to be put before him contains no disproof of that view. Does he believe in a Deity who has given unchanging laws to the Universe ? Then he will find nothing at variance with his belief in an exposition of those laws and an account of the results.

*March*, 1899.

# PART II

## THE KNOWABLE

# CHAPTER 1

## PHILOSOPHY DEFINED

§ 35. AFTER concluding that we cannot know the ultimate nature of that which is manifested to us, there arise the questions—What is it that we know? In what sense do we know it? And in what consists our highest knowledge of it? Having repudiated as impossible the Philosophy which professes to formulate Being as distinguished from Appearance, it becomes needful to say what Philosophy truly is—not simply to specify its limits, but to specify its character within those limits. Given the sphere to which human intelligence is restricted, and there remains to define that product of human intelligence which may still be called Philosophy.

Here, we may fitly avail ourselves of the method followed at the outset—that of separating from conceptions which are partially or mainly erroneous the element of truth they contain. As in the chapter on "Religion and Science," it was inferred that religious beliefs, wrong as they may severally be, nevertheless probably each contain an essential verity, and that this is most likely common to them all; so in this place it is to be inferred that past and present beliefs respecting the nature of Philosophy, are none of them wholly false, and that that in which they are true is that in which they agree. We have here, then, to do what was done there—to compare all opinions of the sane genus; to set aside as more or less discrediting one another those elements in which such opinions differ; to observe what remains after the discordant components have been cancelled; and to find for this remaining component that expression which holds true throughout its divergent forms.

§ 36. Earlier speculations being passed over, we see that among the Greeks, before there had arisen any notion of Philosophy in general, those particular forms of it, from which the general notion was to arise, were hypotheses respecting some universal principle which was the essence of all kinds of being. To the question— "What is that *invariable existence* of which these are *variable states?*" there were sundry answers—Water, Air, Fire. A class of suppositions of this all-embracing character having been propounded, it became possible for Pythagoras to conceive of Philosophy in the abstract, as knowledge the most remote from practical ends; and to define it as "knowledge of immaterial and eternal things": "the cause of the material existence of things" being, in his view, Number. Thereafter, was continued a pursuit of Philosophy as some deepest explanation of the Universe, assumed to be possible, whether actually reached in any case or not. And in the course of this pursuit, various such interpretations were given as that "One is the beginning of all things"; that "the One is God"; that "the One is Finite"; that "the One is Infinite"; that "Intelligence is the governing principle of things"; and so on. From all which it is plain that the knowledge supposed to constitute Philosophy, differed from other knowledge in its exhaustive character.     After the Sceptics had shaken men's faith in their powers of reaching such transcendent knowledge, there grew up a much-restricted conception of Philosophy. Under Socrates, and still more under the Stoics, Philosophy became little else than the doctrine of right living. Not indeed that the proper ruling of conduct, as conceived by sundry of the later Greek thinkers to constitute the subject-matter of Philosophy, answered to what was popularly understood by the proper ruling of conduct. The injunctions of Zeno were not of the same class as those which guided men in their daily observances, sacrifices, customs, all having more or less of religious sanction; but they were principles of action enunciated without reference to times, or persons, or special cases.     What, then, was the constant element in these unlike ideas of Philosophy held by the ancients? Clearly this last idea agrees with the first, in implying that Philosophy seeks for wide and deep truths, as distinguished from the multitudinous detailed truths which the surfaces of things and actions present.

By comparing the conceptions of Philosophy that have been current in modern times, we get a like result. The disciples of

Schelling and Fichte join the Hegelian in ridiculing the so-called Philosophy which has been current in England. Not without reason, they laugh on reading of "Philosophical instruments"; and would deny that any one of the papers in the *Philosophical Transactions* has the least claim to come under such a title. Retaliating on their critics, the English may, and most of them do, reject as absurd the imagined Philosophy of the German schools. They hold that whether consciousness does or does not vouch for the existence of something beyond itself, it at any rate cannot comprehend that something; and that hence, in so far as any Philosophy professes to be an Ontology, it is false. These two views cancel one another over large parts of their areas. The English criticism on the Germans, cuts off from Philosophy all that is regarded as absolute knowledge. The German criticism on the English tacitly implies that if Philosophy is limited to the relative, it is at any rate not concerned with those aspects of the relative which are embodied in mathematical formulæ, in accounts of physical researches, in chemical analyses, or in descriptions of species and reports of physiological experiments. Now what has the too-wide German conception in common with the conception current among English men of science; which, narrow and crude as it is, is not so narrow and crude as their misuse of the word philosophical indicates? The two have this in common, that neither Germans nor English apply the word to unsystematized knowledge—to knowledge quite un-coördinated with other knowledge. Even the most limited specialist would not describe as philosophical, an essay which, dealing wholly with details, manifested no perception of the bearings of those details on wider truths.

The vague idea of Philosophy thus raised may be rendered more definite by comparing what has been known in England as Natural Philosophy with that development of it called Positive Philosophy. Though, as M. Comte admits, the two consist of knowledge essentially the same in kind; yet, by having put this kind of knowledge into a more coherent form, he has given it more of that character to which the term philosophical is applied. Without saying anything about the character of his co-ordination, it must be conceded that, by the fact of its co-ordination, the body of knowledge organized by him has a better claim to the title Philosophy, than has the comparatively-unorganized body of knowledge named Natural Philosophy.

If subdivisions of Philosophy be contrasted with one another, or with the whole, the same implication comes out. Moral Philosophy and Political Philosophy, agree with Philosophy at large in the comprehensiveness of their reasonings and conclusions. Though under the head Moral Philosophy, we treat of human actions as right or wrong, we do not include special directions for behaviour in school, at table, or on the Exchange; and though Political Philosophy has for its topic the conduct of men in their public relations, it does not concern itself with modes of voting or details of administration. Both of these sections of Philosophy contemplate particular instances only as illustrating truths of wide application.

§ 37. Thus every one of these conceptions implies belief in a possible way of knowing things more completely than they are known through simple experiences, mechanically accumulated in memory or heaped up in cyclopædias. Though in the extent of the sphere which they have supposed Philosophy to fill, men have differed and still differ very widely; yet there is a real if unavowed agreement among them in signifying by this title a knowledge which transcends ordinary knowledge. That which remains as the common element in these conceptions of Philosophy, after the elimination of their discordant elements, is—*knowledge of the highest degree of generality*. We see this tacitly asserted by the simultaneous inclusion of God, Nature, and Man, within its scope; or still more distinctly by the division of Philosophy as a whole into Theological, Physical, Ethical, &c. For that which characterizes the genus of which these are species, must be something more general than that which distinguishes any one species.

What must be the shape here given to this conception? Though persistently conscious of a Power manifested to us, we have abandoned as futile the attempt to learn anything respecting that Power, and so have shut out Philosophy from much of the domain supposed to belong to it. The domain left is that occupied by Science. Science concerns itself with the co-existences and sequences among phenomena; grouping these at first into generalizations of a simple or low order, and rising gradually to higher and more extended generalizations. But if so, where remains any subject-matter for Philosophy?

The reply is—Philosophy may still properly be the title retained for knowledge of the highest generality. Science means merely the family of the Sciences—stands for nothing more than the sum of knowledge formed of their contributions; and ignores the knowledge constituted by the *fusion* of these contributions into a whole. As usage has defined it, Science consists of truths existing more or less separated, and does not recognize these truths as entirely integrated. An illustration will make the difference clear.

If we ascribe the flow of a river to the same force which causes the fall of a stone, we make a statement that belongs to a certain division of Science. If, to explain how gravitation produces this movement in a direction almost horizontal, we cite the law that fluids subject to mechanical forces exert re-active forces which are equal in all directions, we formulate a wider truth, containing the scientific interpretations of many other phenomena; as those presented by the fountain, the hydraulic press, the steam-engine, the air-pump. And when this proposition, extending only to the dynamics of fluids, is merged in a proposition of general dynamics, comprehending the laws of movement of solids as well as of fluids, there is reached a yet higher truth; but still a truth that comes wholly within the realm of Science. Again, looking around at Birds and Mammals, suppose we say that air-breathing animals are hot-blooded; and that then, remembering how Reptiles, which also breathe air, are not much warmer than their media, we say, more truly, that animals (bulks being equal) have temperatures proportionate to the quantities of air they breathe; and that then, calling to mind certain large fish, as the tunny, which maintain a heat considerably above that of the water they swim in, we further correct the generalization by saying that the temperature varies as the rate of oxygenation of the blood; and that then, modifying the statement to meet other criticisms, we finally assert the relation to be between the amount of heat and the amount of molecular change—supposing we do all this, we state scientific truths that are successively wider and more complete, but truths which, to the last, remain purely scientific. Once more if, guided by mercantile experiences, we reach the conclusions that prices rise when the demand exceeds the supply; that commodities flow from places where they are abundant to places where they are scarce; that the industries of different localities are determined in their kinds mainly by the facilities which the localities afford for them; and if, studying these generalizations of political economy, we trace them all to the truth that each man seeks satisfaction for his desires in ways costing the smallest efforts—such social phenomena being *resultants* of individual actions so guided; we are still dealing with the propositions of Science only.

How, then, is Philosophy constituted? It is constituted by carrying a stage further the process indicated. So long as these truths are known only apart and regarded as independent, even the most general of them cannot without laxity of speech be called philosophical. But when, having been severally reduced to a mechanical axiom, a principle of molecular physics, and a law of social action, they are contemplated together as corollaries of some ultimate truth, then we rise to the kind of knowledge which constitutes Philosophy proper.

The truths of Philosophy thus bear the same relation to the highest scientific truths, that each of these bears to lower scientific truths. As each widest generalization of Science comprehends and consolidates the narrower generalizations of its own division; so the generalizations of Philosophy comprehend and consolidate the widest generalizations of Science. It is therefore a knowledge the extreme opposite in kind to that which experience first accumulates. It is the final product of that process which begins with a mere colligation of crude observations, goes on establishing propositions that are broader and more separated from particular cases, and ends in universal propositions. Or to bring the definition to its simplest and clearest form:—Knowledge of the lowest kind is *un-unified* knowledge; Science is *partially-unified* knowledge; Philosophy is *completely-unified* knowledge.

§ 38. Such, at least, is the meaning we must here give to the word Philosophy, if we employ it at all. In so defining it, we accept that which is common to the various conceptions of it current among both ancients and moderns—rejecting those ele ments in which these conceptions disagree. In short, we are simply giving precision to that application of the word which has been gradually establishing itself.

Two forms of Philosophy, as thus understood, may be distinguished and dealt with separately. On the one hand, the things contemplated may be the universal truths: all particular truths referred to being used simply for proof or elucidation of these universal truths. On the other hand, setting out with the universal truths, the things contemplated may be the particular truths as interpreted by them. In both cases we deal with the universal truths; but in the one case they are passive and in the other case active—in the one case they form the products of exploration and in the other case the instruments of exploration. These divisions we may appropriately call General Philosophy and Special Philosophy respectively.

The remainder of this volume will be devoted to General Philosophy. Special Philosophy, divided into parts determined by the natures of the phenomena treated, will be the subject-matter of subsequent volumes.

# CHAPTER II

## THE DATA OF PHILOSOPHY

§ 39. Every thought involves a whole system of thoughts and ceases to exist if severed from its various correlatives. As we cannot isolate a single organ of a living body, and deal with it as though it had a life independent of the rest; so, from the organized structure of our cognitions, we cannot cut out one, and proceed as though it had survived the separation. The development of formless protoplasm into an embryo is a specialization of parts, the definiteness of which increases only as fast as their combination increases. Each becomes a distinguishable organ only on condition that it is bound up with others, which have simultaneously become distinguishable organs. Similarly, from the unformed material of consciousness, a developed intelligence can arise only by a process which, in making thoughts defined also makes them mutually dependent—establishes among them certain vital connexions the destruction of which causes instant death of the thoughts. Overlooking this all-important truth, however, speculators have habitually set out with some professedly-simple datum or data; have supposed themselves to assume nothing beyond this datum or these data; and have thereupon proceeded to prove or disprove propositions which were, by implication, already unconsciously asserted along with that which was consciously asserted.

This reasoning in a circle has resulted from the misuse of words: not that misuse commonly enlarged upon—not the misapplication or change of meaning whence so much error arises; but a more radical and less obvious misuse. Only that thought which is directly indicated by each word has been contemplated; while

numerous thoughts indirectly indicated have been left out of
consideration.   Because a spoken or written word can be detached
from all others, it has been inadvertently assumed that the thing
signified by a word can be detached from the things signified by
all other words.          How profoundly this error vitiates the
conclusions of one who makes it, we shall quickly see on taking
a case.   The sceptical metaphysician, wishing his reasonings to be
as rigorous as possible, says to himself—" I will take for granted
only this one thing."   What now are the tacit assumptions
inseparable from his avowed assumption?   The resolve itself
indirectly asserts that there is some other thing, or are some other
things, which he might assume; for it is impossible to think of
unity without thinking of a correlative duality or multiplicity.
In the very act, therefore, of restricting himself, he takes in much
that is professedly left out.   Again, before proceeding he must
give a definition of that which he assumes.   Is nothing unexpressed
involved in the thought of a thing as defined?   There is the
thought of something excluded by the definition—there is, as
before, the thought of other existence.   But there is much more.
Defining a thing, or setting a limit to it, implies the thought of
a limit; and limit cannot be thought of apart from some notion
of quantity—extensive, protensive, or intensive.   Further, definition is impossible unless there enters into it the thought of
difference; and difference, besides being unthinkable without
having two things that differ, implies the existence of other
differences than the one recognized; since without them there
cannot have been formed the general conception of difference.
Nor is this all.   As before pointed out (§ 24) all thought involves
the consciousness of likeness: the one thing avowedly postulated
cannot be known absolutely as one thing, but can be known only
as of such or such kind—only as classed with other things in
virtue of some common attribute.   Thus, along with the single
avowed datum, we have surreptitiously brought in a number of
unavowed data—*existence other than that alleged, quantity, number,
limit, difference, likeness, class, attribute.*   Now in these unacknowledged postulates, we have the outlines of a general theory;
and that theory can be neither proved nor disproved by the
metaphysician's argument.   Insist that his symbol shall be in-

terpreted at every step into its full meaning, with all the complementary thoughts implied by that meaning, and you find already taken for granted in the premises that which in the conclusion is asserted or denied.

In what way, then, must Philosophy set out? The developed intelligence is framed upon certain organized and consolidated conceptions of which it cannot divest itself; and which it can no more stir without using than the body can stir without help of its limbs. In what way, then, is it possible for intelligence, striving after Philosophy, to give any account of these conceptions, and to show either their validity or their invalidity? There is but one way. Those of them which are vital, or cannot be severed from the rest without mental dissolution, must be assumed as true *provisionally*. The fundamental intuitions that are essential to the process of thinking, must be temporarily accepted as unquestionable: *leaving the assumption of their unquestionableness to be justified by the results.*

§ 40. How is it to be justified by the results? As any other assumption is justified—by ascertaining that all the conclusions deducible from it correspond with the facts as directly observed—by showing the agreement between the experiences it leads us to anticipate, and the actual experiences. There is no mode of establishing the validity of any belief except that of showing its congruity with all other beliefs. If we suppose that a mass which has a certain colour and lustre is the substance called gold, how do we proceed to prove that it is gold? We represent to ourselves certain other impressions which gold produces on us, and then observe whether, under the appropriate conditions, this particular mass produces on us such impressions. We remember that gold has a high specific gravity; and if, on poising this substance on the finger, we find that its weight is great considering its bulk, we take the correspondence between the represented impression and the presented impression as further evidence that the substance is gold. Knowing that gold, unlike most metals, is insoluble in nitric acid, we imagine to ourselves a drop of nitric acid placed on the surface of this yellow, glittering, heavy substance, without causing corrosion ; and when, after so placing a drop of nitric acid, no effervescence or other change follows, we hold this agreement between the anticipation and the experience to be an additional reason for thinking that the substance is gold. And if, similarly, the great malleability possessed by gold we find to be paralleled by the great malleability of this substance; if, like gold, it fuses at about 2,000 deg.; crystallizes in octahedrons; is dissolved by selenic acid; and, under all conditions, does what gold does under such conditions; the conviction that it is gold reaches what we regard as the highest certainty—we know it to be gold in the fullest sense of knowing. For, as we here see, our whole knowledge of gold consists in nothing more than the consciousness of a definite set of impressions, standing in definite relations, disclosed under definite conditions; and if, in a present experience, the impressions, relations, and conditions, perfectly correspond with those in past experiences, the cognition has all the validity of which it is capable. So that, generalizing the statement, hypotheses, down even to those simple ones which we make from moment to moment in our acts of recognition, are verified when entire congruity is found between the states of consciousness constituting them, and certain other states of consciousness given in perception, or reflection, or both; and no other knowledge is possible for us than that which consists of the consciousness of such congruities and their correlative incongruities.

Hence Philosophy, compelled to make those fundamental assumptions without which thought is impossible, has to justify them by showing their congruity with all other dicta of consciousness. Debarred as we are from everything beyond the relative, truth, raised to its highest form, can be for us nothing more than perfect agreement, throughout the whole range of our experience, between those representations of things which we distinguish as ideal and those presentations of things which we distinguish as real. If, by discovering a proposition to be untrue, we mean nothing more than discovering a difference between a thing inferred and a thing perceived; then a body of conclusions in which no such difference anywhere occurs, must be what we mean by an entirely true body of conclusions.

And here, indeed, it becomes also obvious that, setting out with these fundamental intuitions provisionally assumed to be true, the process of proving or disproving their congruity with all other dicta of consciousness becomes the business of Philosophy; and the complete establishment of the congruity becomes the same thing as the complete unification of knowledge in which Philosophy reaches its goal.

§ 41. What is this datum, or rather, what are these data, which Philosophy cannot do without? Clearly one primordial datum is involved in the foregoing statement. Already by implication we have assumed that congruities and incongruities exist, and are cognizable by us. We cannot avoid accepting as true the verdict of consciousness that some manifestations are like one another and some are unlike one another. Unless consciousness be a competent judge of the likeness and unlikeness of its states, there can never be established that congruity throughout the whole of our cognitions which constitutes Philosophy; nor can there ever be established that incongruity by which only any hypothesis, philosophical or other, can be shown erroneous.

It is useless to say, as Sir W. Hamilton does, that "consciousness is to be presumed trustworthy until proved mendacious." It cannot be proved mendacious in this, its primordial act; since proof involves a repeated acceptance of this primordial act. Nay more, the very thing supposed to be proved cannot be expressed without recognizing this primordial act as valid; since unless we accept the verdict of consciousness that they differ, mendacity and trustworthiness become identical. Process and product of reasoning both disappear in the absence of this assumption.

It may, indeed, be often shown that what, after careless comparison, were supposed to be like states of consciousness, are really unlike; or that what were carelessly supposed to be unlike, are really like. But how is this shown? Simply by a more careful comparison, mediately or immediately made. And what does acceptance of the revised conclusion imply? Simply that a deliberate verdict of consciousness is preferable to a rash one; or, to speak more definitely—that a consciousness of likeness or difference which survives critical examination must be accepted in place of one that does not survive—the very survival being itself the acceptance.

And here we get to the bottom of the matter.    The permanence of a consciousness of likeness or difference, is our ultimate warrant for asserting the existence of likeness or difference; and, in fact, we mean by the existence of likeness or difference, nothing more than the permanent consciousness of it.    To say that a given congruity or incongruity exists, is simply our way of saying that we invariably have a consciousness of it along with a consciousness of the compared things.    We know nothing more of existence than continued manifestation.

§ 42.  But Philosophy requires for its datum some substantive proposition.    To recognize as unquestionable a certain fundamental *process* of thought is not enough :  we must recognize as unquestionable some fundamental *product* of thought, reached by this process. If Philosophy is completely-unified knowledge—if the unification of knowledge is to be effected only by showing that some ultimate proposition includes and consolidates all the results of experience ; then, clearly, this ultimate proposition which has to be proved congruous with all others, must express a piece of knowledge, and not the validity of an act of knowing.    Having assumed the trustworthiness of consciousness, we have also to assume as trustworthy some deliverance of consciousness.

What must this be ?    Must it not be one affirming the widest and most profound distinction which things present ?    An ultimate principle that is to unify all experience, must be co-extensive with all experience.    That which Philosophy takes as its datum, must be an assertion of some likeness and difference to which all other likenesses and differences are secondary.    If knowing is classifying, or grouping the like and separating the unlike ; and if the unification of knowledge proceeds by arranging the smaller classes of like experiences within the larger, and these within the still larger ; then, the proposition by which knowledge is unified must be one specifying the antithesis between two ultimate classes of experiences, in which all others merge.

Let us consider what these classes are.    In drawing the distinction between them, we cannot avoid using words which have implications wider than their meanings—we cannot avoid arousing thoughts that imply the very distinction which it is the object of the analysis to establish. Keeping this fact in mind, we can do no more than ignore the connotations of the words, and attend only to the things they avowedly denote.

§ 43. Setting out from the conclusion lately reached, that all things known to us are manifestations of the Unknowable, and suppressing every hypothesis respecting that which underlies one or other order of these manifestations; we find that the manifestations, considered simply as such, are divisible into two great classes, called by some *impressions* and *ideas*. The implications of these words are apt to vitiate the reasonings of those who use the words; and it is best to avoid the risk of making unacknowledged assumptions. The term *sensation*, too, commonly used as the equivalent of impression, implies certain psychological theories—tacitly, if not openly, postulates a sensitive organism and something acting upon it; and can scarcely be employed without bringing these postulates into the thoughts and including them in the inferences. Similarly, the phrase *state of consciousness*, as signifying either an impression or an idea, is objectionable. As we cannot think of a state without thinking of something of which it is a state, and which is capable of different states, there is involved a foregone conclusion—an undeveloped system of metaphysics. Here, accepting the inevitable implication that the manifestations imply something manifested, our aim must be to avoid any further implications. Though we cannot exclude further implications from our thoughts, and cannot carry on our argument without tacit recognitions of them, we can at any rate refuse to recognize them in the terms with which we set out. We may do this most effectually by classing the manifestations as *vivid* and *faint* respectively. Let us consider what are the several distinctions that exist between these.

And first a few words on this most conspicuous distinction which these names imply. Manifestations that. occur under the conditions called those of perception (which conditions we must separate from all hypotheses, and regard as themselves a certain group of manifestations) are ordinarily far more distinct than those which occur under the conditions known as those of reflection, or memory, or imagination, or ideation. These vivid manifestations do, indeed, sometimes differ but little from the faint ones. When it is nearly dark we may be unable to decide whether a certain manifestation belongs to the vivid order or the faint order—whether, as we say, we really see something or fancy we see it. In like manner, between a very feeble sound and the imagination of a sound, it is occasionally difficult to discriminate. But these exceptional cases are extremely rare in comparison with the enormous mass of cases in which, from instant to instant, the vivid manifestations distinguish themselves unmistakeably from the faint. Conversely, it now and then happens (though under conditions which we distinguish as abnormal) that manifestations of the faint order become so strong as to be mistaken for those of the vivid order. Ideal sights and sounds are in the insane so much intensified as to be classed with real sights and sounds—ideal and real being here supposed to imply no other contrast than that which we are considering. These cases of illusion, as we call them, bear, however, so small a ratio to the great mass of cases, that we may safely neglect them, and say that the relative faintness of manifestations of the second order is so marked, that we are never in doubt as to their distinctness from those of the first order. Or if we recognize the exceptional occurrence of doubt, the recognition serves but to introduce the significant fact that we have other means of deciding to which order a particular manifestation belongs, when the test of comparative vividness fails us.

Manifestations of the vivid order precede, in our experience, those of the faint order. To put the facts in historical sequence —there is first a presented manifestation of the vivid order, and then, afterwards, may come a represented manifestation that is like it except in being much less distinct. After having those vivid manifestations known as particular places and persons and things, we can have those faint manifestations which we call recollections of the places, persons, and things, but cannot have these previously. Before tasting certain substances and smelling certain perfumes, we are without those faint manifestations called ideas of their tastes and smells ; and where certain orders of the vivid manifestations are shut out (as the visible from the blind and the audible from the deaf) the corresponding faint manifestations never come into

8

existence. It is true that special faint manifestations precede the vivid. What we call a conception of a machine may presently be followed by a vivid manifestation matching it—a so-called actual machine. But in the first place this occurrence of the vivid manifestation after the faint is not either spontaneous or easy like that of the faint after the vivid. And in the second place, though a faint manifestation of this kind may occur before the vivid one answering to it, yet its component parts may not. Without the foregoing vivid manifestations of wheels and bars and cranks, the inventor could have no faint manifestation of his new machine. Thus it cannot be denied that the two orders of manifestations are distinguished from one another as independent and dependent.

Note next that they form concurrent series; or rather let us call them, not series, which implies linear arrangements, but heterogeneous streams or processions. These run side by side; each now broadening and now narrowing, each now threatening to obliterate its neighbour and now in turn threatened with obliteration, but neither ever quite excluding the other from their common channel. Let us watch the mutual actions of the two currents. During what we call states of activity, the vivid manifestations predominate. We simultaneously receive many and varied presentations—a crowd of sights, sounds, resistances, tastes, odours, &c.; some groups of them changing and others temporarily fixed, but altering as we move; and when we compare in its breadth and massiveness this stream of vivid manifestations with the stream of faint ones, these last sink into relative insignificance. They never wholly disappear, however. Always along with the vivid manifestations, even in their greatest obtrusiveness, there goes a thread called thoughts constituted of the faint manifestations. Or if it be contended that the occurrence of a deafening explosion or an intense pain may for a moment exclude every idea, it must yet be admitted that such breach of continuity can never be immediately known as occurring; since the act of knowing is impossible in the absence of ideas. On the other hand, after certain vivid mani-festations which we call the acts of closing the eyes and adjust-ing ourselves so as to enfeeble the vivid manifestations called pressures, sounds, &c., the faint manifestations become relatively predominant. The current of them, no longer obscured by the vivid current, grows distinct, and seems almost to exclude the vivid current. But the vivid manifestations, however small the current of them becomes, still continue: pressure and touch do not wholly disappear. It is only during the state termed sleep, that manifestations of the vivid order cease to be distinguishable as such, and those of the faint order come to be mistaken for them. And even of this we remain unaware till manifestations of the vivid order recur on awaking. We can never infer that manifestations of the vivid order have been absent, until they are again present; and can therefore never directly know them to be absent. Thus, of the two streams of manifestations, each preserves its continuity. As they flow side by side, either trenches on the other; but at no moment can it be said that the one has, then and there, broken through the other.

Besides this longitudinal cohesion there is a lateral cohesion, both of the vivid to the vivid and of the faint to the faint. The components of the vivid series are bound together by ties of co-existence as well as by ties of succession; and the components of the faint series are similarly bound together. Between the degrees of union in the two cases there are, however, marked and very significant differences. Let us observe them. Over a limited area of consciousness, as we name this double stream, lights and shades and colours and outlines constitute a group to which we give a certain name distinguishing it as an object; and while they continue present, these united vivid manifestations remain inseparable. So, too, is it with co-existing groups of manifestations: each persists as a special combination; and most of them preserve unchanging relations with those around. Such of them as do not—such of them as are capable of what we call independent movements, nevertheless show us a constant connexion between certain of the manifestations they include, along with a variable connexion of others. And though, after certain vivid manifestations known as a change in the conditions of perception, there is a change in the proportions among the vivid manifestations constituting any group, their cohesion continues. Turning to the faint manifestations, we see that their lateral cohesions are much less extensive, and in most cases by no means so rigorous. After the group of feelings I call closing my eyes, I can represent an object now standing in a certain place, as standing in some other place, or as absent. While I look at a blue vase, I cannot separate the vivid manifestation of blueness from the vivid manifestation of a particular shape; but, in the absence of these vivid manifestations, I can separate the faint manifestation of the shape from the faint manifestation of blueness, and replace the last by a faint manifestation of redness, and I can also change the shape and the size of the vase to any extent. It is so throughout: the faint manifestations cling together to a certain extent, but most of them may be re-arranged with facility. Indeed none of the *individual* faint manifestations cohere in the same indissoluble way as do the individual vivid manifestations. Though along with a faint manifestation of pressure there is always some faint manifestation of extension, yet no particular faint manifestation of extension is bound up with a particular faint manifestation of pressure. So that whereas in the vivid order the individual manifestations cohere indissolubly, usually in large groups, in the faint order the individual manifestations none of them cohere indissolubly, and are most of them loosely aggregated: the only indissoluble cohesions among them being between certain of their generic forms.

While the components of each current cohere strongly with their neighbours of the same current, most of them do not cohere strongly with those of the other current. Or, more correctly, we may say that the vivid current unceasingly flows on quite undisturbed by the faint current; and that the faint current, though often largely determined by the vivid, and always to some extent carried with it, may yet maintain a substantial independence, letting the vivid current slide by. We will glance at the interactions of the two. Save in peculiar cases hereafter to be dealt with, the faint manifestations fail to modify in the slightest degree the vivid manifestations. Those vivid manifestations, which I know as components of a landscape, as surgings of the sea, as whistlings of the wind, as movements of vehicles and people, are absolutely uninfluenced by the accompanying faint manifestations which I know as my ideas.     On the other hand, the current of faint manifestations is always perturbed by the vivid.  Frequently it consists mainly of faint manifestations which cling to the vivid ones, and are carried with them as they pass—memories and suggestions as we call them.  At other times when, as we say, absorbed in thought, the disturbance of the faint current is but superficial.  The vivid manifestations drag after them such few faint manifestations only as constitute recognitions of them: to each impression adhere certain ideas which make up the interpretation of it as such or such, and sometimes not even this cohesion happens.  But there meanwhile flows on a main stream of faint manifestations wholly unrelated to the vivid manifestations—what we call a reverie, perhaps, or it may be a process of reasoning.  And occasionally, during the state known as absence of mind, this current of faint manifestations so far predominates that the vivid current scarcely affects it at all.     Hence, these concurrent series of manifestations, each coherent with itself longitudinally and transversely, have but a partial coherence with one another.  The vivid series is quite unmoved by its passing neighbour; and though the faint series is always to some extent moved by the adjacent vivid series, and is often carried bodily along with the vivid series, it may nevertheless become in great measure separate.

Yet another all-important difference has to be named.  The conditions under which these two orders of manifestations occur, are unlike; and the conditions of occurrence of each order belong to itself.  Whenever the immediate antecedents of vivid manifestations are traceable, they prove to be other vivid manifestations; and though we cannot say that the antecedents of the faint manifestations always lie wholly among themselves, yet the essential ones do.  These statements need a good deal of explanation.     Changes among the motions and sounds and aspects of what we call objects, are either changes that follow certain other motions, sounds, and aspects, or changes of which the antecedents are unapparent.  Some of the vivid manifestations, however, occur only under conditions that seem of another order.  Those known as colours and visible forms presuppose open eyes.  But what is opening of the eyes, translated into the terms we are here using?

Literally it is an occurrence of certain vivid manifestations. The preliminary idea of opening the eyes does, indeed, consist of faint manifestations, but the act of opening them consists of vivid manifestations. And the like is still more obviously the case with those movements of the eyes and the head which are followed by new groups of vivid manifestations. Similarly with the antecedents to the vivid manifestations which we distinguish as touch and pressure. All the changeable ones have for their conditions of occurrence certain vivid manifestations called sensations of muscular tension. It is true that the conditions to these conditions are manifestations of the faint order—those ideas of muscular actions which precede muscular actions. And here arises a complication, for what is called the body, is present to us as a set of vivid manifestations connected with the faint manifestations in a special way—a way such that in it alone certain vivid manifestations are capable of being produced by faint manifestations. There must be named, too, the kindred exception furnished by the emotions—an exception which, however, serves to enforce the general proposition. For while it is true that the emotions must be classed as vivid manifestations, which admit of being produced by the faint manifestations we call ideas ; it is also true that because the conditions to their occurrence thus exist among the faint manifestations, we regard them as belonging to the same general aggregate as the faint manifestations—do not class them with such other vivid manifestations as colours, sounds, pressures, smells, &c. But omitting these peculiar vivid manifestations which we know as muscular tensions and emotions, we may say of the rest, that their antecedents are manifestations belonging to their own class. In the parallel current we find a parallel truth. Though many manifestations of the faint order are partly caused by manifestations of the vivid order, which call up memories, as we say, and suggest inferences, yet these results mainly depend on certain antecedents belonging to the faint order. A cloud drifts across the Sun, and may or may not change the current of ideas : the inference that it will rain may arise, or the previous train of thought may continue—a difference determined by conditions among the thoughts. Again, such power as a vivid manifestation has of causing certain faint manifestations depends on the pre-existence of appropriate faint manifestations. If I have never heard a curlew, the cry which an unseen one makes, fails to produce an idea of the bird. And on remembering what various trains of thought are aroused by the same sight, we see that the occurrence of each faint manifestation chiefly depends on its relations to other faint manifestations that have gone before or co-exist.

Here we are introduced, lastly, to one of the most important of the differences between those two orders of manifestations. The conditions of occurrence are not distinguished solely by the fact that each set, when identifiable, belongs to its own order of manifestations. They are further distinguished in a very significant way. Manifestations of the faint order have traceable antecedents; can be made to occur by establishing their conditions of occurrence; and can be suppressed by establishing other conditions. But manifestations of the vivid order continually occur without previous presentation of their antecedents; and in many cases they persist or cease in such ways as to show that their antecedents are beyond control. The sensation known as a flash of lightning breaks across the current of our thoughts absolutely without notice. The sounds from a band that strikes up in the street or from a crash of china in the next room, are not connected with any previously-present manifestations, either of the faint order or of the vivid order. Often these vivid manifestations, arising unexpectedly, persist in thrusting themselves across the current of the faint ones, which not only cannot directly affect them, but cannot even indirectly affect them. A wound produced by a blow from behind, is a vivid manifestation the conditions of occurrence of which were neither among the faint nor among the vivid; and the conditions to the persistence of which are bound up with the vivid manifestations in some unmanifested way. So that whereas in the faint order, the conditions of occurrence are always among the pre-existing or co-existing manifestations; in the vivid order, the conditions of occurrence are often neither present nor can be made present.

Let me briefly enumerate these distinctive characters. Manifestations of the one order are vivid and those of the other are faint. Those of the one order are originals, while those of the other are copies. The first form with one another a heterogeneous current that is never broken; and the second also form with one another a heterogeneous current that is never broken: or, to speak strictly, no breakage of either is ever directly known. Those of the first order cohere with one another, not only longitudinally but also transversely; as also do those of the second order with one another. Between manifestations of the first order the cohesions, both longitudinal and transverse, are indissoluble by any direct action of the second order; but between manifestations of the second order, these cohesions are most of them dissoluble with ease. While the members of each current are so coherent with one another that it cannot be broken, the two currents, running side by side, have but little coherence. The conditions under which manifestations of either order occur, themselves belong to that order; but whereas in the faint order the conditions are always present, in the vivid order they are often not present, but lie somewhere outside of the series. Seven separate characters, then, mark off these two orders of manifestations from one another.

§ 44. What is the meaning of this? The foregoing analysis was commenced in the belief that the proposition postulated by Philosophy, must affirm some ultimate classes of likenesses and unlikenesses, in which all other classes merge; and here we have found that all manifestations of the Unknowable are divisible into two such classes. What is the division equivalent to?

Obviously it corresponds to the division between *object* and *subject*. This profoundest distinction among manifestations of the Unknowable we recognize by grouping them into *self* and *not-self*. These faint manifestations, forming a continuous whole differing from the other in the quantity, quality, cohesion, and conditions of existence of its parts, we call the *ego;* and these vivid manifestations, bound together in relatively-immense masses, and having independent conditions of existence, we call the *non-ego.* Or rather, more truly—each order of manifestations carries with it the irresistible implication of some power that manifests itself; and by the words *ego* and *non-ego* respectively, we mean the power that manifests itself in the faint forms, and the power that manifests itself in the vivid forms.

This segregation of the manifestations and coalescence of them into two distinct wholes, is in great part spontaneous, and precedes all deliberate judgments; though it is endorsed by such judgments when they come to be made.   For the manifestations of each order have not simply that kind of union implied by grouping them as belonging to the same class, but they have that much more intimate union implied by cohesion.   Their cohesive union exhibits itself before any acts of classing take place.   So that, in truth, these two orders of manifestations are substantially self-separated and self-consolidated.   The members of each, by clinging to one another and parting from their opposites, themselves form the united wholes known as object and subject.   It is this self-union of their members which gives to these wholes formed of them, their individualities as wholes, and that separateness from each other which transcends judgment; and judgment merely aids by assigning to their respective classes, such manifestations as have not distinctly united themselves with the rest of their kind.

One further perpetually-repeated act of judgment there is, indeed, which strengthens this fundamental antithesis, and gives a vast extension to one term of it.   We continually learn that while the conditions of occurrence of faint manifestations are always to be found, the conditions of occurrence of vivid manifestations are often not to be found.   We also continually learn that vivid manifestations which have no perceivable antecedents among the vivid manifestations, are like certain preceding ones which *had* perceivable antecedents among the vivid manifestations.   Junction of these two experiences produces the irresistible belief that some vivid manifestations have conditions of occurrence existing out of the current of vivid manifestations—existing as potential vivid manifestations capable of becoming actual.   And so we are made conscious of an indefinitely-extended region of power or being, not merely separate from the current of faint manifestations constituting the phenomenal *ego*, but lying beyond the current of vivid manifestations constituting the immediately-present portion of the phenomenal *non-ego*.

§ 45. In a very imperfect way, passing over objections and omitting needful explanations, I have thus indicated the nature and justification of that fundamental belief which Philosophy requires as a datum. I might, indeed, safely have assumed this ultimate truth; which Common Sense asserts, which every step in Science takes for granted, and which no metaphysician ever for a moment succeeded in expelling from consciousness. But as all that follows proceeds upon this postulate, it seemed desirable briefly to show its warrant, with the view of shutting out criticisms which might else be made. It seemed desirable to prove that this deepest cognition is neither, as the idealist asserts, an illusion, nor as the sceptic thinks, of doubtful worth, nor as is held by the natural realist, an inexplicable intuition; but that it is a legitimate deliverance of consciousness elaborating its materials after the laws of its normal action. While, in order of time, the establishment of this distinction precedes all reasoning; and while, running through our mental structure as it does, we are debarred from reasoning about it without taking for granted its existence; analysis nevertheless enables us to justify the assertion of its existence, by showing that it is also the outcome of a primary classification based on accumulated likenesses and accumulated differences. In other words—Reasoning, which is itself but a formation of cohesions among manifestations, here strengthens, by the cohesions it forms, the cohesions which it finds already existing.

Before proceeding a further preliminary is needed. The manifestations of the Unknowable, separated into the two divisions of self and not-self, are re-divisible into certain most general forms, the reality of which Science, as well as Common Sense, from moment to moment assumes. In the chapter on "Ultimate Scientific Ideas," it was shown that we know nothing of these forms, considered in themselves. As, nevertheless, we must continue to use the words signifying them, it is needful to say what interpretations are to be put on these words.

# CHAPTER III

## SPACE, TIME, MATTER, MOTION, AND FORCE

§ 46. THAT sceptical state of mind which the criticisms of Philosophy usually produce is, in great measure, caused by the misinterpretation of words. These have by association acquired meanings quite different from those given to them in philosophical discussion; and the ordinary meanings being unavoidably suggested, there results more or less of that dream-like illusion which is so incongruous with our instinctive convictions. The word *phenomenon* and its equivalent word *appearance*, are in great part to blame for this. In ordinary speech these always imply visual perceptions. Habit almost, if not quite, disables us from thinking of *appearance* except as something seen; and though *phenomenon* has a more generalized meaning, yet we cannot rid it of associations with *appearance*. When, therefore, Philosophy proves that our know-ledge of the external world can be but phenomenal—when it concludes that the things of which we are conscious are appearances; it inevitably suggests an illusiveness like that to which our visual perceptions are so liable. Good pictures show us that the aspects of things may be very nearly simulated by colours on canvas. The looking-glass distinctly proves how deceptive is sight when unverified by touch; as does also the apparent bend in a straight stick inclined in the water. And the cases in which we think we see something which we do not see further shake our faith in vision. So that the implication of uncertainty has infected the very word *appearance*. Hence, Philosophy, by giving it an ex-tended meaning, leads us to think of all our senses as deceiving us in the same way that our eyes do; and so makes us feel ourselves in a world of phantasms. Had *phenomenon* and *appearance* no such misleading associations, little, if any, of this mental confusion would result.  Or if, when discussing the nature of our knowledge, we always thought of tactual impressions instead of visual impressions—if instead of the perceptions of objects yielded by our eyes we always insisted upon thinking of the perceptions yielded by our hands, the idea of unreality would in large measure disappear. Metaphysical criticism would then have merely the effect of proving to us that feelings of touch and pressure produced by an object give us no knowledge of its nature, at the same time that the criticism would by implication admit that there was a something which produced these feelings.  It would prove to us that our knowledge consists simply of the *effects* wrought on our consciousness, and that the *causes* of those effects remain unknown; but it would not in doing this tend in any degree to disprove the existence of such causes: all its arguments tacitly taking them for granted. And when the two were always thought of in this immediate relation, there would be little danger of falling into the insanities of idealism.

Such danger as might remain, would disappear on making a further verbal correction.  We increase the seeming unreality of that phenomenal existence which we can alone know, by contrasting it with a noumenal existence which we imagine would, if we could know it, be more truly real to us.  But we delude ourselves with a verbal fiction.        What is the meaning of the word *real?* In the interpretation given to it, the discussions of philosophy retain one element of the vulgar conception of things while they reject the rest, and create confusion by the inconsistency.  The peasant, on contemplating an object, does not regard that which he is conscious of as something in himself, but believes it to be the external object itself: to him the appearance and the reality are one and the same thing.  The metaphysician, however, while his words imply belief in a reality, sees that consciousness cannot embrace it, but only the appearance of it; and so he transfers the appearance into consciousness and leaves the reality outside.  This reality left outside, he continues to think of much in the same way that the peasant thinks of the appearance.  The *realness* ascribed to it is constantly spoken of as though it were known apart from all acts of consciousness.  It seems to be forgotten that the idea of reality can be nothing more than some mode of consciousness; and that the question to be considered is—What is the relation between this mode and other modes?

By reality we mean *persistence* in consciousness : a persistence which is either unconditional, as our consciousness of space, or which is conditional, as our consciousness of a body while grasping it. The real, as we conceive it, is distinguished solely by the test of persistence; for by this test we separate it from what we call the unreal. Between a person standing before us and the idea of such a person, we discriminate by our ability to expel the idea from consciousness and our inability, while looking at him, to expel the person from consciousness. And when in doubt as to the trust-worthiness of some impression made on our eyes in the dusk, we settle the matter by observing whether the impression persists on closer inspection; and we predicate reality if the persistence is complete. How truly persistence is what we mean by reality, is shown in the fact that, after criticism has proved that the real as presented in perception is not the objectively real, the vague consciousness which we retain of the objectively real, is of something which persists absolutely, under all changes of mode, form, or appearance. And the fact that we cannot form even an indefinite notion of the absolutely real, except as the absolutely persistent, implies that persistence is our ultimate test of the real whether as existing under its unknown form or under the form known to us.

Consequently, the result must be the same to us whether that which we perceive be the Unknowable itself, or an effect invariably wrought on us by the Unknowable. If, under certain conditions furnished by our constitutions, some Power of which the nature is beyond conception, always produces a certain mode of consciousness —if this mode of consciousness is as persistent as would be this Power were it in consciousness; the reality will be to consciousness as complete in the one case as in the other. Were Unconditioned Being itself present in thought, it could but be persistent; and if, instead, there is Being conditioned by the forms of thought, but no less persistent, it must be to us no less real.

Hence there may be drawn these conclusions :—First, that we have an indefinite consciousness of an absolute reality transcending relations, which is produced by the absolute persistence in us of something which survives all changes of relation. Second, that we have a definite consciousness of relative reality, which unceasingly persists in us under one or other of its forms, and under each form so long as the conditions of presentation are fulfilled; and that the relative reality, being thus continuously persistent in us, is as real to us as would be the absolute reality could it be immediately known. Third, that thought being possible only under relation, the relative reality can be conceived as such only in connexion with an absolute reality; and the connexion between the two being absolutely persistent in our consciousness, is real in the same sense as the terms it unites are real.

Thus then we may resume, with entire confidence, those realistic conceptions which Philosophy at first sight seems to dissipate. Though reality under the forms of our consciousness is but a conditioned effect of the absolute reality, yet this conditioned effect standing in indissoluble relation with its unconditioned cause, and being equally persistent with it so long as the conditions persist, is, to the consciousness supplying those conditions, equally real. Much as our visual perceptions, though merely symbols found to be the equivalents of tactual perceptions, are yet so identified with those tactual perceptions that we appear actually to see the solidity and hardness which we do but infer, and thus conceive as solid objects what are only the signs of solid objects; so, on a higher stage, do we deal with these relative realities as though they were the actual existences instead of effects of the actual existences. And we may legitimately continue so to deal with them as long as the conclusions to which they help us are understood as relatives and not absolute.

This general conclusion it now remains to interpret specifically, in its application to each of our ultimate scientific ideas.

§ 47.* We think in relations. We have seen (Chap. iii. Part I) that ultimate modes of being cannot be known or conceived as they exist in themselves, that is, out of *relation* to our conscious-

---

* For the psychological conclusions briefly set forth in this section and the three sections following it, the justification will be found in the writer's *Principles of Psychology.*

ness. We have seen, by analyzing the product of thought, that it always consists of *relations*, and cannot include anything deeper than the most general of these. On analyzing the process of thought, we found that cognition of the Absolute is impossible, because it presents neither *relation* nor its elements—difference and likeness. And lastly, it was shown that though by the relativity of our thought we are eternally debarred from knowing or conceiving Absolute Being; yet that this very *relativity* of our thought, necessitates that vague consciousness of Absolute Being which no mental effort can suppress. That *relation* is the universal form of thought is thus a truth which all kinds of demonstration unite in proving.

By the transcendentalists, certain other elements of consciousness are regarded as forms of thought, or more strictly of intuition, which is the ultimate component of thought. While relation would of necessity be admitted by them to be a universal mental form, they would class with it two others as also universal. Were their doctrine otherwise tenable, however, it must still be rejected if such alleged further forms are interpretable as generated by the primary form. If we think in relations, and if relations have certain universal forms, it is manifest that such universal forms of relations will become universal forms of consciousness. And if these further universal forms are thus explicable, it is superfluous, and therefore unphilosophical, to assign them an independent origin. Now relations are of two orders—relations of sequence, and relations of co-existence; of which the one is original and the other derived. The relation of sequence is given in every change of consciousness. The relation of co-existence, which cannot be originally given in a consciousness of which the states are serial, becomes distinguished only when it is found that certain relations of sequence have their terms presented in consciousness in either order with equal facility; while the others are presented only in one order. Relations of which the terms are not reversible, become recognized as sequences proper; while relations of which the terms occur indifferently in both directions, become recognized as co-existences. Endless experiences, which from moment to moment present both orders of these relations, render the distinction between them perfectly definite; and at the same time generate an abstract conception of each. The abstract of all sequences is Time. The abstract of all co-existences is Space. From the fact that in thought, Time is inseparable from sequence, and Space from co-existence, we do not here infer that Time and Space are original forms of consciousness under which sequences and co-existences are known; but we infer that our conceptions of Time and Space are generated, as other abstracts are generated from other concretes: the only difference being that the organization of experiences has, in these cases, been going on throughout the entire evolution of intelligence.

This synthesis is confirmed by analysis. Our consciousness of Space is a consciousness of co-existent positions. A portion of space can be conceived only by representing its limits as co-existing in certain relative positions; and each of its imagined boundaries, be it line or plane, can be thought of in no other way than as made up of co-existent positions in close proximity. And since a position is not an entity—since the congeries of positions which constitute any conceived portion of space, and mark its bounds, are not sensible existences; it follows that the co-existent positions which make up our consciousness of Space, are not co-existences in the full sense of the word (which implies realities as their terms), but are the blank forms of co-existences, left behind when the realities are absent; that is, are the abstracts of co-existences. The experiences out of which, during the evolution of intelligence, this abstract of all co-existences has been generated, are experiences of individual positions ascertained by touch; and each of such experiences involves the resistance of an object touched, and the muscular tensions which measure this resistance. By countless unlike muscular adjustments, involving unlike muscular tensions, different resisting positions are disclosed; and these, as they can be experienced in one order as readily as another, we regard as co-existing. But since, under other circumstances, the same muscular adjustments do not produce contacts with resisting positions, there result the same states of consciousness *minus* the resistances — blank forms of co-existence from which the co-existent objects before experienced are absent. And from a building up of these, too elaborate to be here detailed, results that abstract of all relations of co-existence which we call Space.  It remains only to point out, as a truth hereafter to be recalled, that the experiences from which the consciousness of Space arises, are experiences of *force*.  A plexus of muscular forces we ourselves exercise constitutes the index of each position as originally disclosed to us; and the resistance which makes us aware of something existing in that position, is an equivalent of the pressure we consciously exert.  Thus, experiences of forces variously correlated, are those from which our consciousness of Space is abstracted.

Our Space-consciousness being thus shown to be purely relative, what are we to say of that which causes it ?  Is there an absolute Space which relative Space in some sort represents ?  Is Space in itself a form or condition of absolute existence, producing in our minds a corresponding form or condition of relative existence ?  These are unanswerable questions.  Our conception of Space is produced by some mode of the Unknowable; and the complete unchangeableness of our conception of it simply implies a complete uniformity in the effects wrought by this mode of the Unknowable upon us.  But therefore to call it a necessary mode of the Unknowable is illegitimate.  All we can assert is that Space is a relative reality; that our consciousness of this unchanging relative reality implies an absolute reality equally unchanging in so far as we are concerned; and that the relative reality may be unhesitatingly accepted in thought as a valid basis for our reasonings; which, when rightly carried on, will bring us to truths that have a like relative reality—the only truths which concern us or can possibly be known to us.

Concerning Time, relative and absolute, a parallel argument leads to parallel conclusions.  These are too obvious to need specifying in detail.

§ 48. Our conception of Matter, reduced to its simplest shape, is that of co-existent positions that offer resistance; as contrasted with our conception of Space, in which the co-existent positions offer no resistance.  We think of Body as bounded by surfaces that resist, and as made up throughout of parts that resist. Mentally abstract the co-existent resistances, and the consciousness

9

of Body disappears, leaving behind it the consciousness of Space. And since the group of co-existing resistant positions gives us impressions of resistance whether we touch its near, its remote, its right, or its left side; it results that as different muscular adjustments indicate different co-existences, we are obliged to conceive every portion of matter as containing more than one resistant position—that is, as occupying Space. Hence the necessity we are under of representing to ourselves the ultimate elements of Matter as being at once extended and resistant: this being the universal form of our sensible experiences of Matter, becomes the form which our conception of it cannot transcend, however minute the fragments which imaginary subdivisions produce.     Of these two inseparable elements, the resistance is primary and the extension secondary.     Occupied extension, or Body, being distinguished in consciousness from unoccupied extension, or Space, by its resistance, this attribute must clearly have precedence in the genesis of the idea.     If, as was argued in the last section, the experiences, mainly ancestral, from which our consciousness of Space is abstracted, can be received only through impressions of resistance made on the organism; the implication is, that experiences of resistance being those from which the conception of Space is generated, the resistance-attribute of Matter must be regarded as primordial and the space-attribute as derivative.     Whence it becomes clear that our experiences of *force*, are those out of which the idea of Matter is built.     Matter as opposing our muscular energies, being immediately present to consciousness in terms of force; and its occupancy of Space being known by an abstract of experiences originally given in terms of force; it follows that forces, standing in certain correlations, form the whole content of our idea of Matter.

Such being our cognition of the relative reality, what are we to say of the absolute reality?     We can only say that it is some mode of the Unknowable, related to the Matter we know as cause to effect.     The relativity of our cognition of Matter is shown alike by the above analysis, and by the contradictions which are evolved when we deal with the cognition as an absolute one (§ 16).     But, as we have lately seen, though known to us only under relation, Matter is as real, in the true sense of that word, as it would be could we know it out of relation; and further, the relative reality which we know as Matter, is necessarily represented to the mind as standing in a persistent or real relation to the absolute reality.    We may therefore deliver ourselves over, without hesitation, to those terms of thought which experience has organized in us.    We need not in our physical, chemical, or other researches, refrain from dealing with Matter as made up of extended and resistant atoms; for this conception, necessarily resulting from our experiences of Matter, is not less legitimate than the conception of aggregate masses as extended and resistant.    The atomic hypothesis, and the kindred hypothesis of an all-pervading ether consisting of units, are simply developments of those universal forms which the actions of the Unknowable have wrought in us. The conclusions logically worked out by their aid are sure to be in harmony with all others which these same forms involve, and will have a *relative* truth that is equally complete.

§ 49.  The conception of Motion, as presented or represented in the developed consciousness, involves the conceptions of Space, of Time, and of Matter.  A something perceived; a series of positions occupied by it in succession; and a group of co-existent positions united in thought with the successive ones—these are the constituents of the idea.  And since, as we have seen, these are severally elaborated from experiences of *force* as given in certain correlations, it follows that from a further synthesis of such experiences, the idea of Motion is also elaborated.  A certain other element in the idea, which is in truth its fundamental element (namely, the necessity which the moving body is under to go on changing its position), results immediately from the earliest experiences of force.  Movements of different parts of the organism in relation to one another, are the first presented in consciousness. These, produced by the actions of the muscles, entail reactions on consciousness in the shape of sensations of muscular tension.  Consequently, each stretching-out or drawing-in of a limb, is originally known as a series of muscular tensions, varying as the position of the limb changes.  And this rudimentary consciousness of Motion, consisting of serial impressions of force, becomes inseparably united with the consciousnesses of Space and Time as fast as these are abstracted from other impressions of force. Or rather, out of this primitive conception of Motion, the adult conception of it is developed simultaneously with the development of the conceptions of Space and Time: all three being evolved from the more multiplied and varied impressions of muscular tension and objective resistance.

That this relative reality answers to some absolute reality, it is needful only for form's sake to assert. What has been said above, respecting the Unknown Cause which produces in us the effects called Matter, Space, and Time, will apply, on simply changing the terms, to Motion.

§§ 50, 51. We come down, then, finally to Force, as the ultimate of ultimates. Though Space, Time, Matter, and Motion, are apparently all necessary data of intelligence, yet a psychological analysis (here indicated only in rude outline) shows us that these are either built up of, or abstracted from, experiences of Force. Matter and Motion as we know them are concretes built up from the *contents* of various mental relations ; while Space and Time are abstracts of the *forms* of these various relations. Deeper down than these, however, are the primordial experiences of Force. A single impression of force is manifestly receivable by a sentient being devoid of mental forms. Grant but sensibility, with no established power of thought, and a force producing some nervous change, will still be presentable at the supposed seat of sensation. Though no single impression of force so received, could itself produce a consciousness (which implies relations between different states), yet a multiplication of such impressions, differing in kind and degree, would give the materials for the establishment of relations, that is, of thought. And if such relations differed in their forms as well as in their contents, the impressions of such forms would be organized simultaneously with the impressions they contained. It needs but to remember that consciousness consists of changes, to see that the ultimate datum of consciousness must be that of which change is the manifestation ; and that thus the force by which we ourselves produce changes, and which serves to symbolize the cause of changes in general, is the final disclosure of analysis.

That this undecomposable mode of consciousness, into which all other modes may be decomposed, cannot be itself the Power manifested to us through phenomena, has been already proved (§ 18). We saw that to assume identity of nature between the cause of changes as it exists absolutely, and that cause of change of which we are conscious in our own muscular efforts, betrays us into alternate impossibilities of thought. Force, as we know it, can be regarded only as a conditioned effect of the Unconditioned Cause —as the relative reality indicating to us an Absolute Reality by which it is immediately produced.

# CHAPTER IV

## THE INDESTRUCTIBILITY OF MATTER

§ 52. Not because the truth is unfamiliar, is it needful here to assert the indestructibility of Matter; but partly because the symmetry of our argument demands enunciation of this truth, and partly because the evidence on which it is accepted must be examined. Could it be shown, or could it with reason be supposed, that Matter, either in its aggregates or in its units, ever becomes non-existent, it would be needful either to ascertain under what conditions it becomes non-existent, or else to confess that Science and Philosophy are impossible. For if, instead of having to deal with fixed quantities and weights, we had to deal with quantities and weights which are apt, wholly or in part, to be annihilated, there would be introduced an incalculable element, fatal to all positive conclusions. Clearly, therefore, the proposition that matter is indestructible must be deliberately considered.

So far from being admitted as a self-evident truth, this would, in primitive times, have been rejected as a self-evident error. There was once universally current a notion that things could vanish into nothing, or arise out of nothing. If men did not believe this in the strict sense of the word (which would imply that the process of creation or annihilation was clearly represented in consciousness), they still believed that they believed it; and how nearly, in their confused thoughts, the one was equivalent to the other, is shown by their conduct. Nor, indeed, have dark ages and inferior minds alone betrayed this belief. In its dogmas respecting the beginning and end of the world, the current theology clearly implies it; and it may be questioned whether Shakespeare, in his poetical anticipation of a time when all things shall disappear and "leave not a wrack behind," was not under its influence.    The accumulation of experiences, however, and still more the organization of experiences, has slowly reversed this conviction.   All apparent proofs that something can come out of nothing a wider knowledge has one by one cancelled.   The comet which is suddenly discovered and nightly waxes larger is proved not to be a newly-created body, but a body which was until lately beyond the range of vision.   The cloud formed a few minutes ago in the sky consists not of substance that has just begun to be, but of substance that previously existed in a transparent form.   And similarly with a crystal or a precipitate in relation to the fluid depositing it.   Conversely, the seeming annihilations of matter turn out to be only changes of state.   It is found that the evaporated water, though it has become invisible, may be brought by condensation to its original shape.   Though from a discharged fowling-piece the gunpowder has disappeared, there have appeared in place of it certain gases which, in assuming a larger volume, have caused the explosion.       Not, however, until the rise of quantitative chemistry, could the conclusion suggested by such experiences be harmonized with all the facts.   When, having ascertained not only the combinations formed by various sub-stances, but also the proportions in which they combine, chemists were enabled to account for the matter that had made its appearance or become invisible, scepticism was dissipated.   And of the general conclusion thus reached, the exact analyses daily made, by which the same portion of matter is pursued through numerous disguises and finally separated, furnish never-ceasing confirmations.

Such has become the effect of this specific evidence, joined to that general evidence which the continued existence of familiar objects gives us, that the Indestructibility of Matter is now held by many to be a truth of which the negation is inconceivable.

§ 53.   This last fact raises the question whether we have any higher warrant for this fundamental belief than the warrant of conscious induction.   Before showing that we have a higher warrant, some explanations are needful.

The consciousness of logical necessity, is the consciousness that a certain conclusion is implicitly contained in certain premises explicitly stated. If, contrasting a young child and an adult, we see that this consciousness of logical necessity, absent from the one is present in the other, we are taught that there is a *growing up to* the recognition of certain necessary truths, merely by the unfolding of the inherited intellectual forms and faculties.

To state the case more specifically :—Before a truth can be known as necessary, two conditions must be fulfilled. There must be a mental structure capable of grasping the terms of the proposition and the relation alleged between them; and there must be such definite and deliberate mental representation of these terms, as makes possible a clear consciousness of this relation. Non-fulfilment of either condition may cause non-recognition of the necessity of the truth. Let us take cases.

The savage who cannot count the fingers on one hand, can frame no definite thought answering to the statement that 7 and 5 are 12; still less can he frame the consciousness that no other total is possible.

The boy adding up figures inattentively, says to himself that 7 and 5 are 11; and may repeatedly bring out a wrong result by repeatedly making this error.

Neither the non-recognition of the truth that 7 and 5 are 12, which in the savage results from undeveloped mental structure, nor the assertion, due to the boy's careless mental action, that they make 11, leads us to doubt the necessity of the relation between these two separately-existing numbers and the sum they make when existing together. Nor does failure from either cause to apprehend the necessity of this relation, make us hesitate to say that when its terms are distinctly represented in thought, its necessity will be seen ; and that, apart from multiplied experiences, this necessity becomes cognizable when structures and functions are so far developed that groups of 7 and 5 and 12 can be mentally grasped.

Manifestly, then, there are recognitions of necessary truths, as such, which accompany mental evolution. And there are ascending gradations in these recognitions. A boy who has intelligence enough to see that things which are equal to the same thing are equal to one another, may be unable to see that ratios which are severally equal to certain other ratios that are unequal to each other, are themselves unequal; though to a more developed mind this last axiom is no less obviously necessary than the first.

All this which holds of logical and mathematical truths, holds, with change of terms, of physical truths. There are necessary truths in Physics for the apprehension of which, also, a developed and disciplined intelligence is required; and before such intelligence arises, not only may there be failure to apprehend the necessity of them, but there may be vague beliefs in their contraries. Up to comparatively recent times, all mankind were in this state of incapacity respecting physical axioms; and the mass of mankind are so still. Effects are expected without causes of fit kinds; or effects extremely disproportionate to causes are looked for; or causes are supposed to end without effects.* But though many are unable to grasp physical axioms, it no more follows that physical axioms are not knowable *à priori* by a developed intellect, than it follows that logical relations are not necessary, because undeveloped intellects cannot perceive their necessity.

It is thus with the notions which have been current respecting the creation and annihilation of Matter. In the first place, there has been a confounding of two radically-different things—disappearance of Matter from a visible form, say by evaporation, and passage of Matter from existence into non-existence. Until this confusion is avoided, the belief that Matter can be annihilated readily obtains currency. In the second place, the currency of it continues so long as there is not power of introspection enough to make manifest what results from the attempt to annihilate Matter in thought. But when the vague ideas arising in a nervous structure imperfectly organized, are replaced by the clear ideas arising in a definite nervous structure; this definite structure, moulded by experience into correspondence with external things, makes necessary

---

* I knew a lady, who contended that a dress folded up tightly weighed more than when loosely folded up; and who, under this belief, had her trunks made large that she might diminish the charge for freight! Another, whom I know, ascribes the feeling of lightness which accompanies vigour, to actual decrease of weight; believes that by stepping gently, she can press less upon the ground; and, when cross-questioned, asserts that, if placed in scales, she can make herself lighter by an act of will!

in thought the relations answering to uniformities in things. Hence, among others, the conception of the Indestructibility of Matter.

For self-analysis shows this to be a datum of consciousness. Conceive space to be cleared of all bodies save one. Now imagine the remaining one not to be removed from its place, but to lapse into nothing while standing in that place. You fail. The space which was solid you cannot conceive becoming empty, save by transfer of that which made it solid. What is termed the ultimate incompressibility of Matter is an admitted law of thought. However small the bulk to which we conceive a piece of matter reduced, it is impossible to conceive it reduced into nothing. While we can represent to ourselves its parts as approximated, we cannot represent to ourselves the quantity of matter as made less. To do this would be to imagine some of the parts compressed into nothing, which is no more possible than to imagine compression of the whole into nothing.        Our inability to conceive Matter becoming non-existent, is consequent on the nature of thought. Thought consists in the establishment of relations. There can be no relation established, and therefore no thought framed, when one of the related terms is absent from consciousness. Hence it is impossible to think of something becoming nothing, for the same reason that it is impossible to think of nothing becoming something—the reason, namely, that nothing cannot become an object of consciousness. The annihilation of Matter is unthinkable for the same reason that the creation of Matter is unthinkable.

It must be added that no experimental verification of the truth that Matter is indestructible, is possible without a tacit assumption of it. For all such verification implies weighing, and weighing assumes that the matter forming the weight remains the same.

§ 54. And here we are introduced to that which it most concerns us to observe—the nature of the perceptions by which the permanence of Matter is perpetually illustrated. These perceptions under all their forms simply reveal this—that the force which a given quantity of matter embodies remains always the same under the same conditions. A toy, which long unseen produces in us a set of visual and tactual feelings like those produced in child-hood, is recognized as the same because it has the *power* of affecting us in the same ways. The downward strain of some sovereigns, which the bank-clerk weighs to save himself the trouble of counting, proves the special amount of a special kind of Matter; and the goldsmith uses the same test when the shape of the Matter has been changed by a workman. So, too, with special properties. Whether a certain crystal is or is not diamond is decided by its resistance to abrasion and the degree to which it bends light out of its course. And so the chemist when a piece of substance lately visible and tangible has been reduced to an invisible, intangible gas, but has the same weight, or when the quantity of a certain element is inferred from its ability to neutralize a given quantity of some other element, he refers to the amount of *action* which the Matter exercises as his measure of the amount of Matter.

Thus, then, by the Indestructibility of Matter, we really mean the indestructibility of the *force* with which Matter affects us. And this truth is made manifest not only by analysis of the *à posteriori* cognition, but equally so by analysis of the *à priori* one.\*

---

\* Lest he should not have observed it, the reader must be warned that the terms "*à priori* truth" and "necessary truth," as used in this work, are to be interpreted not in the old sense, as implying cognitions wholly independent of experiences, but as implying cognitions that have been rendered organic by immense accumulations of experiences, received partly by the individual, but mainly by all ancestral individuals whose nervous systems he inherits. On referring to the *Principles of Psychology* (§§ 426–433), it will be seen that the warrant alleged for one of these irreversible ultimate convictions is that, on the hypothesis of Evolution, it represents an immeasurably-greater accumulation of experiences than can be acquired by any single individual.

# CHAPTER V

## THE CONTINUITY OF MOTION

§ 55. LIKE the Indestructibility of Matter, the Continuity of Motion, or, more strictly, of that something which has Motion for one of its sensible forms, is a truth on which depends the possibility of exact Science, and therefore of a Philosophy which unifies the results of exact Science. Motions, visible and invisible, of masses and of molecules, form the larger half of the phenomena to be interpreted; and if such motions might either proceed from nothing or lapse into nothing, there could be no scientific interpretation of them.

This second fundamental truth, like the first, is not self-evident to primitive men nor to the uncultured among ourselves. Contrariwise, to uninstructed minds the opposite seems self-evident. The facts that a stone thrown up soon loses its ascending motion, and that after the blow its fall gives to the Earth, it remains quiescent, apparently prove that the principle of activity * which the stone manifested may disappear absolutely. Accepting the dicta of unaided perception, all men once believed, and most believe still, that motion can pass into nothing, and ordinarily does so pass. But the establishment of certain facts having opposite implications, led to inquiries which have proved these appearances to be illusive. The discovery that the celestial motions do not diminish, raised the suspicion that a moving body, when not interfered with, will go on for ever without change of velocity; and suggested the question whether bodies which lose their motion, do not at the same time communicate as much motion to

* Throughout this chapter I use this phrase, not with any metaphysical meaning, but merely to avoid foregone conclusions.

other bodies. It was a familiar fact that a stone would glide further over a smooth surface, as that of ice, presenting no small objects to which it could part with its motion by collision, than over a surface strewn with such small objects; and that a stick hurled into the air would travel a far greater distance than if hurled into a dense medium like water. Thus the primitive notion that moving bodies have an inherent tendency to stop—a notion which the Greeks did not get rid of, and which lasted till the time of Galileo—began to give way. It was further shaken by such experiments as those of Hooke, which proved that a top spins the longer in proportion as it is prevented from communicating motion to surrounding matter.

To explain here all disappearances of visible motions is out of the question. It must suffice to state, generally, that the molar motion which disappears when a bell is struck by its clapper, reappears in the bell's vibrations and in the waves of air they produce; that when a moving mass is stopped by coming against a mass that is immovable, the motion which does not show itself in sound shows itself in molecular motion; and that when bodies rub against one another, the motion lost by friction is gained in the motion of molecules. But one aspect of this general truth, as it is displayed in the motions of masses, we must carefully contemplate; for, otherwise, the doctrine of the Continuity of Motion will be misapprehended.

§ 56. As expressed by Newton, the first law of motion is that " every body must persevere in its state of rest, or of uniform motion in a straight line, unless it be compelled to change that state by forces impressed upon it."

With this truth may be associated the truth that a body describing a circular orbit round a centre which detains it by a tractive force, moves in that orbit with undiminished velocity.

The first of these abstract truths is never realized in the concrete, and the second of them is but approximately realized. Uniform motion in a straight line implies the absence of a resisting medium; and it further implies the absence of forces, gravitative or other, exercised by neighbouring masses: conditions never fulfilled. So, too, the maintenance of a circular orbit by any celestial body, implies that there are no perturbing bodies, and that there is an exact adjustment between its velocity and the tractive force of its primary : neither requirement ever being conformed to. In actual orbits, sensibly elliptical as they are, the velocity is sensibly variable. And along with great eccentricity there goes great variation.

With the case of those celestial bodies which, moving in eccentric orbits, display at one time little motion and at another much motion, may be associated as partially analogous the case of the pendulum. With speed now increasing and now decreasing, the pendulum alternates between extremes at which motion ceases.

How shall we so conceive these allied phenomena as to express rightly the truth common to them ? The first law of motion, nowhere literally fulfilled, is yet, in a sense, implied by these facts which seem at variance with it. Though in a circular orbit the direction of the motion is continually being changed, yet the velocity remains unchanged. Though in an elliptical orbit there is now acceleration and now retardation, yet the average speed is constant through successive revolutions. Though the pendulum comes to a momentary rest at the end of each swing, and then begins a reverse motion, yet the oscillation, considered as a whole, is continuous : friction and atmospheric resistance being absent, this alternation of states would go on for ever.

What, then, do these cases show us in common ? That which vision familiarizes us with in Motion, and that which has thus been made the dominant element in our conception of Motion, is not the element of which we can allege continuity. If we regard Motion simply as change of place, then the pendulum shows us both that the rate of this change may vary from instant to instant, and that, ceasing at intervals, it may be afresh initiated.

But if what we may call the translation-element in Motion is not continuous, what is continuous ? If, like Galileo, we watch a swinging chandelier, and observe, not the isochronism of its oscillations but the recurring reversal of direction, we are impressed with the fact that though, at the end of each swing, the translation through space ceases, yet there is something which does not cease ; for the translation recommences in the opposite direction. And on remembering that when a violent push was given to the chandelier it described a larger arc, and was a longer time before the resistance of the air brought it to rest, we are shown that what continues to exist during its alternating movements is some correlative of the muscular effort which put it in motion. The truth forced on our attention is that translation through space is not itself an *existence ;* and that hence the cessation of Motion, considered simply as translation, is not the cessation of an existence, but is the cessation of a certain *sign of an existence.*

Still there remains a difficulty. If that element in the chandelier's motion of which alone we can allege continuity, is the correlative of the muscular effort which moved the chandelier, what becomes of this element at either extreme of the oscillation? Arrest the chandelier in the middle of its swing, and it gives a blow to the hand—exhibits some principle of activity such as muscular effort can give. But touch it at either turning point and it displays no such principle of activity. This has disappeared just as much as the translation through space has disappeared. How, then, can it be alleged that though the Motion through space is not continuous, the principle of activity implied by the Motion is continuous?

Unquestionably the facts show that the principle of activity continues to exist under some form. When not perceptible it must be latent. How is it latent? A clue to the answer is gained on observing that though the chandelier when seized at the turning point of its swing, gives no impact in the direction of its late movement, it forthwith begins to pull in the opposite direction; and on observing, further, that its pull is great when the swing has been made extensive by a violent push. Hence the loss of visible activity at the highest point of the upward motion, is accompanied by the production of an invisible activity which generates the subsequent motion downwards. To conceive this latent activity gained as an existence equal to the preceptible activity lost is not easy; but we may help ourselves so to conceive it by considering cases of another class.

§ 57. When one who pushes against a door that has stuck fast, produces by great effort no motion, but eventually by a little greater effort bursts the door open, swinging it back and tumbling headlong into the room, he has evidence that the first muscular strain which did not produce transfer of matter through space, was yet equivalent to a certain amount of such transfer. Again, when a railway-porter gradually stops a detached carriage by pulling at the buffer, he shows us that (supposing friction, &c., absent) the slowly-diminished motion of the carriage over a certain space, is the equivalent of the constant backward strain put upon the carriage while it is travelling through that space. Carrying with us the conception thus reached, we will now consider a case which makes it more definite.

When used as a plaything, a ball fastened to the end of an india-rubber string yields a clear idea of the correlation between perceptible activity and latent activity. If, retaining one end of the string, a boy throws the ball from him horizontally, its motion is resisted by the increasing strain on the string; and the string, stretched more and more as the ball recedes, presently brings it to rest. Where now exists the principle of activity which the moving ball displayed? It exists in the strained thread of india-rubber. Under what form of changed molecular state it exists we need not ask. It suffices that the string is the seat of a tension generated by the motion of the ball, and equivalent to it. When the ball has been arrested the stretched string begins to generate in it an opposite motion, and continues to accelerate that motion until the ball comes back to the point at which the stretching of the string commenced—a point at which, but for loss by atmospheric resistance and molecular redistribution, its velocity would be equal to the original velocity. Here the truth that the principle of activity, alternating between visible and invisible modes, does not cease to exist when the translation through space ceases to exist, is readily comprehensible; and it becomes easy to understand the corollary that at each point in the path of the ball, the quantity of its perceptible activity, *plus* the quantity which is latent in the stretched string, yields a constant sum.

Aided by this illustration, we can vaguely conceive what happens between bodies connected, not by a stretched string, but by a traction exercised by an invisible agency. It matters not to our general conception that the intensity of this traction varies in a different manner: decreasing as the square of the distance increases, but being practically constant for terrestrial distances

itself as strain. And this principle of activity, now shown by translation, now by strain, and often by the two together, is alone that which in Motion we can call continuous.

§ 58. What is this principle of activity? Vision gives us no idea of it. If by a mirror we cast the image of an illuminated object on to a dark wall, and then suddenly changing the attitude of the mirror make the reflected image pass from side to side, no thought arises that there is present in the image a principle of activity. Before we can conceive the presence of this, we must regard the visual impression as symbolizing something tangible. Sight of a moving body suggests a principle of activity which would be appreciable by skin and muscles were the body laid hold of. This principle of activity which Motion shows us is the objective correlate of our subjective sense of effort. By pushing and pulling we get feelings which, generalized and abstracted, yield our ideas of resistance and tension. Now displayed by changing position and now by unchanging strain, this principle of activity is ultimately conceived by us under the single form of its equivalent muscular effort. So that the continuity of Motion, as well as the indestructibility of Matter, is really known to us in terms of Force. Here, however, the Force is of the kind known as Energy— a word applied to the force, molar or molecular, possessed by matter in action, as distinguished from the passive force by which matter maintains its shape and occupies space: a force which physicists appear to think needs no name.

§ 59. And now we reach the truth to be here especially noted. All proofs of the Continuity of Motion involve the postulate that the quantity of Energy is constant. Observe what results when we analyze the reasonings by which the Continuity of Motion is shown.

A particular planet is identified by its constant power to affect our eyes in a special way. Further, such planet has not been *seen* to move by the astronomer; but its motion is *inferred* from a comparison of its present position with the position it before occupied. This comparison proves to be a comparison between the different impressions produced on him by the different adjustments of his observing instruments. And the validity of the inferences drawn depends on the truth of the assumption that these masses of matter, celestial and terrestrial, continue to affect his senses in the same ways under the same conditions.      On going a step further back, it turns out that difference in the adjustment of his observing instrument, and by implication in the planet's position, is meaningless until shown to correspond with a certain calculated position which the planet must occupy, supposing that no motion has been lost. And if, finally, we examine the implied calculation, we find that it takes into account those accelerations and retardations which ellipticity of the orbit involves, as well as those variations of motion caused by adjacent planets—we find, that is, that the motion is concluded to be indestructible not from the uniform velocity of the planet, but from the constant quantity of motion exhibited after allowances have been made for the motions communicated to, or received from, other celestial bodies. And when we ask how this is estimated, we discover that the estimate assumes certain laws of force or energy ; which laws, one and all, embody the postulate that energy cannot be destroyed.

Similarly with the à priori conclusion that Motion is continuous. That which defies suppression in thought (disciplined thought, of course), is the force which the motion indicates. We can imagine retardation to result from the actions of other bodies. But to imagine this we must imagine loss of some of the energy implied by the motion. We are obliged to conceive this energy as impressed in the shape of reaction on the bodies causing the retardation. And the motion communicated to them, we are compelled to regard as a product of the communicated energy. We can mentally diminish the velocity or space-element of motion, by diffusing the momentum or force-element over a larger mass of matter ; but the quantity of this force-element is unchangeable in thought.*                        .

* This exposition differs in its point of view from the expositions ordinarily given ; and some of the words employed, such as *strain*, have somewhat larger implications. Unable to learn anything about the nature of Force, physicists have, of late years, formulated ultimate physical truths in such ways as often tacitly to exclude the consciousness of Force : conceiving cause, as Hume proposed, in terms of antecedence and sequence only. "Potential energy," for

example, is defined as constituted by such relations in space as permit masses to generate in one another certain motions, but as being in itself nothing. While this mode of conceiving the phenomena suffices for physical inquiries, it does not suffice for the purposes of philosophy. In the *Principles of Psychology*, §§ 347–350, I have shown that our ideas of Body, Space, Motion, are derived from our ideas of muscular tension, which are the ultimate symbols into which all our other mental symbols are interpretable. Hence to formulate phenomena in the proximate terms of Body, Space, Motion, while discharging from the concepts the consciousness of Force, is to acknowledge the superstructure while ignoring the foundation.

When, in 1875, I recast the foregoing chapter, and set forth more fully the doctrine contained in the answering chapters of preceding editions, I supposed myself to be alone in dissenting from the prevailing doctrine. But a year after, in the *Philosophical Magazine* for October, 1876, I was glad to see the same view enunciated and defended by Dr. Croll, in an essay "On the Transformation of Gravity." I commend his arguments to those who are not convinced by the arguments used above.

Let me add a remark concerning the nature of the question at issue. It is assumed that, as a matter of course, it is a question falling within the sphere of the mathematicians and physicists. I demur to the assumption. It is a question falling within the sphere of the psychologists—a question concerning the right interpretation of our ideas.

# CHAPTER VI

## THE PERSISTENCE OF FORCE *

§ 60. In the foregoing two chapters, manifestations of force of two fundamentally-different classes have been dealt with—the force by which matter demonstrates itself to us as existing, and the force by which it demonstrates itself to us as acting.

Body is distinguishable from space by its power of affecting our senses, and, in the last resort, by its opposition to our efforts. We can conceive of body only by joining in thought extension and resistance: take away resistance, and there remains only space. In what way this force which produces space-occupancy is conditioned we do not know. The mode of force which is revealed to us only by opposition to our own powers, may have for one of its factors the mode of force which reveals itself by the changes initiated in our consciousness. That the space a body occupies is in part determined by the degree of that activity of its molecules known

---

* Some explanation of this title is needful. In the text itself are given the reasons for using the word "force" instead of the word "energy"; and here I must say why I think "persistence" preferable to "conservation." Some two years ago (this was written in 1861) I expressed to my friend Prof. Huxley, my dissatisfaction with the (then) current expression—"Conservation of Force": assigning as reasons, first, that the word "conservation" implies a conserver and an act of conserving; and, second, that it does not imply the existence of the force before the particular manifestation of it which is contemplated. And I may now add, as a further fault, the tacit assumption that, without some act of conservation, force would disappear. All these implications are at variance with the conception to be conveyed. In place of "conservation" Prof. Huxley suggested *persistence*. This meets most of the objections; and though it may be urged that it does not directly imply pre-existence of the force at any time manifested, yet no word less faulty in this respect can be found. In the absence of a word coined for the purpose, it seems the best; and as such I adopt it.

as heat, is a familiar truth. Moreover, such molecular rearrangement as occurs when water is changed into ice, is shown to be accompanied by an evolution of force which may burst the containing vessel and give motion to the fragments. Nevertheless, the forms of our experience oblige us to distinguish between two modes of force; the one not a worker of change and the other a worker of change, actual or potential. The first of these—the space-occupying kind of force—has no specific name.

For the second kind of force, the specific name now accepted is "Energy." That which in the last chapter was spoken of as perceptible activity, is called by physicists, "actual energy"; and that which was there spoken of as latent activity, they call "potential energy." While including the mode of activity shown in molar motion, Energy includes also the several modes of activity into which molar motion is transformable—heat, light, &c. It is the common name for the power shown alike in the movements of masses and in the movements of molecules. To our perceptions this second kind of force differs from the first kind as being not intrinsic but extrinsic.

In aggregated matter as presented to sight and touch, this antithesis is, as above implied, much obscured. Especially in a compound substance, both the latent energy locked up in the chemically-combined molecules and the actual energy made perceptible to us as heat, complicate the manifestations of intrinsic force by the manifestations of extrinsic force. But the antithesis, here partially hidden, is clearly seen on reducing the data to their lowest terms—a unit of matter, or atom, and its motion. The force by which it exists is *passive but independent*; while the force by which it moves is *active but dependent* on its past and present relations to other atoms. These two cannot be identified in our thoughts. For as it is impossible to think of motion without something that moves, so it is impossible to think of energy without something possessing the energy.

While recognizing this fundamental distinction between that *intrinsic* force by which body manifests itself as occupying space, and that *extrinsic* force distinguished as energy, I here treat of them together as being alike persistent. And I thus treat of them together partly because, in our consciousness of them, there

is the same essential element. The sense of effort is our subjective symbol for objective force in general, passive and active.
Power of resisting that which we know as our own muscular strain,
is the ultimate element in our idea of body as distinguished from
space; and any motor energy which we give to body, or receive
from it, is thought of as equal to a certain amount of muscular
strain. The two consciousnesses differ essentially in this, that
the feeling of effort common to them is in the last case joined
with consciousness of change of position, but in the first case
is not.*

There is, however, a further and more important reason for here
dealing with the proposition that Force under each of these forms
persists. We have to examine its warrant.

§ 61. A little more patience is asked. We must reconsider
the reasoning by which the indestructibility of Matter and the
continuity of Motion are established, that we may see how
impossible it is to arrive by parallel reasoning at the Persistence
of Force.

In all three cases the question is one of quantity:—Does
the Matter, or Motion, or Force, ever diminish in quantity?
Quantitative science implies measurement, and measurement
implies a unit of measure. The units of measure from which
all others of any exactness are derived, are units of linear exten-

---

* Concerning the fundamental distinction here made between the space-
occupying kind of force, and the kind of force shown by various modes of
activity, I am, as in the last chapter, at issue with some of my scientific friends.
They do not admit that the conception of force is involved in the conception of
a unit of matter. From the psychological point of view, however, Matter, in
all its properties, is the unknown cause of the sensations it produces in us; of
which the one which remains when all others are absent, is resistance to our
efforts—a resistance we are obliged to symbolize as the equivalent of the
muscular force it opposes. In imagining a unit of matter we may not ignore
this symbol, by which alone a unit of matter can be figured in thought as an
existence. It is not allowable to speak as though there remained a conception
of an existence when that conception has been eviscerated—deprived of the element
of thought by which it is distinguished from empty space. Divest the conceived unit of matter of the objective correlate to our subjective sense of effort,
and the entire fabric of physical conceptions disappears.

sion.　Our units of linear extension are the lengths of masses of matter, or the spaces between marks made on the masses, and we assume these lengths, or these spaces between marks, to remain unchanged while the temperature is unchanged.　From the standard-measure preserved at Westminster, are derived the measures for trigonometrical surveys, for geodesy, the measurement of terrestrial arcs, and the calculations of astronomical distances, dimensions, &c., and therefore for Astronomy at large. Were these units of length, original and derived, irregularly variable, there could be no celestial dynamics, nor any of that verification yielded by it of the constancy of the celestial masses and of their energies.　Hence, persistence of the space-occupying species of force cannot be proved, for the reason that it is tacitly assumed in every experiment or observation by which it is proposed to prove it.　　　The like holds of the force distinguished as energy.　The endeavour to establish this by measurement, takes for granted both the persistence of the intrinsic force by which body manifests itself as existing, and the persistence of the extrinsic force by which body acts.　For it is from these equal units of linear extension, through the medium of the equal-armed lever or scales, that we derive our equal units of weight, or gravitative force; and only by means of these can we make those quantitative comparisons by which the truths of exact science are reached.　Throughout the investigations leading the chemist to the conclusion that of the carbon which has disappeared during combustion, no portion has been lost, what is his repeatedly-assigned proof?　That afforded by the scales.　In what terms is the verdict of the scales given?　In grammes—in units of weight—in units of gravitative force.　And what is the total content of the verdict?　That as many units of gravitative force as the carbon exhibited at first, it exhibits still.　The validity of the inference, then, depends entirely upon *the constancy of the units of force.*　If the force with which the portion of metal called a gramme-weight tends towards the Earth, has varied, the inference that matter is indestructible is vicious.　Everything turns on the truth of the assumption that the gravitation of the weights is persistent; and of this no proof is assigned, or can be assigned.　　　In the reasonings of the astronomer there is a like implication, from which we may draw the like conclusion. No problem in celestial dynamics can be solved without the assumption of some unit of force. This unit need not be, like a pound or a ton, one of which we can take direct cognizance. It is requisite only that the mutual attraction which some two of the bodies concerned exercise at a given distance, shall be taken as one; so that the other attractions with which the problem deals, may be expressed in terms of this one. Such unit being assumed, the motions which the respective masses will generate in one another in a given time, are calculated; and compounding these with the motions they already have, their places at the end of that time are predicted. The prediction is verified by observation. From this, either of two inferences may be drawn. Assuming the masses to be unchanged, their energies may be proved undiminished; or assuming their energies undiminished, the masses may be proved unchanged. But the validity of one or other inference depends wholly on the truth of the assumption that the unit of force is unchanged. Let it be supposed that the gravitation of the two bodies towards each other at the given distance has varied, and the conclusions drawn are no longer true.          Nor is it only in their concrete data that the reasonings of terrestrial and celestial physics assume the Persistence of Force. The equality of action and reaction is taken for granted from beginning to end of either argument; and to assert that action and reaction are equal and opposite, is to assert that Force persists. The implication is that there cannot be an isolated force, but that any force manifested implies an equal antecedent force from which it is derived, and against which it is a reaction.

We might indeed be certain, even in the absence of any such analysis as the foregoing, that there must exist some principle which, as being the basis of science, cannot be established by science. All reasoned-out conclusions whatever must rest on some postulate. As before shown (§ 23), we cannot go on merging derivative truths in those wider truths from which they are derived, without reaching at last a widest truth which can be merged in no other, or derived from no other. And the relation in which it stands to the truths of science in general, shows that this truth transcending demonstration is the Persistence of Force. To this an ultimate analysis brings us down, and on this a rational synthesis must build up.

§ 62. But now what is the force of which we predicate persistence? That which the word ordinarily stands for is the consciousness of muscular tension—the feeling of effort which we have either when putting something in motion or when resisting a pressure. This feeling, however, is but a symbol.

In § 18 it was said that though, since action and reaction are equal and opposite, we are obliged to think of the downward pull of a weight as equal to the upward pull which supports it, and though the thought of equality suggests kinship of nature, yet, as we cannot ascribe feeling to the weight, we are obliged to admit that Force as it exists beyond consciousness has no likeness to force as we conceive it, though there is between them the kind of equivalence implied by simultaneous variation. The effort of one who throws a cricket ball is followed by the motion of the ball through space, and its momentum is re-transformed into muscular strain in one who catches it. What the force was when it existed in the flying cricket ball it is impossible to imagine: we have no terms of thought in which to represent it. And it is thus with all the transformations of energy taking place in the world around. Those illustrations given in § 66, showing the changes of form which energy undergoes and the equivalence between so much of it in one form and so much in another, fail to enlighten us respecting the energy itself. It assumes under this or that set of conditions this or that shape, and the quantity of it is not altered during its transformations. For that interpretation of things which is alone possible for us this is all we require to know—that the force or energy manifested, now in one way now in another, persists or remains unchanged in amount. But when we ask what this energy is, there is no answer save that it is the noumenal cause implied by the phenomenal effect.

Hence the force of which we assert persistence is that Absolute Force we are obliged to postulate as the necessary correlate of the force we are conscious of. By the Persistence of Force, we really mean the persistence of some Cause which transcends our knowledge and conception. In asserting it we assert an Unconditioned Reality, without beginning or end.

Thus, quite unexpectedly, we come down once more to that ultimate truth in which, as we saw, Religion and Science coalesce —the continued existence of an Unknowable as the necessary correlative of the Knowable.

# CHAPTER VII

## THE PERSISTENCE OF RELATIONS AMONG FORCES '

§ 63. THE first deduction to be drawn from the ultimate universal truth that force persists is that the relations among forces persist. Supposing a given manifestation of force, under a given form and given conditions, be either preceded by or succeeded by some other manifestation, it must, in all cases where the form and conditions are the same, be preceded by or succeeded by such other manifestation. Every antecedent mode of the Unknowable must have an invariable connexion, quantitative and qualitative, with that mode of the Unknowable which we call its consequent.

For to say otherwise is to deny the persistence of force. If in any two cases there is exact likeness not only between those conspicuous antecedents which we call the causes, but also between those accompanying antecedents which we call the conditions, we cannot affirm that the effects will differ, without affirming either that some force has come into existence or that some force has ceased to exist. If the co-operative forces in the one case are equal to those in the other, each to each, in distribution and amount; then it is impossible to conceive the product of their joint action in the one case as unlike that in the other, without conceiving one or more of the forces to have increased or diminished in quantity; and this is conceiving that force is not persistent.

To impress the truth thus enunciated under its most abstract form, some illustrations will be desirable.

§ 64. Let two bullets, equal in weights and shapes, be projected with equal energies; then, in equal times, equal distances must be travelled by them.   The assertion that one of them will describe an assigned space sooner than the other, though their initial momenta were alike and they have been equally resisted (for if they are unequally resisted the antecedents differ) is an assertion that equal quantities of force have not done equal amounts of work ; and this cannot be thought without thinking that some force has disappeared into nothing or arisen out of nothing.        Assume, further, that during its flight one of them has-been drawn by the Earth a certain number of inches out of its original line of movement ; then the other, which has moved the same distance in the same time, must have fallen just as far towards the Earth.   No other result can be imagined without imagining that equal attractions acting for equal times, have produced unequal effects ; which involves the inconceivable proposition that some action has been created or annihilated.        Again, one of the bullets having penetrated the target to a certain depth, penetration by the other bullet to a smaller depth, unless caused by greater local density in the target, cannot be mentally represented.   Such a modification of the consequents without modification of the antecedents is thinkable only through the impossible thought that something has become nothing or nothing has become something.

It is thus not with sequences only, but also with simultaneous changes and permanent co-existences.   Given charges of powder alike in quantity and quality, fired from barrels of the same structure, and propelling bullets of equal weights, sizes, and forms, similarly rammed down ; * and it is a necessary inference that the concomitant actions which make up the explosion, will bear to one another like relations of quantity and quality in the two cases. The proportions among the different products of combustion will be equal.   The several amounts of energy taken up in giving momentum to the bullet, heat to the gases, and sound on their escape, will preserve the same ratios.   The quantities of light and smoke in the one case will be what they are in the other ; and the two recoils will be alike.   For no difference of relation among these concurrent phenomena can be imagined as arising, without imagining it as arising by the creation or annihilation of energy.

* This was written while muzzle-loading was still usual.

That which holds between these two cases must hold among any number of cases; and that which here holds between comparatively simple antecedents and consequents, must hold however involved the antecedents become and however involved the consequents become.

§ 65. Thus Uniformity of Law, resolvable as we find it into the persistence of relations among forces, is a corollary from the persistence of force. The general conclusion that there exist constant connexions among phenomena, ordinarily regarded as an inductive conclusion only, is really a conclusion deducible from the ultimate datum of consciousness.

More than this may be said. Every apparent inductive proof of the uniformity of law itself takes for granted both the persistence of force and the persistence of relations among forces. For in the exact sciences, in which alone we may seek relations definite enough to prove uniformity, any alleged demonstration must depend on measurement; and as we have already seen, measurement, whether of matter or force, assumes that both are persistent in assuming that the measures have not varied. While at the same time every determination of the relations among them—in amount, proportion, direction, or what not—similarly implies measurement, the validity of which as before implies the persistence of force.

That uniformity of law thus follows inevitably from the persistence of force, will become more and more clear as we advance. The next chapter will indirectly supply abundant illustrations of it.

# CHAPTER VIII

## THE TRANSFORMATION AND EQUIVALENCE OF FORCES

§ 66. When, to the unaided senses, Science began to add supplementary senses in the shape of measuring instruments, men began to perceive various phenomena which eyes and fingers could not distinguish. Of known forms of force, minuter manifestations became appreciable; and forms of force before unknown were rendered cognizable and measurable. Where forces had apparently ended in nothing, and had been carelessly supposed to have actually done so, instrumental observation proved that effects had in every instance been produced: the forces having reappeared in new shapes. Hence has at length arisen the inquiry whether the force displayed in each surrounding change, does not in the act of expenditure undergo metamorphosis into an equivalent amount of some other force or forces. And to this inquiry experiment is giving an affirmative answer, which becomes daily more decisive. Séguin, Mayer, Joule, Grove, and Helmholtz, are more than others to be credited with the enunciation of this doctrine. Let us glance at the evidence on which it rests.

Motion, wherever we can directly trace its genesis, we find had pre-existed as some other mode of force. Our own voluntary acts have always certain sensations of muscular tension as their antecedents. When, as in letting fall a relaxed limb, we are conscious of a bodily movement requiring no effort, the explanation is that the effort was exerted in raising the limb to the position whence it fell. In this case, as in the case of an inanimate body descending to the Earth, the force accumulated by the downward motion si equal to the force previously expended in the act of elevation. Conversely, Motion that is arrested produces, under

different circumstances, heat, electricity, magnetism, light.  From
the warming of the hands by rubbing them together, up to the
ignition of a railway-brake by intense friction—from the lighting
of detonating powder by percussion, up to the setting on fire a
block of wood by a few blows from a steam-hammer; we have
abundant instances in which heat arises as Motion ceases.  It is
uniformly found that the heat generated is great in proportion
as the Motion lost is great; and that to diminish the arrest of
motion by diminishing the friction, is to diminish the quantity
of heat evolved.  The production of electricity by Motion is
illustrated equally in the boy's experiment with rubbed sealing-wax,
in the common electrical machine, and in the apparatus for exciting
electricity by the escape of steam.  Wherever there is friction
between heterogeneous bodies electrical disturbance is one of the
consequences.  Magnetism may result from Motion either immediately, as through percussion on steel, or mediately as through
electric currents previously generated by Motion.  And similarly,
Motion may create light; either directly, as in the minute
incandescent fragments struck off by violent collisions, or indirectly,
as through the electric spark.  "Lastly, Motion may be again
reproduced by the forces which have emanated from Motion; thus,
the divergence of the electrometer, the revolution of the electrical
wheel, the deflection of the magnetic needle, are, when resulting
from frictional electricity, palpable movements reproduced by the
intermediate modes of force, which have themselves been originated
by motion."

That mode of force which we distinguished as Heat, is now
regarded as molecular motion—not motion as displayed in the
changed relations of sensible masses to one another, but as possessed
by the units of which such sensible masses consist.  Omitting cases
in which there is structural rearrangement of the molecules, heated
bodies expand; and expansion is interpreted as due to movements
of the molecules in relation to one another: wider oscillations.
That radiation through which anything of higher temperature than
things around it, communicates Heat to them, is clearly a species
of motion.  Moreover, the evidence afforded by the thermometer
that Heat thus diffuses itself, is simply a movement caused in the
mercurial column.  And that the molecular motion which we call

Heat, may be transformed into visible motion, familiar proof is given by the steam-engine; in which "the piston and all its concomitant masses of matter are moved by the molecular dilatation of the vapour of water." Where Heat is absorbed without apparent result, modern inquiries have detected unobtrusive modifications: as in glass, the molecular state of which is so far changed, that a polarized ray of light passing through it becomes visible, which it does not when the glass is cold; or as on polished metallic surfaces, which are altered in molecular structure by radiations from objects very close to them. The transformation of Heat into electricity occurs when dissimilar metals touching each other are heated at the point of contact: electric currents being so produced. Solid, incombustible matter put into heated gas, as lime into the oxy-hydrogen flame, becomes incandescent; and so exhibits the conversion of Heat into light. The production of magnetism by Heat, if it cannot be proved to take place directly, may be proved to take place indirectly through the agency of electricity. And through the same agency may be established the correlation of Heat and chemical affinity—a correlation which is directly shown by the marked influence Heat exercises on chemical composition and decomposition.

The transformations of Electricity into other modes of force are clearly demonstrable. Produced by the motion of heterogeneous bodies in contact, Electricity, through attractions and repulsions, will immediately reproduce motion in neighbouring bodies. In this case a current of Electricity magnetizes a bar of soft iron; and in that case the rotation of an equipped magnet generates currents of Electricity. Here is the cell of a battery in which, from the play of chemical affinities, an electric current results; and there, in the adjacent cell, is an electric current effecting chemical decomposition. In the conducting wire we witness the transformation of Electricity into heat; while in electric sparks and in the voltaic arc we see light produced. Molecular arrangement, too, is changed by Electricity: as instance the transfer of matter from pole to pole of a battery; the fractures caused by the disruptive discharge; the formation of crystals under the influence of electric currents. And then that, conversely, Electricity is directly generated by rearrangement of the molecules

11

of matter, is shown when a storage-battery or accumulator is used.

How from Magnetism the other physical forces result, must be next briefly noted—briefly, because in each successive case the illustrations become in great part the obverse forms of those before given. That Magnetism produces motion is the ordinary evidence we have of its existence. In the magneto-electric machine a rotating magnet evolves electricity; and the electricity so evolved may immediately after exhibit itself as heat, light, or chemical affinity. Faraday's discovery of the effect of Magnetism on polarized light, as well as the discovery that change of magnetic state is accompanied by heat, point to further like connexions. Lastly, experiments show that the magnetization of a body alters its internal structure; and that, conversely, the alteration of its internal structure, as by mechanical strain, alters its magnetic condition.

Improbable as it seemed, it is now proved that from Light also may proceed the like variety of agencies. Rays of light change the atomic arrangements of particular crystals. Certain mixed gases, which do not otherwise combine, combine in the sunshine. In some compounds light produces decomposition. Since the inquiries of photographers have drawn attention to the subject, it has been shown that "a vast number of substances, both elementary and compound, are notably affected by this agent, even those apparently the most unalterable in character, such as metals." And when a daguerreotype plate is connected with a proper apparatus "we get chemical action on the plate, electricity circulating through the wires, magnetism in the coil, heat in the helix, and motion in the needles."

The genesis of all other modes of force from Chemical Action, scarcely needs pointing out. The ordinary accompaniment of chemical combination is heat; and when the affinities are intense, light also is produced. Chemical changes involving alteration of bulk cause motion, both in the combining elements and in adjacent masses of matter: witness the propulsion of a bullet by the explosion of gunpowder. In the galvanic battery we see electricity resulting from chemical composition and decomposition. While through the medium of this electricity, Chemical Action produces magnetism.

These facts, the larger part of which are culled from Grove's work on *The Correlation of Physical Forces*, show that each force is transformable, directly or indirectly, into the others. In every change Force (or Energy, as in these cases it is called) undergoes metamorphosis; and from the new form or forms it assumes, may subsequently result either the previous one or any of the rest, in endless variety of order and combination. It is further now manifest that the physical forces stand not simply in qualitative correlations with one another, but also in quantitative correlations. Besides proving that one mode of force may be transformed into another mode, experiments show that from a definite amount of one, the amounts of others that arise are definite. Ordinarily it is difficult to show this; since it mostly happens that the transformation of any force is not into some one of the rest but into several of them : the proportions being determined by ever-varying conditions. But in certain cases positive results have been reached. Mr. Joule has ascertained that the fall of 772 lbs. through one foot, will raise the temperature of a pound of water one degree of Fahrenheit. Dulong, Petit, and Neumann, have proved a relation in amount between the affinities of combining bodies and the heat evolved during their combination. Between chemical action and voltaic electricity, a quantitative connexion has been established by Faraday. The well-determined relations between the amounts of heat generated and of water turned to steam, or still better the known expansion produced in steam by each additional degree of heat, may be cited in further evidence. Hence it is no longer doubted that among the several forms which force assumes, the quantitative relations are fixed.

§ 67. Throughout the Cosmos this truth must invariably hold. Every change, or group of changes, going on in it, must be due to forces affiliable on the like or unlike forces previously existing; while from the forces exhibited in such change or changes must be derived others more or less transformed. And besides recognizing this necessary linking of the forces at any time manifested with those preceding and succeeding them, we must recognize the amounts of these forces as necessarily producing such and such quantities of results, and as necessarily limited to those quantities.

That unification of knowledge which is the business of Philosophy, is but little furthered by the establishment of this truth under its general form. We must trace it out under its leading special forms. Changes, and the accompanying transformations of forces, are everywhere in progress, from the movements of stars to the currents of commodities; and to comprehend the great fact that forces, unceasingly metamorphosed, are nowhere increased or decreased, it is requisite to contemplate the changes of all kinds going on around, that we may learn whence arise. the forces they show and what becomes of these forces. Of course if answerable at all, these questions can be answered only in the rudest way. The most we can hope is to establish a qualitative correlation that is indefinitely quantitative—quantitative to the extent of implying something like a due proportion between causes and effects.

Let us, then, consider the several classes of phenomena which the several concrete sciences deal with.

§ 68. The antecedents of those forces which our Solar System displays, belong to a past of which we can never have anything but inferential knowledge. Many and strong as are the reasons for believing the Nebular Hypothesis, we cannot yet regard it as more than an hypothesis. If, however, we assume that the matter of our Solar System was once diffused and had irregularities of shape and density such as existing nebulæ display, or resulted from the coalescence of moving nebulous masses, we have, in the momenta of its parts, original and acquired forces adequate to produce the motions now going on.

Various stages in the formation of spiral nebulæ imply that rotation in many cases results from concentration: whether always, there is no proof; for large nebulæ are too diffused, small ones too dense, and others are seen too much edgeways, to yield evidence. But in the absence of adverse pre-arrangement some rotation may safely be inferred. So far as the evidence carries us, we perceive some quantitative relation between the motions generated and the gravitative forces expended in generating them. In the Solar System the outermost planets, formed from that matter which has travelled the shortest distance towards the

common centre of gravity, have the smallest velocities.  Doubtless this is explicable on the teleological hypothesis, since it is a
condition to equilibrium.   But without insisting that this is beside
the question, it will suffice to point out that the like cannot be
said of the planetary rotations.   No such final cause can be assigned for the rapid axial movement of Jupiter and Saturn, or the
slow axial movement of Mars.   If, however, we look for the
natural antecedents of these gyrations which all planets exhibit,
the nebular hypothesis furnishes them ; and they bear manifest
quantitative relations to the rates of motions.   For the planets
that turn on their axes with extreme rapidity are those having
large orbits — those of which the once-diffused components,
probably formed into broad rings, moved to their centres of
aggregation through immense spaces, and so acquired high
velocities.   While, conversely, the planets which rotate with
relatively small velocities, are those formed out of small nebulous
rings.

"But what," it may be asked, "has in such case become of all
that motion which ended in the aggregation of this diffused matter
into solid bodies ?"   The answer is that it has been radiated in
the form of heat and light ; and this answer the evidence, so far as
it goes, confirms.   Geologists and physicists agree in concluding
that the heat of the Earth's interior is but a remnant of the heat
which once made molten the whole mass.   The mountainous surfaces of the Moon and of Venus, indicating, as they do, crusts which
have, like our own, been corrugated by contraction, imply that
these bodies, too, have undergone refrigeration.   Lastly, we have
in the Sun a still-continued production of the heat and light which
result from the arrest of diffused matter moving towards a common
centre of gravity.           Here also, as before, a quantitative relation is traceable.   Mars, the Earth, Venus, and Mercury, which
severally contain comparatively small amounts of matter whose
contripetal motion has been destroyed, have already lost nearly all
the produced heat ; while the great planets, Jupiter and Saturn,
imply by their low specific gravity, as well as by the perturbations
of their surfaces, that they still retain much heat.   And then the
Sun, a thousand times as great in mass as the largest planet, and
having to give off an enormously greater quantity of heat and light

due to that loss of molar motion which concentration entails, is still radiating with great intensity.

§ 69. Those forces which have wrought the surface of our planet into its present shape, are traceable to the primordial source just assigned. Geologic changes are either direct or indirect results of the unexpended heat caused by nebular condensation. They are commonly divided into igneous and aqueous—heads under which we may most conveniently consider them.

All those disturbances known as earthquakes, all those elevations and subsidences which they severally produce, all those accumulated effects of many such elevations and subsidences exhibited in ocean-basins, islands, continents, table-lands, mountain-chains, and all those formations which are distinguished as volcanic, geologists now regard as modifications of the Earth's crust caused by the actions and reactions of its interior. Even supposing that volcanic eruptions, extrusions of igneous rock, and upheaved mountain-chains, could be otherwise satisfactorily accounted for, it would be impossible otherwise to account for those wide-spread elevations and depressions whence continents and oceans result. Such phenomena as the fusion or agglutination of sedimentary deposits, the warming of springs, the sublimation of metals into the fissures where we find them as ores, may be regarded as positive results of the residuary heat of the Earth's interior; while fractures of strata and alterations of level are its negative results, since they ensue on its escape. The original cause of all these effects is still, however, as it has been from the first, the gravitating movement of the Earth's matter towards the Earth's centre; seeing that to this is due both the internal heat itself and the collapse which takes place as it is radiated into space.

To the question—Under what forms previously existed the force which works out the geological changes classed as aqueous, the answer is less obvious. The effects of rain, of rivers, of winds, of waves, of marine currents, do not manifestly proceed from one general source. Analysis, nevertheless, proves that they have a common genesis. If we ask,—Whence comes the power of the river-current, bearing sediment down to the sea? the reply is,— The gravitation of water throughout the tract which this river drains. If we ask,—How came the water to be dispersed over this tract? the reply is,—It fell in the shape of rain. If we ask,—How came the rain to be in that position whence it fell? the reply is,— The vapour from which it was condensed was drifted there by the winds. If we ask,—How came this vapour to be at that height? .the reply is,—It was raised by evaporation. And if we ask,— What force thus raised it? the reply is,—The Sun's heat. Just that amount of gravitative force which the Sun's heat overcame in raising the molecules of water, is given out again in the fall of those molecules to the same level. Hence the denudations effected by rain and rivers, during the descent of this condensed vapour to the level of the sea, are indirectly due to the radiated energy of the Sun. Similarly with the winds that transport the vapours hither and thither. Consequent as atmospheric currents are on differences of temperature (either general, as between the equatorial and polar regions, or special as between tracts of the Earth's surface having unlike physical characters) all such currents are due to that source from which the irregularly distributed heat proceeds. And if the winds thus originate, so too do the waves raised by them on the sea's surface. Whence it follows that whatever changes waves produce—the wearing away of cliffs, the breaking down of rocks into shingle, sand, and mud—are also traceable to the solar rays as their primary cause. The same may be said of ocean-currents. Generated as the larger ones are by the excess of heat which the ocean in tropical climates acquires from the Sun; and determined as the smaller ones are in part by local shapes of land; it follows that the distribution of sediment and other geological processes which these marine currents effect, are affiliable upon the energy the Sun radiates. The only aqueous agency otherwise originating is that of the tides—an agency which, equally with the others, is traceable to unexpended celestial motion. But making allowance for the changes this works, we conclude that the slow wearing down of continents and gradual filling up of seas, effected by rain, rivers, winds, waves, and ocean-streams, are the indirect effects of solar heat.

Thus we see that while the geological changes classed as igneous, arise from the still-progressing motion of the Earth's substance to its centre of gravity; the antagonistic changes classed as aqueous, arise from the still-progressing motion of the Sun's substance towards its centre of gravity.

§ 70. That the forces exhibited in vital actions, vegetal and animal, are similarly derived, is. an obvious deduction from the facts of organic chemistry. Let us note first the physiological generalizations; and then the generalizations which they necessitate.

Plant-life is all directly or indirectly dependent on the heat and light of the Sun—directly dependent in the immense majority of plants, and indirectly dependent in plants which, as the fungi, flourish in the dark : since these, growing at the expense of decaying organic matter, mediately draw their forces from the same original source. Each plant owes the carbon and hydrogen of which it mainly consists, to the carbon dioxide and water contained in the surrounding air and earth. These must, however, be decomposed before their carbon and hydrogen can be assimilated. To overcome the affinities which hold their elements together, requires the expenditure of energy; and this energy is supplied by the Sun. When, under fit conditions, plants are exposed to the solar rays, they give off oxygen and accumulate carbon and hydrogen. In darkness this process ceases. It ceases, too, when the quantities of light and heat received are greatly reduced, as in winter. Conversely, it is active when the light and heat are great, as in summer. And the like relation is seen in the fact that while plant-life is luxuriant in the tropics, it diminishes in temperate regions, and disappears as we approach the poles. Thus the irresistible inference is that the forces by which plants grow and carry on their functions, are forces which previously existed as solar radiations.

That in the main, the processes of animal life are opposite to those of vegetal life is a truth long current among men of science. Chemically considered, vegetal life is chiefly a process of de-oxidation, and animal life chiefly a process of oxidation: chiefly, we must say, because in so far as plants are expenders of force for the purposes of organization, they are oxidizers: and animals, in some of their minor processes, are probably de-oxidizers. But with this qualification, the general truth is that while the plant, decomposing carbon dioxide and water and liberating oxygen, builds up the detained carbon and hydrogen (along with a little nitrogen and small quantities of other elements) into stem, branches, leaves, and seeds; the animal, consuming these branches, leaves, and seeds, and absorbing oxygen, re-composes carbon dioxide and water, forming also certain nitrogenous compounds in minor amounts. And while the decomposition effected by the plant is at the expense of energies emanating from the Sun, the re-composition effected by the animal is at the profit of these energies, which are liberated during the combination of such elements. Thus the movements, internal and external, of the animal, are re-appearances in new forms of a power absorbed by the plant under the shape of light and heat. Just as the solar forces expended in raising vapour from the sea's surface, are given out again in the fall of rain and rivers to the same level, and in the accompanying transfer of solid matters; so, the solar forces that in the plant raised certain chemical elements to a condition of unstable equilibrium, are given out again in the actions of the animal during the fall of these elements to a condition of stable equilibrium.

Besides thus tracing a qualitative correlation between these two great orders of organic activity, as well as between both of them and inorganic activities, we may rudely trace a quantitative correlation. Where vegetal life is abundant, we usually find abundant animal life; and as we advance from torrid to temperate and frigid climates, the two decrease together. Speaking generally, the animals of each class reach larger sizes in regions where vegetation is luxuriant, than in those where it is sparse.

Certain facts of development in both plants and animals, illustrate still more directly the truth we are considering. In pursuance of a suggestion made by Mr. (afterwards Sir William) Grove, Dr. Carpenter pointed out that a connexion between physical and vital forces is exhibited during incubation. The transformation of the unorganized contents of an egg into the organized chick is a question of heat · withhold heat and the process does not commence; supply heat and it goes on while the temperature is maintained, but ceases when the egg is allowed to cool. The developmental changes can be completed only by keeping the temperature with tolerable constancy at a definite height for a definite time; that is—only by supplying a definite quantity of heat. Though the proclivities of the molecules determine the typical structure assumed, yet the energy supplied by the thermal undulations gives them the power of arranging themselves into that structure. In the metamorphoses of insects we may discern parallel facts. The hatching of their eggs is determined by temperature, as is also the evolution of the pupa into the imago; and both are accelerated or retarded according as heat is artificially supplied or withheld. It will suffice just to add, that the germination of plants presents like relations of cause and effect, as every season shows.

Thus then the various changes exhibited by the organic creation, whether considered as a whole, or in its two great divisions, or in its individual members, conform, so far as we can ascertain, to the general principle.

§ 71. Even after all that has been said in the foregoing part of this work, many will be alarmed by the assertion that the forces which we distinguish as mental, come within the same generalization. Yet there is no alternative but to make this assertion : the facts which justify, or rather which necessitate, it being abundant and conspicuous. At the same time they are extremely involved. The essential correlations occur in organs which are mostly invisible, and between forces or energies quite other than those which are apparent. Let us first take a superficial view of the evidence.

The modes of consciousness called pressure, motion, sound, light, heat, are effects produced in us by agencies which, as otherwise expended, crush or fracture pieces of matter, generate vibrations in surrounding objects, cause chemical combinations, and reduce substances from a solid to a liquid form. Hence if we regard the changes of relative position, of aggregation, or of chemical union, thus arising, as being transformed manifestations of certain energies; so, too, must we regard the sensations which such energies produce in us. Any hesitation to admit this must disappear on remembering that the last correlations, like the first, are not qualitative only but quantitative. Masses of matter which, by scales or dynamometer, are shown to differ greatly in weight, differ as greatly in the feelings of pressure they produce on our bodies. In arresting moving objects, the strains we are conscious of are proportionate to the momenta of such objects as otherwise measured. The impressions of sounds given to us by vibrating strings, bells, or columns of air, are found to vary in strength with the amount of force applied. Fluids or solids proved to be markedly contrasted in temperature by the different degrees of expansion they produce in the mercurial column, produce in us correspondingly different degrees of the sensation of heat. And unlike intensities in our impressions of light, answer to unlike effects as measured by photometers.

Besides the correlation and equivalence between external physical forces and the mental forces generated by them under the form of sensations, there appears to be a correlation and equivalence between sensations and those physical forces which, in the shape of bodily actions, result from them. In addition to the excitements of secreting organs, sometimes traceable, there arise contractions of the involuntary muscles. Sensations increase the action of the heart, and recent experiments imply that the muscular fibres of the arteries are at the same time contracted. The respiratory muscles, too, are stimulated. The rate of breathing is visibly and audibly augmented both by pleasurable and painful excitements of the nerves, if these reach any intensity. When the quantity of sensation is great, it generates contractions of the voluntary muscles, as well as of the involuntary ones. Violent pains cause violent struggles. The start that follows a loud sound, the wry face produced by an extremely disagreeable taste, the jerk with which the hand or foot is snatched out of very hot water, exemplify the genesis of motions by feelings; and in these cases it is manifest that the quantity of bodily action is proportionate to the quantity of sensation. Even where pride causes suppression of the screams and groans expressive of great pain (also indirect results of muscular contraction), we may still see in the clenching of the hands, the knitting of the brows, and the setting of the teeth, that the bodily actions excited are as great, though less obtrusive in their results.    If we take emotions instead of sensations, we find the correlation and equivalence similarly suggested. Emotions of moderate intensity, like sensations of moderate intensity, generate little beyond excitement of the heart and vascular system, joined sometimes with increased action of glandular organs. But as the emotions rise in strength, the muscles of the face, body, and limbs, begin to move. Of examples may be mentioned the frowns, dilated nostrils, and stampings of anger; the contracted brows, and wrung hands, of grief; the laughs and leaps of joy; the frantic struggles of terror or despair. Passing over cases in which extreme agitation causes fainting, we see that whatever be the kind of emotion, there is a manifest relation between its amount and the amount of muscular action induced, from the fidgetiness of impatience up to the almost convulsive movements accompanying great mental agony. To these several orders of evidence must be joined the further order, that between feelings and those voluntary motions which result from them, there comes the sensation of muscular tension, standing in manifest correlation with both—a correlation that is distinctly quantitative: the sense of strain varying, other things equal, directly as the quantity of momentum generated.

§ 71a. But now, reverting to the caution which preceded these two paragraphs, we have to note, first, that the facts do not prove transformation of feeling into motion but only a certain constant ratio between feeling and motion; and then we have further to note that what seems a direct quantitative correlation is illusory. For example, tickling is followed by almost uncontrollable movements of the limbs; but obviously there is no proportion between the amount of force applied to the surface and the amount of feeling or the amount of motion: rather there is an inverse proportion, for while a rough touch does not produce the effect a gentle one does. Even when it is recognized that the feeling is not the correlate of the external touching action but of a disturbance in certain terminal tactile structures, it still remains demonstrable that there is no necessary relation between the amount of such disturbance and the amount of feeling produced; for under some conditions muscular motion results without the intercalation of any feeling. When the spinal cord has been so injured as to cut off all nervous communication between the lower part of the body and the brain, tickling the sole of the foot produces convulsion of the leg more violent than it would do were it accompanied by sensation: there is a reflex transmission of the stimulus and genesis of motion without passage through consciousness. Cases of another class show that between central feelings or emotions and the muscular movements they initiate there are no fixed ratios: instance the sense of effort felt in making a small movement by one who is exhausted, or the inability of an enfeebled patient to raise a limb from the bed however strong the desire to do it. So that neither the feelings peripherally initiated nor those centrally initiated, though they are correlated with motions, are quantitatively correlated. Even still more manifest becomes the lack, of direct relation, either qualitative or quantitative, between outer stimuli and inner feelings, or between such inner feelings and muscular motions, when we contemplate the complex kinds of mental processes. The emotions and actions of a man who has been insulted are clearly not equivalents of the sensations produced by the words in his ears; for the same words otherwise arranged, would not have caused them. The thing said bears to the mental action it excites, much the same relation that the pulling of a trigger bears to the subsequent explosion—does not produce the power but merely liberates it. Whence, then, arises this immense amount of nervous energy which a whisper or a glance may call forth?

Evidently we shall go utterly wrong if the problem of the transformation and equivalence of forces is dealt with as though an organism were simple and passive instead of being complex and active. In the living body there are already going on multitudinous transformations of energy very various in their natures, and between any physical action falling on it and any motion which follows, there are intercalated numerous changes of kind and quantity. The fact of chief significance for us here, is that organization is, under one of its aspects, a set of appliances for the multiplication of energies — appliances which, by their successive actions, make the energy eventually given out enormous as compared with the energy which liberated it. A physical stimulus affecting an organ of sense, is in some cases multiplied by local nervous agents; the augmented energy is again multiplied in some part of the spinal cord or in some higher ganglion; and this, usually again multiplied in the cerebrum and discharged to the muscles, is there enormously multiplied in the contracting fibres. Of these transformations only some carried on centrally have accompanying states of consciousness; so that, manifestly, there can be no quantitative equivalence either between the sensation and the original stimulus, or between it and the eventual motion. All we can say is that, other things equal, the three vary together; so that if in one case the successive stages of increase are 1, 9, 27, 270, they will in another case be 2, 18, 54, 540. This kind of correlation is all which the foregoing facts imply. But now let us glance at the indirect evidences which confirm the view that mental and physical forces are connected, though in an indirect way.

Nowadays no one doubts that mental processes and the resulting actions are contingent on the presence of a nervous system; and that, greatly obscured as it is by numerous and involved conditions, a general relation may be traced between the size of this system and the quantity of mental action as measured by its results. Further, this nervous apparatus has a chemical constitution on which its activity depends; and there is one element in it between the amount of which and the amount of function performed there is an ascertained connexion: the proportion of phosphorus present in the brain being the smallest in infancy, old age, and idiotcy, and the greatest during the prime of life. Note, next, that the evolution of thought and emotion varies, other things equal, with the supply of blood to the brain. On the one hand, an arrest of the cerebral circulation from stoppage of the heart, immediately entails unconsciousness. On the other hand, excess of cerebral circulation (unless it is such as to cause undue pressure) results in unusual excitement. Not the quantity only, but also the condition, of the blood passing through the brain, influences the mental manifestations. The arterial currents must be duly aerated, to produce the normal amount of cerebration. If the blood is not allowed to exchange its carbon dioxide for oxygen, there results asphyxia, with its accompanying stoppage of ideas and feelings. That the quantity of consciousness is, other things equal, determined by the constituents of the blood, is unmistakably seen in the exaltation which certain vegeto-alkalies commonly produce when taken into it. The gentle exhilaration which tea and coffee create is familiar to all; and though the gorgeous imaginations and intense feelings produced by opium and hashish, have been experienced by few (in this country at least), the testimony of those who have experienced them is sufficiently conclusive. Yet another proof that the genesis of the mental energies depends on chemical change, is afforded by the fact that the effete products separated from the blood by the kidneys vary in character with the amount of cerebral action. Excessive activity of mind is accompanied by excretion of an unusual quantity of the alkaline phosphates.

§ 71*b*. But now after recognizing the classes of facts which unite to prove that the law of metamorphosis, and in a partial way the law of equivalence, holds between physical energies and nervous energies, let us enter upon the ultimate question—What is the nature of the relation between nervous energies and mental states? how are we to conceive molecular changes in the brain as producing feelings, or feelings as producing molecular changes which end in motion?

In his lecture on Animal Automatism, Prof. Huxley set forth the proofs that alike in animals and in Man, the great mass of those complex actions which we associate with purpose and intelligence may be performed automatically; and contended that the consciousness which ordinarily accompanies them is outside the series of changes constituting the nervous co-ordination—does not form a link in the chain but is simply a "concomitant" or a "collateral product." In so far as it correlates the nervous actions by which our bodily and mental activities are carried on, with physical forces in general, Prof. Huxley's conclusion accords with the conclusions above set forth; but in so far as it regards the accompanying states of consciousness as collateral products only, and not as factors in any degree, differs from them. Here I cannot do more than indicate the set of evidences by which I think my own conclusion is supported if not justified.

One of them we have in the facts of habit, which prove that states of consciousness, which were at first accompaniments of sensory impressions and resulting motions, gradually cease to be concomitants. The little boy who is being taught to read has definite perceptions and thoughts about the form and sound of each letter, but in maturity all these have lapsed, so that only the words are consciously recognized: each letter produces its effect automatically. So, too, the girl learning to knit is absorbed in thinking of each movement made under the direction of her eyes, but eventually the movements come to be performed almost like those of a machine while her mind is otherwise occupied. Such cases seem at variance with the belief that consciousness is outside the lines of nervous communication, and suggest, rather, that it exists in any line of communication in course of establishment and disappears when the communication becomes perfect. If it is not a link in the line, it is not easy to see how these changes can arise.

Sundry facts appear to imply that consciousness is needful as an initiator in cases where there are no external stimuli to set up the co-ordinated nervous changes: the nervous structures, though capable of doing everything required if set going, are not set going unless there arises an idea. Now this implies that an idea, or co-ordinated set of feelings, has the power of working changes in the nervous centres and setting up motions: the state of consciousness is a *factor*.

Then what we may call passive emotions—emotions which do not initiate actions—apparently imply that between feelings and nervous changes there is not merely a concomitance but a physical *nexus*. Intense grief or anxiety in one who remains motionless, is shown to be directly dependent on nervous changes by the fact that there is an unusual excretion of phosphates by the kidneys. Now unless we suppose that in such cases there is great activity of certain nervous plexuses ending in nothing, we must say that the feeling is a product of the molecular changes in them.

Once more there is the question—If feeling is not a factor how is its existence to be accounted for? To any one who holds in full the Cartesian doctrine that animals are automata, and that a howl no more implies feeling than does the bark of a toy dog, I have nothing to say. But whoever does not hold this is obliged to hold that as we ascribe anger and affection to our fellow men, though we literally know no such feelings save in ourselves, so must we ascribe them to animals under like conditions. If so, however—if feelings are not factors and the appropriate actions might be automatically performed without them—then, on the supernatural hypothesis it must be assumed that feelings were given to animals for no purpose, and on the natural hypothesis it must be assumed that they have arisen to do nothing.

§ 71c. But whether feeling is only a concomitant of certain nervous actions, or whether it is, as concluded above, a factor in such actions, the connexion between the two is inscrutable. If we suppose that in which consciousness inheres to be an immaterial something, not implicated in these nervous actions but nevertheless affected by them in such way as to produce feeling, then we are obliged to conceive of certain material changes—molecular motions—as producing changes in something in which there is nothing to be moved; and this we cannot conceive. If, on the other hand, we regard this something capable of consciousness, as so related to certain nervous changes that the feelings arising in it join them in producing muscular motions, then we meet the same difficulty under its converse aspect. We have to think of an immaterial something—a something which is not molecular motion—which is capable of affecting molecular motions : we have to endow it with the power to work effects which, so far as our knowledge goes, can be worked only by material forces. So that this alternative, too, is in the last resort inconceivable.

The only supposition having consistency is that that in which consciousness inheres is the all-pervading ether. This we know can be affected by molecules of matter in motion and conversely can affect the motions of molecules; as witness the action of light on the retina. In pursuance of this supposition we may assume that the ether which pervades not only all space but all matter, is, under special conditions in certain parts of the nervous system, capable of being affected by the nervous changes in such way as to result in feeling, and is reciprocally capable under these conditions of affecting the nervous changes. But if we accept this explanation we must assume that the potentiality of feeling is universal, and that the evolution of feeling in the ether takes place only under the extremely complex conditions occurring in certain nervous centres. This, however, is but a semblance of an explanation, since we know not what the ether is, and since, by the confession of those most capable of judging, no hypothesis that has been framed accounts for all its powers. Such an explanation may be said to do no more than symbolize the phenomena by symbols of unknown natures.

Thus though the facts oblige us to say that physical and psychical actions are correlated, and in a certain indirect way quantitatively correlated, so as to suggest transformation, yet how the material affects the mental and how the mental affects the material, are mysteries which it is impossible to fathom. But they are not profounder mysteries than the transformations of the physical forces into one another. They are not more completely beyond our comprehension than the natures of Mind and Matter. They have simply the same insolubility as all other ultimate questions. We can learn nothing more than that here is one of the uniformities in the order of phenomena.

§ 72. If the general law of transformation and equivalence holds of the forces we class as vital and mental, it must hold also of those which we class as social. Whatever takes place in a society results either from the undirected physical energies around, from these energies as directed by men, or from the energies of the men themselves.

While, as among primitive tribes, men's actions are mainly independent of one another, social forces can scarcely be said to exist: they come into existence along with co-operation. The effects which can be achieved only by the joint actions of many, we may distinguish as social. At first these are obviously due to accumulated individual efforts, but as fast as societies become large and highly organized, they acquire such separateness from individual efforts as to give them a character of their own. The network of roads and railways and telegraph wires—agencies in the formation of which individual labours were so merged as to be practically lost—serve to carry on a social life that is no longer thought of as caused by the independent doings of citizens. The prices of stocks, the rates of discount, the reported demand for this or that commodity, and the currents of men and things setting to and from various localities, show us large movements and changes scarcely at all affected by the lives and deaths and deeds of persons. But these and multitudinous social activities displayed in the growth of towns, the streams of traffic in their

Of the physical forces that are directly transformed into social ones, the like is to be said. Currents of air and water, which before the use of steam were the only agents brought in aid of muscular effort for performing industrial processes, are, as we have seen, generated by solar heat. And the inanimate power that now, to so vast an extent, supplements human labour, is similarly derived. Sir John Herschel was the first to recognize the truth that the force impelling a locomotive, originally emanated from the Sun. Step by step we go back—from the motion of the piston to the evaporation of the water; thence to the heat evolved during the burning of coal; thence to the assimilation of carbon by the plants of whose imbedded products coal consists; thence to the carbon di-oxide from which their carbon was obtained; and thence to the rays of light which effected the de-oxidation. Solar forces millions of years ago expended on the Earth's vegetation, and since locked up in deep-seated strata, now smelt the metals required for our machines, turn the lathes by which the machines are shaped, work them when put together, and distribute the fabrics they produce. And since economy of labour makes possible a larger population, gives a surplus of human power that would else be absorbed in manual occupations, and thus facilitates the development of higher kinds of activity; these social forces which are directly correlated with physical forces anciently derived from the Sun, are only less important than those of which the correlates are the vital forces recently derived from it.

§ 73. Many who admit that among physical phenomena at large, transformation of forces is now established, will probably say that inquiry has not yet gone far enough to enable us to assert equivalence. And in respect of the forces classed as vital, mental, and social, the evidence assigned they will consider by no means conclusive even of transformation, much less of equivalence.

But the universal truth above followed out under its various aspects, is a corollary from the persistence of force. From the proposition that force can neither come into existence nor cease to exist, the several foregoing conclusions inevitably follow. Each manifestation of force can be interpreted only as the effect of some antecedent force: no matter whether it be an inorganic action, an animal movement, a thought, or a feeling. Either bodily and mental energies, as well as inorganic ones, are quantitatively correlated to certain energies expended in their production, and to certain other energies which they initiate; or else nothing must become something and something must become nothing. The alternatives are, to deny the persistence of force, or to admit that from given amounts of antecedent energies neither more nor less than certain physical and psychical changes can result.       This corollary cannot indeed be made more certain by accumulating illustrations.   Whatever proof of correlation and equivalence is reached by experimental inquiry, is based on measurement of the forces expended and the forces produced.   But, as was shown in the last chapter, any such process implies the use of some unit of force which is assumed to remain constant; and its constancy can be assumed only as being a corollary from the persistence of force.   How then can any reasoning based on this corollary, prove the equally direct corollary that when a given quantity of force ceases to exist under one form, an equal quantity must come into existence under some other form or forms?

"What, then," it may be asked, "is the use of investigations by which transformation and equivalence of forces is sought to be inductively established?   If the correlation cannot be made more certain by them than it is already, does not their uselessness necessarily follow?"   No.  They are of value as disclosing the many particular implications which the general truth does not specify.  They are of value as teaching us how much of one mode of force is the equivalent of so much of another mode.  They are of value as determining under what conditions each metamorphosis occurs.  And they are of value as leading us to inquire in what shape the remnant of force has escaped, when the apparent results are not equivalent to the cause.

# CHAPTER IX

## THE DIRECTION OF MOTION

§ 74. THE Absolute Cause of changes, no matter what may be their special natures, is not less incomprehensible in respect of the unity or duality of its action, than in all other respects. Are phenomena due to the variously-conditioned workings of a single force, or are they due to the conflict of two forces? Whether everything is explicable on the hypothesis of universal pressure, whence so-called tension results differentially from inequalities of pressure; or whether things are to be explained on the hypothesis of universal tension, from which pressure is a differential result; or whether, as most physicists hold, pressure and tension everywhere co-exist; are questions which it is impossible to settle. Each of these three suppositions makes the facts comprehensible only by postulating an inconceivability. To assume a universal pressure, confessedly requires us to assume an infinite plenum—an unlimited space full of something which is everywhere pressed by something beyond; and this assumption cannot be mentally realized. That universal tension is the agency is an idea open to a parallel and equally fatal objection. And verbally intelligible as is the pro-position that pressure and tension everywhere co-exist, yet we cannot truly represent to ourselves one ultimate unit of matter as drawing another while resisting it.

Nevertheless, this last belief we are compelled to entertain. Matter cannot be conceived except as manifesting forces of attrac-tion and repulsion. In our consciousness, Body is distinguished from Space by its opposition to our muscular energies; and this opposition we feel under the twofold form of a cohesion which hinders our efforts to rend, and a resistance which hinders our efforts to compress. Without resistance there can be nothing but empty extension. Without cohesion there can be no resistance. Probably this conception of antagonistic forces originates from the antagonism of our flexor and extensor muscles. But be this as it may, we are obliged to think of all objects as made up of parts that attract and repel one another, since this is the form of our experience of all objects.

By a higher abstraction results the conception of attractive and repulsive forces pervading space. We cannot dissociate force from occupied extension, or occupied extension from force, because we have never an immediate consciousness of either in the absence of the other. Nevertheless, we have abundant proof that force is exercised through what appears to our senses a vacuity. Mentally to represent this exercise, we are hence obliged to fill the apparent vacuity with a species of matter—an ethereal medium. The constitution we assign to this ethereal medium, however, is necessarily an abstract of the impressions received from tangible bodies. The opposition to pressure which a tangible body offers to us, is not shown in one direction only, but in all directions; and so likewise is its tenacity. Suppose countless lines radiating from its centre, and it resists along each of these lines and coheres along each of these lines. Hence the constitution of those ultimate units through the instrumentality of which phenomena are interpreted. Be they molecules of ponderable matter or molecules of ether, the properties we conceive them to possess are nothing else than these perceptible properties idealized. Centres of force attracting and repelling one another in all directions, are simply insensible portions of matter having the endowments common to sensible portions of matter—endowments of which we cannot by any mental effort divest them. In brief, they are the invariable elements of the conception of matter, abstracted from its variable elements—size, form, quality, &c. And so to interpret manifestations of force which cannot be tactually experienced, we use the terms of thought supplied by our tactual experiences; and this for the sufficient reason that we must use these or none.

It needs scarcely be said that these universally co-existent forces of attraction and repulsion, must not be taken as realities, but as our symbols of the reality. They are the forms under which the workings of the Unknowable are cognizable by us—modes of the Unconditioned as presented under the conditions of our consciousness. How these ideas stand related to the absolute truth we cannot know, but we may unreservedly surrender ourselves to them as relatively true, and may proceed to evolve a series of deductions having a like relative truth.

§ 75. Universally co-existent forces of attraction and repulsion imply certain laws of direction of all movement. Where attractive forces alone are concerned, or rather are alone appreciable, movement takes place in the direction of their resultant ; which may, in a sense, be called the line of greatest traction. Where repulsive forces alone are concerned, or rather are alone appreciable, movement takes place along their resultant ; which is usually known as the line of least resistance. And where both attractive and repulsive forces are concerned, and are appreciable, movement takes place along the resultant of the tractions and resistances. Strictly speaking this last is the sole law ; since, by the hypothesis, both forces are everywhere in action. But very frequently the one kind of force is so immensely in excess, that the effect of the other kind may be left out of consideration. Practically, we may say that a body falling to the Earth follows the line of greatest traction ; since, though the resistance of the air must, if the body be irregular, cause some divergence from this line (quite perceptible with feathers and leaves), yet, ordinarily, the divergence is so slight that we may disregard it. In the same manner, though the courses taken by steam from an exploding boiler, differ somewhat from those which it would take were gravitation out of the question ; yet, as gravitation affects its courses only infinitesimally, we are justified in saying that the escaping steam goes along lines of least resistance. Motion, then, always follows the line of greatest traction, or the line of least resistance, or the resultant of the two ; and though the last is alone strictly true, the others are in many cases sufficiently near the truth for practical purposes.

Motion set up in any direction is itself a cause of further motion in that direction, since it is the manifestation of a surplus force in that direction. This holds equally with the transit of matter through space, the transit of matter through matter, and the transit through matter of any kind of vibration. In the case of matter moving through space, this principle is expressed in the law of inertia—a law which all the calculations of physical astronomy assume. In the case of matter moving through matter, we trace the same truth under the familiar experience that any breach made by one solid through another, or any channel formed by a fluid through a solid, becomes a route along which, other things equal, subsequent movements of like nature most readily take place. And in the case of motion passing through matter under the form of an impulse communicated from part to part, the facts of magnetization appear to imply that the establishment of undulations along certain lines, determines their continuance along those lines.

It further follows from the conditions, that the direction of movement can rarely if ever be perfectly straight. For matter in motion to pursue continuously the exact line in which it sets out, the forces of attraction and repulsion must be symmetrically disposed around its path; and the chances against this are infinitely great. It may be added that in proportion as the forces at work are numerous and varied, the line a moving body describes is necessarily complex: witness the contrast between the flight of an arrow and the gyrations of a stick tossed about by breakers.

As a step towards unification of knowledge, we have now to trace these general laws throughout the various orders of changes which the Cosmos exhibits.

§ 76. In the Solar System the principles thus briefly summarized are every instant exemplified. Each planet and satellite has a momentum which would, if acting alone, carry it forward in the direction it is at any instant pursuing—a momentum which would make a straight line its line of least resistance. Each planet and satellite, however, is drawn by a force which, if it acted alone, would take it in a straight line towards its primary. And the resultant of these two forces is that curve which it describes—a curve consequent on the unsymmetrical distribution of the forces around. When more closely examined, its path supplies further illustrations. For it is not an exact circle or ellipse, which it would be were the tangential and centripetal forces the only ones concerned. Adjacent members of the Solar System, ever varying in their relative positions, cause perturbations; that is, slight divergences from that circle or ellipse which the two chief forces would produce. These perturbations severally show us in minor degrees, how the line of movement is the resultant of all the forces engaged; and how this line becomes more complicated in proportion as the forces are multiplied.

If instead of the motions of the planets and satellites as wholes, we consider the motions of their parts, we meet with comparatively complex illustrations. Every portion of the Earth's substance in its daily rotation, describes a curve which is in the main a resultant of that resistance which checks its nearer approach to the centre of gravity, that momentum which would carry it off at a tangent, and those forces of gravitation and cohesion which keep it from being so carried off. When with this axial motion is contemplated the orbital motion, the course of each part is seen to be a much more involved one. And we find it to have a still greater complication on taking into account that lunar attraction which mainly produces the tides and the precession of the equinoxes.

§ 77. We come next to terrestrial changes: present ones as observed, and past ones as inferred by geologists. Let us set out with the unceasing movements in the Earth's atmosphere; descend to the slow alterations in progress on its surface; and then to the still slower ones going on beneath.

Masses of air, absorbing heat from surfaces warmed by the Sun, expand, and ascend: the resistance being less than the resistance to lateral movement. Adjacent atmospheric masses, moving in the directions of the diminished resistance, displace the expanded air. When, again, by the ascent of heated air from great tracts like the torrid zone, there is produced at the upper surface of the atmosphere a protuberance—when the air forming this protuberance overflows laterally towards the poles; it does so because, while the tractive force of the Earth is nearly the same, the lateral resistance is diminished. And throughout the course of each current thus generated, as well as throughout the course of each counter-current flowing into the space vacated, the direction is always the resultant of the Earth's tractive force and the resistance offered by the surrounding masses of air : modified only by conflict with other currents similarly generated, and by collision with prominences on the Earth's crust.     The movements of water, in both its gaseous and liquid states, furnish further examples. Evaporation is the escape of particles of water in the direction of least resistance ; and as the resistance (which is due to gaseous pressure) diminishes, the evaporation increases.   On the other hand condensation, which takes place when any portion of atmospheric vapour has its temperature much lowered, may be interpreted as a diminution of the mutual pressure among the condensing particles, while the pressure of surrounding particles remains the same ; and so is a motion taking place in the direction of lessened resistance. In the course followed by the resulting raindrops, we have one of the simplest instances of the joint effect of the two antagonist forces. The Earth's attraction, and the resistance of atmospheric currents ever varying in direction and intensity, give us their resultants, lines which incline to the horizon in countless different degrees and undergo perpetual variations.   In the course the raindrops take while trickling over the surface, in every rill, in every larger stream, and in every river, we see them descending as straight as the antagonism of surrounding objects permits.  So far from a cascade furnishing an exception, it furnishes but another illustration. For though all solid obstacles to a vertical fall of the water are removed, yet the water's horizontal momentum is an obstacle ; and the parabola in which the stream leaps from the projecting ledge, is generated by the combined gravitation and momentum.

The Earth's solid crust undergoes changes which supply another group of illustrations.  The denudation of lands and the depositing of the removed sediment in new strata at the bottoms of seas and lakes, is a process throughout which motion is obviously determined in the same way as is that of the water effecting the transport. Again, though we have no direct inductive proof that the forces classed as igneous, expend themselves along lines of least resistance, yet what little we know of them is in harmony with the belief that they do so.  Earthquakes continually revisit the same localities, and special tracts undergo for long periods together successive elevations or subsidences : facts which imply that already-fractured portions of the Earth's crust are those most prone to yield under the pressure caused by further contractions. The distribution of volcanoes along certain lines, as well as the frequent recurrence of eruptions from the same vents, are facts of like meaning.

§ 78. That organic growth takes place in the direction of least resistance is a proposition set forth and illustrated by Mr. James Hinton, in the *Medico-Chirurgical Review* for October, 1858. After detailing a few of the early observations which led him to this generalization, he formulates it thus :— •

"Organic form is the result of motion."

" Motion takes the direction of least resistance."

"Therefore organic form is the result of motion in the direction of least resistance."

After an elucidation and defence of this position, Mr. Hinton proceeds to interpret, in conformity with it, sundry phenomena of development. Speaking of plants, he says :—

"The formation of the root furnishes a beautiful illustration of the law of least resistance, for it grows by insinuating itself, cell by cell, through the interstices of the soil ; it is by such minute additions that it increases, winding and twisting whithersoever the obstacles it meets in its path determine, and growing there most, where the nutritive materials are added to it most abundantly. As we look on the roots of a mighty tree, it appears to us as if they had forced themselves with giant violence into the solid earth. But it is not so ; they were led on gently, cell added to cell, softly as the dews descended, and the loosened earth made way. Once formed, indeed, they expand with an enormous power, but the spongy condition of the growing radicles utterly forbids the supposition that they are forced into the earth. Is it not probable, indeed, that the enlargement of the roots already formed may crack the surrounding soil, and help to make the interstices into which the new rootlets grow ? * * *

"Throughout almost the whole of organic nature the spiral form is more or less distinctly marked. Now, motion under resistance takes a spiral direction, as may be seen by the motion of a body rising or falling through water. A bubble rising rapidly in water describes a spiral closely resembling a corkscrew, and a body of moderate specific gravity dropped into water may be seen to fall in a curved direction, the spiral tendency of which may be distinctly observed. * * * In this prevailing spiral form of organic bodies, therefore, it appears to me, that there is presented a strong *prima facie* case for the view I have maintained. * * * The spiral form of the branches of many trees is very apparent, and the universally spiral arrangement of the leaves around the stem of plants needs only to be referred to. * * * The heart commences as a spiral turn, and in its perfect form a manifest spiral may be traced through the left ventricle, right ventricle, right auricle, left auricle and appendix. And what is the spiral turn in which the heart commences but a necessary result of the lengthening, under a limit, of the cellular mass of which it then consists? * * *

"Every one must have noticed the peculiar curling up of the young leaves of the common fern. The appearance is as if the leaf were rolled up, but in truth this form is merely a phenomenon of growth. The curvature results from the increase of the leaf, it is only another form of the wrinkling up, or turning at right angles by extension under limit.

"The rolling up or imbrication of the petals in many flower-buds is a similar thing; at an early period the small petals may be seen lying side by side; afterwards growing within the capsule, they become folded round one another. * * *

"If a flower-bud be opened at a sufficiently early period, the stamens will be found as if moulded in the cavity between the pistil and the corolla, which cavity the anthers exactly fill; the stalks lengthen at an after period. I have noticed also in a few instances, that in those flowers in which the petals are imbricated, or twisted together, the pistil is tapering as growing up between the petals; in some flowers which have the petals so arranged in the bud as to form a dome (as the hawthorn; e.g.), the pistil is flattened at the apex, and in the bud occupies a space precisely limited by the stamens below, and the enclosing petals above and at the sides. I have not, however, satisfied myself that this holds good in all cases."

Without endorsing all Mr. Hinton's illustrations, his conclusion may be accepted as a large instalment of the truth. But in the case of organic growth, as in all other cases, the line of movement is in strictness the resultant of tractive and resistant forces; and the tractive forces here form so considerable an element that the formula is not complete without them. The shapes of plants are manifestly modified by gravitation. The direction of each branch is not what it would have been in the absence of the pull exercised by the Earth; and every flower and leaf is somewhat altered in the course of development by the weight of its parts. Though in animals such effects are less conspicuous, yet the instances in which flexible organs have their directions in great measure determined by gravity justify the assertion that throughout the whole organism the forms of parts must be affected by this force.

The organic movements which constitute growth, are not, however, the only organic movements to be interpreted. There are also those which constitute function; and throughout these the same general principles are discernible. That the vessels and ducts along which blood, lymph, bile, and all the secretions, find their ways, are channels of least resistance, is an illustration almost too conspicuous to be named. Less conspicuous, however, is the truth that the currents setting along these vessels are affected by the tractive force of the Earth: witness varicose veins; witness the relief to an inflamed part obtained by raising it; witness the congestion of head and face produced by stooping. And in the facts that dropsy in the legs gets greater by day and decreases at night, while, conversely, that œdematous fulness under the eyes common in debility grows worse during the hours of reclining and decreases after getting up, we see how the transudation of liquid through the walls of the capillaries, varies according as change of position changes the effect of gravity in different parts of the body.

It may be well just to note the bearing of the principle on the development of species. From a dynamic point of view, "natural selection" implies structural changes along lines of least resistance. The multiplication of any kind of plant or animal in localities that are favourable to it, is a growth where the antagonistic forces are less than elsewhere. And the preservation of varieties which succeed better than their allies in coping with surrounding conditions, is the continuance of vital movements in those directions where the obstacles to them are most eluded.

§ 79. Throughout mental phenomena the law enunciated is not readily established. In a large part of them, as those of thought and emotion, there is no perceptible movement. Even in sensation and action, which show us in one part of the body an effect produced by a force applied to another part, the intermediate movement is inferential only. Some suggestions may be made however.

A stimulation implies a force added to, or evolved in, that part of the organism which is its seat; while a mechanical movement implies an expenditure or loss of force in that part of the organism which is its seat: implying some tension of molecular state between the two localities. Hence if, in the life of a minute animal, there are circumstances involving that a stimulation in one particular place is habitually followed by a contraction in another particular place—if there is thus a repeated motion through some line of least resistance between these places; what must be the result as respects the line? If this line—this channel—is affected by the discharge—if the obstructive action of the tissues traversed, involves any reaction upon them, deducting from their obstructive power; then a subsequent motion between these two points will meet with less resistance along this channel than the previous motion met with, and will consequently take this channel still more decidedly. Every repetition will further diminish the resistance offered; and thus will gradually be formed a permanent line of communication, differing greatly from the surrounding tissue in respect of the ease with which force traverses it. Hence in small creatures may result rudimentary nervous connexions.          Only an adumbration of nervous processes, thus hinted as conforming to the general law, is here possible. But the effects of associations between impressions and motions, as seen in habits, all yield illustrations. In knitting, in reading aloud, in the performance of the skilled pianist who talks while he plays, we have examples of the way in which channels of nervous communication are eventually made so permeable by perpetual discharges along them as to bring about a state almost automatic or reflex: illustrating at once the fact that molecular motion follows lines of least resistance, and the fact that motion along such lines, by diminishing the resistance, further facilitates the motion. Though qualifications arising in the same manner as those indicated in the last chapter, complicate these nervo-motor processes in ways which cannot here be followed, they do not conflict with the law set forth. Moreover they are congruous with the principle that in proportion to the frequency with which any external connexion of phenomena is experienced, will be the strength of the answering internal connexion of nervous states. In this way will arise all degrees of cohesion among nervous states, as there are all degrees of commonness among the surrounding co-existences and sequences that generate them. Whence must result a general correspondence between associated ideas and associated actions in the environment.*

---

* This paragraph is a re-statement, somewhat amplified, of an idea set forth in the *Medico-Chirurgical Review* for January, 1859 (pp. 189 and 190), and contains the germ of the intended fifth part of the *Principles of Psychology*, which was withheld for reasons given in the preface to that work.

The relation between emotions and actions may be similarly construed. Observe what happens with emotions which are undirected by volitions. As was pointed out in the last chapter, there result movements of the involuntary and voluntary muscles, that are great in proportion as the emotions are strong. It remains here to add that the order in which these muscles are affected conforms to the principle. A pleasurable or painful feeling of but slight intensity does little more than increase the action of the heart. Why? For the reason that the relation between nervous excitement and cardiac contraction, being common to every species of feeling, is the one of most frequent repetition; that hence the nervous connexion, offering the least resistance to a discharge, is the one along which a feeble force produces motion. A stronger sentiment affects not only the heart but the muscles of the face, and especially those around the mouth. Here the like explanation applies; since these muscles, being both comparatively small and, for purposes of speech, perpetually used, offer less resistance than other voluntary muscles to the nervo-motor forces. By a further increase of emotion the respiratory and vocal muscles become perceptibly excited. Finally, under violent passion, the muscles of the trunk and limbs are strongly contracted. The single instance of laughter, which is an undirected discharge of feeling that affects first the muscles round the mouth, then those of the vocal and respiratory apparatus, then those of the limbs, and then those of the spine, suffices to show that when no special route is opened for it, a force evolved in the nervous centres produces motion along channels which offer the least resistance, and if it is too great to escape by these, produces motion along channels offering successively greater resistance.*

Probably it will be thought impossible to extend this reasoning so as to include voluntary acts. Yet we are not without evidence that the transition from special desires to special muscular motions conforms to the same principle. The mental antecedents of a voluntary movement are such as temporarily make the line through which this movement is initiated the line of least resist-

* For details see a paper on "The Physiology of Laughter," published in *Macmillan's Magazine* for March, 1860, and reprinted in *Essays*, vol. II.

ance. For a volition, suggested as it is by some previous thought joined with it by associations that determine the transition, is itself a representation of the movements which are willed, and of their sequences. But to represent in consciousness certain of our own movements, is partially to arouse the sensations accompanying such movements, inclusive of those of muscular tension—is partially to excite the appropriate motor nerves and all the other nerves implicated. That is to say, the volition is itself an incipient discharge along a line which previous experiences have rendered a line of least resistance. And the passing of volition into action is simply a completion of the discharge.

One corollary must be noted; namely, that the particular set of movements by which an object of desire is reached are usually movements implying the smallest total of forces to be overcome. As the motion initiated by each feeling takes the line of least resistance, it is inferable that a group of feelings constituting a more or less complex desire will initiate motions along a series of lines of least resistance ; that is, the desired end will be achieved with the smallest effort. Doubtless through want of knowledge or want of skill or want of resolution to make immediate exertion, a man often takes the more laborious of two courses. But it remains true that, relatively to his mental state at the time, his course is the easiest to him—the one least resisted by the aggregate of his feelings.

§ 80. As with individual men so is it with aggregations of men. Social changes take directions that are due to the joint actions of citizens, determined as are those of all other changes wrought by composition of forces.

Thus when we note the direction of a nation's growth, we find it to be that in which the aggregate of opposing forces is least. Its units have energies to be expended in self-maintenance and reproduction. These energies are met by various antagonistic energies—those of geologic origin, those of climate, of wild animals, of other human races with whom there is enmity or competition. And the tracts the society spreads over, are those in which there is the smallest total of antagonisms while they yield the best supply of food and other materials which further the genesis of energies. For these reasons it happens that fertile

13

valleys, where water and vegetal products abound, are early peopled. Sea shores, too, supplying much easily-gathered food, are lines along which mankind have commonly spread. The general fact that, so far as we can judge from the traces left by them, large societies first appeared in those warm regions where the fruits of the earth are obtainable with comparatively little exertion, and where the cost of maintaining bodily heat is but slight, is a fact of like meaning. And to these instances may be added the allied one daily furnished by emigration, which we see going on towards countries presenting the fewest obstacles to the self-preservation of individuals, and therefore to national growth.     Similarly with that resistance to the movements of a society which neighbouring societies offer. Each of the tribes or nations inhabiting any region increases in numbers until it outgrows its means of subsistence. In each there is thus a force ever pressing outwards on to adjacent areas—a force antagonized by like forces in the tribes or nations occupying those areas. And the wars that result—the conquests of weaker tribes or nations, and the overrunning of their territories by the victors, are instances of social movements taking place in the directions of least resistance. Nor do the conquered peoples, when they escape extermination or enslavement, fail to show us movements which are similarly determined. For, migrating as they do to less fertile regions—taking refuge in deserts or among mountains—moving in directions where the resistances to social growth are comparatively great; they still do this only under an excess of pressure in all other directions : the physical obstacles to self-preservation they encounter being really less than the obstacles offered by the enemies from whom they fly.

Internal social movements also may be thus interpreted. Localities naturally fitted for producing particular commodities— that is, localities in which such commodities are got at the least cost of energy—that is, localities in which the desires for these commodities meet with the least resistance ; become localities devoted to the obtainment of these commodities. Where soil and climate render wheat a profitable crop, or a crop from which the greatest amount of life-sustaining power is gained by a given quantity of effort, the growth of wheat becomes a dominant industry. Where wheat cannot be economically produced, oats, or rye, or maize, or potatoes, or rice, is the agricultural staple. Along sea shores men support themselves with least effort by catching fish, and hence fishing becomes the occupation. And in places which are rich in coal or metallic ores, the population, finding that labour expended in raising these materials brings a larger return of food and clothing than when otherwise expended, becomes a population of miners.     This last instance introduces us to the phenomena of exchange, which equally illustrate the general law. For the practice of barter begins as soon as it facilitates the fulfilment of men's desires, by diminishing the exertion needed to reach the objects of those desires. When instead of growing his own corn, weaving his own cloth, sewing his own shoes, each man began to confine himself to farming, or weaving, or shoemaking, it was because each found it more laborious to make everything he wanted, than to make a great quantity of one thing and barter the surplus for other things. Moreover, in deciding what commodity to produce, each citizen was, as he is at the present day, guided in the same manner. In choosing those forms of activity which their special circumstances and special faculties dictate, the social units severally move towards the objects of their desires in the directions which present to them the fewest obstacles.     The process of transfer, which commerce presupposes, supplies another series of examples. So long as the forces to be overcome in procuring any necessary of life in the district where it is consumed, are less than the forces to be overcome in procuring it from an adjacent district, exchange does not take place. But when the adjacent district produces it with an economy that is not outbalanced by cost of transit—when the distance is so small and the route so easy that the labour of conveyance *plus* the labour of production is less than the labour of production in the consuming district, transfer commences. Movement in the direction of least resistance is also seen in the establishment of the channels along which intercourse takes place. At the outset, when goods are carried on the backs of men and horses, the paths chosen are those which combine shortness with levelness and freedom from obstacles—those which are achieved with the smallest exertion. And in the subsequent formation of each highway, the course taken is that which deviates horizontally from a straight line so far only as is needful to avoid vertical deviations entailing greater labour in draught. The smallest total of obstructive forces determines the route, even in seemingly exceptional cases; as where a detour is made to avoid the opposition of a landowner. All subsequent improvements, ending in macadamized roads, canals, and railways, which reduce the antagonism of friction and gravity to a minimum, exemplify the same truth. After there comes to be a choice of roads between-one point and another, we still see that the road chosen is that along which the cost of transit is the least: cost being the measure of resistance. When there arises a marked localization of industries, the relative growths of the populations devoted to them may be interpreted on the same principle. The influx of people to each industrial centre is determined by the payment for labour, that is—by the quantity of commodities which a given amount of effort will obtain. To say that artisans flock to places where, in consequence of facilities for production, an extra proportion of produce can be given in the shape of wages, is to say that they flock to places where there are the smallest obstacles to the support of themselves and families; and so growth of the social organism takes place where the resistance is least.

Nor is the law less clearly to be traced in those functional changes daily going on. The flow of capital into businesses yielding the largest returns, the buying in the cheapest market and selling in the dearest, the introduction of more economical modes of manufacture, the development of better agencies for distribution, exhibit movements taking place in directions where they are met by the smallest totals of opposing forces. For if we analyze each of these changes—if instead of interest on capital we read surplus of products which remains after maintenance of labourers —if we thus interpret large interest or large surplus to imply labour expended with the greatest results and if labour expended with the greatest results means muscular action so directed as to evade obstacles as far as possible; we see that all these commercial phenomena imply complicated motions set up along lines of least resistance.

Social movements of these various orders severally conform to the two derivative principles named at the outset. In the first place, we see that, once set up in given directions, such movements, like all others, tend to produce continuance in these directions. A commercial mania or panic, a current of commodities, a social custom, a political agitation, or a popular delusion, maintains its course long after its original cause has ceased, and requires antagonistic forces to arrest it. In the second place, it is to be noted that in proportion to the complexity of social forces is the tortuousness of social movements. The involved series of various processes through which a man is returned to Parliament, or through which afterwards, by an Act he finally gets passed, certain doings of his fellow citizens are changed, show this.

§ 81. And now of the general truth above set forth what is our ultimate evidence? Must we accept it simply as an empirical generalization? or may it be established as a corollary from a still deeper truth? The reader will anticipate the answer.

Suppose several tractive forces, variously directed, to be acting on a given body. By what is known as the composition of forces, there may be found for any two of these a single force of such amount and direction as to produce on the body an exactly equal effect. Such a resultant force, as it is called, may be found for any pair of forces throughout the group. Similarly, for any pair of resultants a single resultant may be found. And by repeating this course, all of them may be reduced to two. If these two are equal and opposite—that is, if there is no line of greatest traction, motion does not arise. If they are opposite but not equal, motion arises in the direction of the greater. If they are neither equal nor opposite, motion arises in the direction of their resultant. For in either of these cases there is an unantagonized force in one direction. And this residuary force must move the body in the direction in which it is acting. To assert the contrary is to assert that a force can be expended without effect; and this involves a denial of the persistence of force. If in place of tractions we take resistances, the argument equally holds; and it holds also where both tractions and resistances are concerned. Thus the law that motion follows the line of greatest traction, or the line of least resistance, or the resultant of the two, is a necessary deduction from that primordial truth which transcends proof.

Reduce the proposition to its simplest form, and its truth becomes still more obvious. Suppose two weights suspended over a pulley, or suppose two men pulling against each other. The heavier weight will descend, and the stronger man will draw the weaker towards him. If asked how we know which is the heavier weight or the stronger man, we can only reply that it is the one producing motion in the direction of its pull. But if of ₊two opposing tractions we can know one as greater than the other only by the motion it generates in its own direction, then the assertion that motion occurs in the direction of greatest traction is a truism. When, going a step further back, we seek a warrant for the assumption that of the two conflicting forces, the one which produces motion in its own direction is the greatest, we find no other than the consciousness that such part of the greater force as is unneutralized by the lesser, must produce its effect—the consciousness that this residuary force cannot disappear, but must manifest itself in some equivalent change—the consciousness that force is persistent. Here too, as before, it may be remarked that no number of varied illustrations, like those of which this chapter mainly consists, can give greater certainty to the conclusion thus immediately drawn from the ultimate datum of consciousness. For in all cases, as in the simple ones just given, we can identify the greatest force only by the resulting motion.

From this same primordial truth, too, may be deduced the principle that motion once set up along any line, becomes itself a cause of subsequent motion along that line. The mechanical axiom that, if left to itself, matter moving in any direction will continue in that direction with undiminished velocity, is but an indirect assertion of the persistence of that kind of force called energy; since it is an assertion that the energy manifested in the transfer of a body along a certain length of a certain line in a certain time cannot disappear without producing some equal manifestation: a manifestation which, in the absence of conflicting forces, must be a further transfer in the same direction at the same velocity. In the case of matter traversing matter a like inference is necessitated. Here however the actions are complicated. A liquid that follows a certain channel through or over a solid, as water along the Earth's surface, loses part of its motion in the shape of heat, through friction and collision with the matters forming its bed. A further amount may be absorbed in overcoming the forces it liberates; as when it loosens a mass which falls into its channel. But after these deductions, any further deduction from the energy embodied in the motion of the water, is at the expense of a reaction on the channel which diminishes its obstructive power: such reaction being shown in the motion acquired by the detached portions carried away. The cutting out of river courses perpetually illustrates this truth. Still more involved is the case of motion passing through matter by impulse from part to part; as a nervous discharge through animal tissue. There are conceivable anomalies. Some chemical change wrought along the route traversed, may render it less fit than before for conveying a current. Or some obstructive form of force may be generated; as in metals, the conducting power of which is, for the time, decreased by the heat which the electric current produces. The real question is, however, what structural modification, if any, is produced throughout the matter traversed, apart from *incidental* disturbing forces—apart from everything but the *necessary* resistance of the matter: that, namely, which results from the inertia of its units. If we confine our attention to that part of the motion which, escaping transformation, continues its course, then the persistence of force necessitates that as much of it as is taken up in changing the positions of the units, must leave these by so much less able to obstruct subsequent motion in the same direction.

Thus in all the changes displayed by the Solar System, in all those which are going on in the Earth's crust, in all processes of organic development and function, in all mental actions and the effects they work on the body, and in all modifications of structure and activity in societies, the implied movements are of necessity determined in the manner above set forth. The truth set forth holds not only of one class, or of some classes, of phenomena, but it is among those universal truths by which our knowledge of phenomena in general is unified.

# CHAPTER X

## THE RHYTHM OF MOTION

§ 82. When the pennant of a vessel lying becalmed shows the coming breeze, it does so by gentle undulations which travel from its fixed to its free end. Presently the sails begin to flap; and their blows against the mast increase in rapidity as the breeze rises. Even when, being fully bellied out, they are in great part steadied by the strain of the yards and cordage, their free edges tremble with each stronger gust. And should there come a gale, the jar that is felt on laying hold of the shrouds shows that the rigging vibrates; while the whistle of the wind proves that in it, also, rapid undulations are generated. Ashore the conflict between the current of air and the things it meets results in a like rhythmical action. The leaves all shiver in the blast; each branch oscillates; and every exposed tree sways to and fro. The blades of grass and dried bents in the meadows, and still better the stalks in the neighbouring corn-fields, exhibit the same rising and falling movements. Nor do the more stable objects fail to do the like, though in a less manifest fashion; as witness the shudder that may be felt throughout a house during the paroxysms of a violent storm. Streams of water produce in opposing objects the same general effects as do streams of air. Submerged weeds growing in the middle of a brook, undulate from end to end. Branches brought down by the last flood, and left entangled at the bottom where the current is rapid, are thrown into a state of up and down movement that is slow or quick in proportion as they are large or small; and where, as in great rivers like the Mississippi, whole trees are thus held, the name "sawyers," by which they are locally known, sufficiently describes the rhythm produced in them. Note, again, the effect of the antagonism between the current and its channel. In shallow places, where the action of the bottom on the water flowing over it is visible, we see a ripple produced—a series of undulations. If we study the action and reaction going on between the moving fluid and its banks, we still find the principle illustrated, though in a different way. For in every rivulet, as in the mapped-out course of every great river, the bends of the stream from side to side throughout its tortuous course constitute a lateral undulation—an undulation so inevitable that even an artificially-straightened channel is eventually changed into a serpentine one. Kindred phenomena may be observed when the water is stationary and the solid matter moving. A stick drawn laterally through the water with much force, proves by the throb which it communicates to the hand that it is in a state of vibration. Even where the moving body is massive, it only requires that great force should be applied to get a sensible effect of like kind: instance the screw of a screw-steamer (of the primitive type), which instead of a smooth rotation falls into a rapid rhythm that sends a tremor through the whole vessel. The sound produced when a bow is drawn over a violin string shows us vibrations accompanying the movement of a solid over a solid. In lathes and planing machines, the attempt to take off a thick shaving causes a violent jar of the whole apparatus, and the production of a series of waves on the iron or wood that is cut. Every boy in scraping his slate-pencil finds it scarcely possible to help making a ridged surface. If you roll a ball along the ground or over the ice, there is always more or less up and down movement —a movement that is visible while the velocity is considerable, but becomes too small and rapid to be seen by the unaided eye as the velocity diminishes. However smooth the rails, and however perfectly built the carriages, a railway train inevitably acquires oscillations, both lateral and vertical. Even where a moving mass is suddenly arrested by collision, the law is still illustrated; for both the body striking and the body struck are made to tremble; and trembling is rhythmical movement. Little as we habitually observe it, it is yet certain that the impulses our actions impress from moment to moment on surrounding objects, are propagated through them in vibrations. It needs but to look through a telescope of high power, placed on a table, to be convinced that each pulsation of the heart gives a jar to surrounding things.　　Motions of another order—those namely of the ethereal medium—teach us the same thing. Every fresh discovery confirms the hypothesis that light consists of undulations, and that the rays of heat have a like fundamental nature: their undulations differing from those of light only in their comparative lengths. Nor do the movements of electricity fail to furnish us with illustrations, though of a different order. The northern aurora may often be observed to pulsate with waves of greater brightness; and the electric discharge through a vacuum shows by its stratified appearance that the current is not uniform, but comes in gushes of greater and lesser intensity.　　Should it be said that there are some motions, as those of projectiles, which are not rhythmical, the reply is that the exception is apparent only, and that these motions would be rhythmical if they were not interrupted. It is common to assert that the trajectory of a cannon ball is a parabola; and it is true that (omitting atmospheric resistance) the curve described differs so slightly from a parabola that it may practically be regarded as one. But, strictly speaking, it is a portion of an extremely eccentric ellipse, having the Earth's centre of gravity for its remoter focus; and but for its arrest by the substance of the Earth, the cannon ball would travel round that focus and return to the point whence it started, again to repeat this slow rhythm. Indeed, while seeming to do the reverse, the discharge of a cannon furnishes one of the best illustrations of the principle enunciated. The explosion produces violent undulations in the surrounding air. The whizz of the shot, as it flies towards its mark, is due to another series of atmospheric undulations. And the eccentric movement round the Earth's centre, which the cannon ball is beginning to perform, being checked by solid matter, is transformed into a rhythm of another order; namely, the vibration which the blow sends through neighbouring bodies.*

Rhythm is very generally not simple but compound. There are

* After having for some years supposed myself alone in the belief that all motion is rhythmical, I discovered that my friend Professor Tyndall also held this doctrine.

usually at work various forces, causing undulations differing in rapidity; and hence besides the primary rhythms there arise secondary rhythms, produced by the periodic coincidence and opposition of the primary ones. Double, triple, and even quadruple rhythms, are thus generated. One of the simplest instances is afforded by what in acoustics are known as "beats": recurring intervals of sound and silence which are perceived when two notes of nearly the same pitch are struck together, and which are due to the alternate correspondence and antagonism of the atmospheric waves. In like manner the phenomena due to what is called interference of light result from the periodic agreement and disagreement of ethereal undulations—undulations which, by alternately intensifying and neutralizing each other, produce intervals of increased and diminished light. On the sea-shore may be noted sundry instances of compound rhythms. We have that of the tides, in which the daily rise and fall undergoes a fortnightly increase and decrease, due to the alternate coincidence and antagonism of the solar and lunar attractions. We have again that which is perpetually furnished by the surface of the sea: every large wave bearing smaller ones on its sides, and these still smaller ones, with the result that each flake of foam, along with the portion of water bearing it, undergoes minor ascents and descents of several orders while it is being raised and lowered by the greater billows. A different and very interesting example of compound rhythm, occurs in the little rills which, at low tide, run over the sand out of the shingle banks above. Where the channel of one of these is narrow and the stream runs strongly, the sand at the bottom is raised into a series of ridges corresponding to the ripple of the water. On watching, it will be seen that these ridges are being raised higher and the ripple growing stronger; until at length, the action becoming violent, the whole series of ridges is suddenly swept away, the stream runs smoothly, and the process commences afresh.

Rhythm results wherever there is a conflict of forces not in equilibrium. If the antagonist forces at any point are balanced, there is rest; and in the absence of motion there can of course be no rhythm. But if instead of a balance there is an excess of force in one direction—if, as necessarily follows, motion is set up in that direction; then for the motion to continue uniformly in that direction, the moving matter must, notwithstanding its unceasing change of place, present unchanging relations to the sources of force by which its motion is produced and opposed. This however is impossible. Every further transfer through space, by altering the ratio between the forces concerned, must prevent uniformity of movement. And if the movement cannot be uniform, then (save where it is destroyed, or rather transformed, as by the collision of two bodies travelling through space in a straight line towards each other) the only alternative is rhythm.

A secondary conclusion must not be omitted. In the last chapter we saw that motion is never absolutely rectilinear; and here it remains to add that, as a consequence, rhythm is necessarily incomplete. A truly rectilinear rhythm can arise only when the opposing forces are in exactly the same line, and the probabilities against this are infinitely great. To generate a perfectly circular rhythm, the two forces concerned must be exactly at right angles to each other, and must have exactly a certain ratio; and against this the probabilities are likewise infinitely great. All other proportions and directions of the two forces (omitting such as produce parabolas or hyperbolas) will produce an ellipse of greater or less eccentricity. And when, as always happens, above two forces are engaged, the curve described must be more complex, and cannot exactly repeat itself. So that throughout nature, this action and reaction of forces never brings about a complete return to a previous state. Where the movement is that of some aggregate whose units are partially independent, regularity is no longer traceable. And on the completion of any periodic change, the degree in which the state arrived at differs from the state departed from is marked in proportion as the influences at work are numerous.

§ 83. That spiral arrangement common among the more structured nebulæ, shows us the progressive establishment of revolution, and therefore of rhythm, in those remote spaces which the nebulæ occupy. Double stars, moving in more or less eccentric orbits round common centres of gravity in periods some of which are now ascertained, exhibit settled rhythmical actions in distant parts of our Sidereal System.

The periodicities of the planets, satellites, and comets, familiar
though they are, must be named as so many grand illustrations of
this general law of movement.  But besides the revolutions of these
bodies in their orbits (all more or less eccentric), the Solar System
presents us with rhythms of a less manifest and more complex
kind.  In each planet and satellite there is the revolution of the
nodes—a slow change in the position of the orbit-plane, which
after completing itself commences afresh.  There is the gradual
alteration in the length of the axis major of the orbit, and also of
its eccentricity: both of which are rhythmical alike in the sense
that they alternate between maxima and minima, and in the sense
that the progress from one extreme to the other is not uniform,
but is made with fluctuating velocity.  Then, too, there is the
revolution of the line of apsides round the heavens—not regularly,
but through complex oscillations.  And, further, we have changes
in the directions of the planetary axes—that known as nutation,
and that larger gyration which, in the case of the Earth, causes the
precession of the equinoxes.          These rhythms, already more
or less compound, are compounded with one another.  One of the
simplest re-compoundings is seen in the secular acceleration and
retardation of the moon, consequent on the varying eccentricity of
the Earth's orbit.  Another, having more important consequences,
results from the changing direction of the axis of rotation in a
planet having a decidedly eccentric orbit.  The Earth furnishes the
best example.  During a certain long period it presents more of its
northern than of its southern hemisphere to the Sun at the time
of nearest approach to him; and then again, during a like period,
presents more of its southern hemisphere than of its northern: a
recurring coincidence which involves an epoch of 21,000 years,
during which each hemisphere goes through a cycle of temperate
seasons and seasons that are extreme in their heat and cold.  Nor
is this all.  There is even a variation of this variation.  For the
summers and winters of the whole Earth become more or less
strongly contrasted, as the eccentricity of its orbit increases or
decreases.  Hence during the increase of the eccentricity, the
epochs of moderately contrasted seasons and epochs of strongly
contrasted seasons, through which alternately each hemisphere
passes, must grow more and more different in the degrees of their

contrasts; and contrariwise during decrease of the eccentricity. So that in those movements of the Earth which determine the varying quantities of light and heat which any portion of it receives from the Sun, there goes on a quadruple rhythm: that causing day and night; that causing summer and winter; that causing the changing position of the axis at perihelion and aphelion, taking 21,000 years to complete; and that causing the variation of the orbit's eccentricity, gone through in millions of years.

§ 84. Those terrestrial processes directly depending on the solar heat, of course exhibit a rhythm that corresponds to the periodically changing amount of heat which each part of the Earth receives. The simplest, though the least obtrusive, instance is supplied by the magnetic variations. In these there is a diurnal increase and decrease, an annual increase and decrease, and a decennial increase and decrease: the latter answering to a period during which the solar spots become alternately abundant and scarce. And besides known variations there are probably others corresponding to the astronomical cycles just described. More obvious examples are furnished by the movements of the ocean and the atmosphere. Marine currents from the equator to the poles above, and from the poles to the equator beneath, show us an unceasing backward and forward motion throughout this vast mass of water —a motion varying in amount according to the seasons, and compounded with smaller like motions of local origin. The similarly-caused general currents in the air, have similar annual variations similarly modified. Irregular as they are in detail, we still see in the monsoons and other tropical atmospheric disturbances, or even in our autumn equinoctial gales and spring east winds, a periodicity sufficiently decided. Again, we have an alternation of times during which evaporation predominates with times during which condensation predominates; shown in the tropics by strongly marked rainy seasons and seasons of drought, and in the temperate zones by changes of which the periodicity is less definite. The diffusion and precipitation of water furnish us with examples of rhythm of a more rapid kind. During wet weather lasting over some weeks, the tendency to condense, though greater than the tendency to evaporate, does not show itself in continuous rain; but the period is made up of rainy days and days which are wholly or partially fair. Nor is it in this rude alternation only that the law is manifested. During any day throughout this wet weather a minor rhythm is often traceable; and especially so when the tendencies to evaporate and to condense are nearly balanced. Among mountains this minor rhythm and its causes may be studied to advantage. Moist winds, which do not precipitate their contained water in passing over the comparatively warm lowlands, lose so much heat when they reach the cold mountain peaks, that condensation rapidly takes place. Water, however, in passing from the gaseous to the liquid state, gives out heat; and therefore the resulting clouds are warmer than the air that precipitates them, and much warmer than the high rocky surfaces round which they fold themselves. Hence in the course of the storm, these high rocky surfaces are raised in temperature, partly by radiation from the enwrapping cloud, partly by contact of the falling rain-drops. Consequently they no longer lower so much the temperature of the air passing over them, and cease to precipitate its contained water. The clouds break; the sky begins to clear; and a gleam of sunshine promises that the day is going to be fine. But the small supply of heat which the cold mountain's tops have received is soon lost: especially when partial dispersion of the clouds permits radiation into space. Very soon, therefore, these elevated surfaces, becoming as cold as at first, begin again to condense the vapour in the air above, and there comes another storm, followed by the same effects as before. In lower lands this action and reaction is less conspicuous, because the contrast of temperatures is less marked. Even here, however, it may be traced, not only on showery days, but on days of continuous rain; for in these we do not see uniformity: always there are fits of harder and gentler rain.

Of course these meteorologic rhythms involve corresponding rhythms in the changes wrought by wind and water on the Earth's surface. Variations in the quantities of sediment brought down by rivers that rise and fall with the seasons, must cause variations in the resulting strata—alternations of colour or quality in the successive laminæ. Beds formed from the detritus of shores worn down and carried away by the waves must similarly show periodic differences answering to the periodic winds of the locality. In so far as frost influences the rate of denudation, its recurrence is a factor in the rhythm of sedimentary deposits. And the geological changes produced by glaciers must similarly have their alternating periods of greater and less intensity.

There is some evidence that modifications in the Earth's crust due to igneous action have an indefinite periodicity. Volcanic eruptions are not continuous but intermittent, and, as far as the data enable us to judge, have something like an average rate of recurrence, as witness the case of Kilauea; which rate is complicated by rising into epochs of greater activity and falling into epochs of comparative quiescence. So too, according to Mallet, is it with earthquakes and the elevations or depressions caused by them. Sedimentary formations yield indirect evidence. At the mouth of the Mississippi the alternation of strata gives decisive proof of successive sinkings of the surface, that have taken place at tolerably equal intervals. Everywhere in the extensive groups of comformable strata that imply small subsidences recurring with a certain average frequency, we see a rhythm in the action and reaction between the Earth's crust and its contents—a rhythm compounded with those slower ones shown in the termination of groups of strata, and the commencement of other groups not conformable to them.

§ 85. Perhaps nowhere are illustrations of rhythm so numerous and so manifest as among the phenomena of life. Plants do not, indeed, usually show us any decided periodicities, save those determined by day and night and by the seasons. But in animals we have a great variety of movements in which the alternation of opposite extremes goes on with all degrees of rapidity. The swallowing of food is effected by a wave of constriction passing along the œsophagus; its digestion is largely aided by a muscular action of the stomach that is also undulatory; and the peristaltic motion of the intestines is of like nature. The blood obtained from this food is propelled in pulses, and is aerated by lungs that alternately contract and expand. All locomotion results from oscillating movements. Even where it is apparently continuous, as in many minute forms, the microscope proves the vibration of cilia to be the agency by which the creature is moved smoothly forwards.

Primary rhythms of the organic actions are compounded with secondary ones of longer duration. We see this in the periodic need for food, and in the periodic need for repose. Each meal induces a more rapid rhythmic action of the digestive organs ; the pulsation of the heart is accelerated ; the inspirations become more frequent. During sleep, on the contrary, these several movements slacken. So that in the course of the twenty-four hours, those small undulations of which the different kinds of organic action are constituted, undergo one long wave of increase and decrease, complicated with several minor waves. Experiments have shown that there are still slower rises and falls of functional activity. Waste and assimilation are not balanced by every meal, but one or other maintains for some time a slight excess ; so that a person in ordinary health undergoes an increase and decrease of weight during recurring intervals of tolerable equality. There are oscillations of vigour too. Even men in training cannot be kept stationary at their highest power, but when they have reached it begin to retrograde. Further evidence of rhythm in the vital movements is furnished by invalids. Sundry disorders are named from the intermittent character of their symptoms. Even where the periodicity is not very marked it is mostly traceable. Patients rarely if ever become uniformly worse ; and convalescents have usually their days of partial relapse or of less decided advance.

Aggregates of living creatures illustrate the general truth in other ways. If each species of organism be regarded as a whole, it displays two kinds of rhythm. Life, as it exists in every member of such species, is an extremely complex kind of movement, more or less distinct from the kinds of movement which constitute life in other species. This extremely complex kind of movement begins, rises to its climax, declines, and ceases in death. And every individual in each generation thus exhibits a wave of that peculiar activity characterizing the species as a whole. The other form of rhythm is seen in that variation of number which each tribe of animals and plants undergoes. Throughout the unceasing conflict between the tendency of a species to increase and the antagonistic tendencies, there is never an equilibrium : one always

14

predominates. In the case even of a cultivated plant or domesticated animal, where artificial means are used to maintain the supply at a uniform level, oscillations of abundance and scarcity cannot be avoided. And among creatures uncared for by man, such oscillations are usually more marked. After a race of organisms has been greatly thinned by enemies or innutrition, its surviving members become more favourably circumstanced than usual. During the decline in their numbers their food has grown relatively abundant, while their enemies have somewhat diminished from want of prey. The conditions thus remain for some time favourable to their increase, and they multiply rapidly. By-and-by their food is rendered relatively scarce, at the same time that their enemies have become more numerous; and the destroying influences being thus in excess, their number begins to diminish again. Yet one more rhythm, extremely slow, may be traced in the phenomena of Life under their most general aspect. The researches of palæontologists show that there have been going on, during the vast period of which our sedimentary rocks bear record, successive changes of organic forms. Species have appeared, become abundant, and then disappeared. Genera, at first constituted of but few species, have for a time gone on growing more multiform, and then have declined in the number of their subdivisions: leaving at last but one or two, or none at all. During longer epochs whole orders have thus arisen, culminated, and dwindled away. And even those wider divisions containing many orders have similarly undergone a gradual rise, a high tide, and a long-continued ebb. The stalked *Crinoidea*, for example, which during the carboniferous epoch became abundant, have almost disappeared: only a few species being extant. Once a large family, the *Brachiopoda* have now become rare. The shelled Cephalopods, at one time dominant among the inhabitants of the ocean, both in number of forms and of individuals, are in our day nearly extinct. And after an "age of reptiles" has come an age in which reptiles have been in great measure supplanted by mammals. Thus Life on the Earth has not progressed uniformly, but in immense undulations.

§ 86. It is not manifest that changes of consciousness are in any sense rhythmical. Yet here, too, analysis proves both that the mental state existing at any moment is not uniform, but is decomposable into rapid oscillations, and also that mental states pass through longer intervals of increasing and decreasing intensity. Though while attending to any single sensation, or any group of related sensations constituting the consciousness of an object, we seem to remain in a persistent and homogeneous condition of mind, self-examination shows that this apparently unbroken mental state is traversed by many minor states, in which various other sensations and perceptions are rapidly presented and disappear. As thinking consists in the establishment of relations, it follows that continuance of it in any one state to the entire exclusion of other states, would be a cessation of thought, that is, of consciousness. So that any seemingly uniform feeling, say of pressure, really consists of portions of that feeling perpetually recurring after momentary intrusions of other feelings and ideas—quick thoughts concerning the place where it is felt, the external object producing it, its consequences, &c. Much more conspicuous rhythms, having longer waves, are seen during the outflow of emotion into dancing, poetry, and music. The current of mental energy expended in one of these modes of bodily action, is not continuous but falls into successive pulses. The measure of a dance is produced by the alternation of strong muscular contractions with weaker ones; and, save in measures of the simplest order, such as are found among barbarians and children, this alternation is compounded with longer rises and falls in the degree of muscular excitement. Poetry is a form of speech in which the emphasis is regularly recurrent, that is—in which the muscular effort of pronunciation has definite periods of greater and less intensity: periods that are complicated with others answering to the successive verses. Music more variously exemplifies the law. There are the recurring bars, in each of which there is a primary and a secondary beat. There is the alternate increase and decrease of muscular strain implied by the ascents and descents to the higher and lower notes—ascents and descents composed of smaller waves, breaking the rises and falls of the larger ones, in a mode peculiar to each melody. And then we have, further, the alternations of *piano* and *forte* passages. That these several kinds of rhythm, characterizing æsthetic expression, are not, in the common sense of the word, artificial, but are intenser forms of an undulatory movement habitually generated by feeling in its bodily discharge, is shown by the fact that they are all traceable in ordinary speech; which in every sentence has its primary and secondary emphases, and its cadence containing a chief rise and fall complicated with subordinate rises and falls.          Still longer undulations may be observed by every one in himself and in others, on occasions of extreme pleasure or extreme pain.  During hours in which bodily pain never actually ceases, it has its variations of intensity —fits or paroxysms; and then after these intervals of suffering there usually come intervals of comparative ease.  Moral pain has the like smaller and larger waves.  One possessed by intense grief does not utter continuous moans, or shed tears with an equable rapidity; but these signs of passion come in recurring bursts.  Then after a time during which such stronger and weaker waves of emotion alternate, there comes a calm—a time of comparative deadness; after which dull sorrow rises afresh into acute anguish, with its series of paroxysms.  Similarly great delight, as shown by children who display it without control, undergoes variations in intensity: there are fits of laughter and dancing about, separated by pauses in which smiles, and other slight manifestations of pleasure, suffice to discharge the lessened excitement.          Nor are there wanting evidences of mental undulations greater in length than any of these.  We continually hear of moods which recur at intervals. Many persons have their days of vivacity and days of depression. Others have periods of industry following periods of idleness; and times at which particular subjects or tastes are cultivated with zeal, alternating with times at which they are neglected.  Respecting which slow oscillations the only qualification to be made is, that being affected by numerous influences they are irregular.

§ 87.  In nomadic societies the changes of place, determined by exhaustion or failure of the supply of food, are periodic; and in many cases recur with the seasons.  Each tribe that has become partially fixed in its locality, goes on increasing until, under pressure of hunger, there results migration of some part of it—a process repeated at intervals.  From such excesses of population, and such waves of migration, come conflicts with other tribes;

which are also increasing and tending to diffuse themselves. Their antagonisms result not in a uniform motion, but in an intermittent one. War, exhaustion, recoil—peace, prosperity, and renewed aggression :—see here the alternation as occurring among both savage and civilized peoples. And irregular as is this rhythm, it is not more so than the different sizes of the societies, and the involved causes of variation in their strengths, would lead us to anticipate.

Passing from external to internal social changes, we meet this backward and forward movement under many forms. In commercial currents it is especially conspicuous. Exchange during early times is carried on mainly at fairs, held at long intervals. The flux and reflux of people and commodities which each of these exhibits, becomes more frequent as national development brings greater social activity. The rapid rhythm of weekly markets begins to supersede the slow rhythm of fairs. And eventually exchange becomes at some places so active, as to bring about daily meetings of buyers and sellers—a daily wave of accumulation and distribution of cotton, or corn, or capital.          In production and consumption there are undulations almost equally obvious. Supply and demand are never completely adjusted, but each, from time to time in excess, leads presently to excess of the other. Farmers who have one season grown wheat abundantly, are disgusted with the consequent low price, and next season, sowing a much smaller quantity, bring to market a deficient crop; whence follows a converse effect. Consumption undergoes parallel undulations that need not be specified. The balancing of supplies between different districts, too, entails oscillations. A place at which some necessary of life is scarce, becomes a place to which currents of it are set up from other places where it is relatively abundant; and these currents lead to a wave of accumulation where they meet—a glut: whence follows a recoil—a partial return of the currents.          But the undulatory character of these actions is best seen in the rises and falls of prices. These, when tabulated and reduced to diagrams, show us in the clearest manner how commercial movements are compounded of oscillations of various magnitudes. The price of consols or the price of wheat, as thus represented, is seen to undergo vast ascents and descents having highest and lowest points that are reached only in the course of years. These largest waves of variation are broken by lesser ones extending over periods of months. On these come others severally having a week or two's duration. And were the changes marked in greater detail, we should see the smaller undulations that take place each day, and the still smaller ones which brokers telegraph from hour to hour. The whole outline would show a complication like that of a vast ocean-swell, having on its surface large billows, which themselves bear waves of moderate size, covered by wavelets, that are roughened by a minute ripple. Similar diagrammatic representations of births, marriages, and deaths, of disease, of crime, of pauperism, exhibit involved conflicts of rhythmical motions throughout society under these several aspects.

There are like traits in social changes of more complex kinds. Both in England and on the Continent the actions and reactions of political progress are now generally recognized. Religion has its periods of exaltation and depression—generations of belief and self-mortification, following generations of indifference and laxity. There are poetical epochs, and epochs in which the sense of the beautiful seems almost dormant. Philosophy, after having been awhile dominant, lapses for a long season into neglect, and then again slowly revives. Each concrete science has its eras of deductive reasoning, and its eras in which attention is chiefly directed to collecting and colligating facts. And that in such minor phenomena as those of fashion, there are oscillations from one extreme to the other, is a trite observation.

As may be foreseen, social rhythms well illustrate the irregularity that results from combination of many causes. Where the variations are those of one simple element in national life, as the supply of a particular commodity, we do indeed witness a return, after many involved movements, to a previous state—the price becomes what it was before: implying a like relative abundance. But where the action is one into which many factors enter, there is never a complete recurrence. A political reaction never brings round just the old form of things. The rationalism of the present day differs widely from the rationalism of the last century. And though fashion from time to time revives extinct types of dress, these always reappear with decided modifications.

§ 88. Rhythm being thus manifested in all forms of movement, we have reason to suspect that it is determined by some primordial condition to action in general. The tacit implication is that it is deducible from the persistence of force. This we shall find to be the fact.

When the prong of a tuning-fork is pulled on one side by the finger, some extra tension is produced among its cohering particles, which resist any force that draws them out of their state of equilibrium. As much force as the finger exerts, so much opposing force arises among the cohering particles. Hence, when the prong is liberated, it is urged back by a force equal to that used in deflecting it. When, therefore, the prong reaches its original position, the force impressed during its recoil, has generated in it a corresponding amount of momentum—an amount nearly equivalent to the force originally impressed (nearly, we must say, because a certain portion has gone in giving motion to the air, and a certain other portion has been transformed into heat). This momentum carries the prong beyond the position of rest, nearly as far as it was originally drawn in the reverse direction; until at length, being gradually used up in producing an opposing tension among the particles, it is all lost. This opposing tension then generates a second recoil, and so on continually: the vibration eventually ceasing only because at each movement a certain amount of force goes in creating atmospheric and ethereal undulations. Now evidently this repeated action and reaction is a consequence of the persistence of force. The force exerted by the finger in bending the prong cannot disappear. Under what form then does it exist? It exists under the form of that cohesive tension which it has generated among the particles. This cohesive tension cannot cease without an equivalent result. What is its equivalent result? The momentum generated in the prong while being carried back to its position of rest. This momentum too—what becomes of it? It must either continue as momentum, or produce some correlative force of equal amount. It cannot continue as momentum, since change of place is resisted by the cohesion of the parts; and thus it gradually disappears by being transformed into tension among these parts. This is retransformed into the equivalent momentum; and so on continuously.          If, instead of motion that is directly antagonized by the cohesion of matter, we consider motion through space, as of a comet, the same truth presents itself under another form. Though while it is approaching the Sun no opposing force seems at work, and therefore no cause of rhythm, yet its own accumulated momentum must eventually carry the moving body beyond the attracting body; and so must become a force in conflict with that which generated it. This force cannot be destroyed, but it can have its direction changed by the still continued attraction: the result being that a passage round the attracting body is followed by a retreat during which this embodied force, gradually becoming non-apparent, is transformed into gravitative strain, until all of it having been thus transformed there begins a return from aphelion.

Before ending, two qualifications must be made. As the rhythm of motion itself postulates continuity of motion, it cannot be looked for when motion has suddenly become invisible. A hint tacitly given in § 82 implies that what we may call a fragmentary motion—a motion which under its perceptible form is suddenly brought to an end—cannot under that form exhibit rhythm: instance the stoppage of a hammer by an anvil. In such cases, however, we observe that this non-continuous motion is transformed into motions that are continuous and rhythmical—the sound-waves, the ether-waves of the heat generated, and the waves of vibration sent through the mass struck: the rhythms of these motions continuing as long as the motions themselves do.

The other qualification is that the motions shall be those occurring within a *closed system*, such as is constituted by our own Sun, planets, satellites, and periodic comets. If a body approaching a centre of attraction from remote space, has any considerable proper motion not towards that centre, this body, passing round it, may take a course which negatives return—an hyperbola. I say an hyperbola because the chances against a parabolic course are infinity to one.

But bearing in mind these two qualifications, of which the last may be considered almost nominal, we may conclude that under the conditions existing within our Solar System and among terrestrial phenomena, rhythm, everywhere arising from the play of antagonist forces, is a corollary from the persistence of force.

# CHAPTER XI

RECAPITULATION, CRITICISM, AND RECOMMENCEMENT

§ 89. LET us pause awhile to consider how far the contents of the foregoing chapters go towards forming a body of knowledge answering to the definition of Philosophy.

In respect of its generality, the proposition enunciated and exemplified in each chapter is of the required kind—is a proposition transcending those class-limits which Science, as currently understood, recognizes. "The Indestructibility of Matter" is a truth not belonging to mechanics more than to chemistry—a truth assumed alike by molecular physics and the physics that deals with sensible masses—a truth which the astronomer and the biologist equally take for granted. Not merely do those divisions of Science which deal with the movements of celestial and terrestrial bodies postulate "The Continuity of Motion," but it is no less postulated in the physicist's investigations into the phenomena of light and heat, and is tacitly, if not avowedly, implied in the generalizations of the higher sciences. So, too, "The Persistence of Force," involved in each of the preceding propositions, is co-extensive with them, as is also its corollary, "The Persistence of Relations among Forces." These are not highly general truths; they are universal truths. Passing to the deductions drawn from them, we see the same thing. That force is transformable, and that between its correlates there exist quantitative equivalences, are ultimate facts not to be classed with those of mechanics, or thermology, or electricity, or magnetism; but they are illustrated throughout phenomena of every order. Similarly, the law that motion follows the line of least resistance or the line of greatest traction or the resultant of the two, we found to be an all-pervading law; conformed to alike by each planet in its orbit, and by the moving matters, aërial, liquid, and solid, on its surface—conformed to no less by every organic movement and process than by every inorganic movement and process. And so, likewise, it has been shown that rhythm is exhibited universally, from the slow gyrations of double stars down to the inconceivably rapid oscillations of molecules— from such terrestrial changes as those of recurrent glacial epochs down to those of the winds and tides and waves; and is no less conspicuous in the functions of living organisms, from pulsations of the heart up to paroxysms of the emotions.

These truths have the character which constitutes them parts of Philosophy. They are truths which unify concrete phenomena belonging to all divisions of Nature; and so must be components of that all-embracing conception of things which Philosophy seeks.

§ 90. But now what parts do these truths play in forming such a conception? Does any one of them singly convey an idea of the Cosmos: meaning by that word the totality of the manifestations of the Unknowable? Do all of them taken in succession yield us an adequate idea of this kind? Do they even when thought of in combination compose anything like such an idea? To each of these questions the answer must be—No.

Neither these truths nor any other such truths, separately or jointly, constitute that integrated knowledge in which Philosophy finds its goal. It has been supposed by one thinker that when Science has reduced all more complex laws to some most simple law, as of molecular action, knowledge will have reached its limit. Another authority holds that all minor facts are so merged in the major fact that the force everywhere in action is nowhere lost, that to express this is to express "the constitution of the universe." But either conclusion implies a misapprehension of the problem.

For these are all analytical truths, and no analytical truth, nor any number of analytical truths, will make up that synthesis of thought which alone can be an interpretation of the synthesis of things. The decomposition of phenomena into their elements is but a preparation for understanding phenomena in their state of composition, as actually manifested. To have ascertained the laws of the factors is not to have ascertained the laws of their co-operation. The thing to be expressed is the joint product of the factors under all its various aspects. A clear comprehension of this matter is important enough to justify some further exposition.

§ 91. Suppose a chemist, a geologist, and a biologist, have given the deepest explanations furnished by their respective sciences, of the processes going on in a burning candle, in a region changed by earthquake, and in a growing plant. To the assertion that their explanations are not the deepest possible, they will probably rejoin—"What would you have? What remains to be said of combustion when light and heat and the dissipation of substance have all been traced down to the liberation of molecular motion as their common cause? When all the actions accompanying an earthquake are explained as consequent upon the slow loss of the Earth's internal heat, how is it possible to go lower? When the influence of light on the oscillations of molecules has been proved to account for vegetal growth, what is the imaginable further *rationale?* You ask for a synthesis. You say that knowledge does not end with the resolution of phenomena into the actions of certain factors, each conforming to ascertained laws; but that the laws of the factors having been ascertained, there comes the chief problem—to show how from their joint action result the phenomena in all their complexity. Well, do not the above interpretations satisfy this requirement? Do we not, starting with the molecular motions of the elements concerned in combustion, build up synthetically an explanation of the light, and the heat, and the produced gases, and the movements of the produced gases? Do we not, setting out from the still-continued radiation of the Earth's heat, construct by synthesis a clear conception of its nucleus as contracting, its crust as collapsing, as becoming shaken and fissured and contorted and burst through by lava? And is it not the same with the chemical changes and accumulation of matter in the growing plant?"

To all which the reply is, that the ultimate interpretation to be reached by Philosophy, is a universal synthesis comprehending and consolidating such special syntheses. The synthetic explanations which Science gives, even up to the most general, are more or less

independent of one another.   Must there not be a deeper explanation including them?   Is it to be supposed that in the burning
candle, in the quaking Earth, and in the organism that is increasing, the processes as wholes are unrelated to one another?   If it be
admitted that each of the factors concerned always operates in
conformity to a law, is it to be concluded that their co-operation
conforms to no law?   These various changes, artificial and natural,
organic and inorganic, which for convenience sake we distinguish,
are not from the highest point of view to be distinguished; for
they are all changes going on in the same Cosmos, and forming
parts of one vast transformation.   The play of forces is essentially
the same in principle throughout the whole region explored by our
intelligence ; and though, varying infinitely in their proportions
and combinations, they work out results everywhere different, yet
there cannot but be among these results a fundamental community.
The question to be answered is—what is the common element in
the histories of all concrete processes?

§ 92.   To resume, then, we have now to seek a law of composition of phenomena, co-extensive with those laws of their components
set forth in the foregoing chapters.   Having seen that matter is
indestructible, motion continuous, and force persistent—having
seen that forces perpetually undergo transformations, and that
motion, following the line of least resistance, is always rhythmic,
it remains to find the formula expressing the combined consequences of the laws thus separately formulated.

Such a formula must be one that specifies the course of the
changes undergone by both the matter and the motion.   Every
transformation implies re-arrangement of parts; and a definition
of it, while saying what has happened to the sensible or insensible
portions of substance concerned, must also say what has happened
to the movements, sensible or insensible, which the re-arrangement
of parts implies.   Further, unless the transformation always goes
on in the same way and at the same rate, the formula must specify
the conditions under which it commences, ceases, and is reversed.

The law we seek, therefore, must be the law of *the continuous
redistribution of matter and motion.*   Absolute rest and permanence do not exist.   Every object, no less than the aggregate

of all objects, undergoes from instant to instant some alteration of state. Gradually or quickly it is receiving motion or losing motion, while some or all of its parts are simultaneously changing their relations to one another. And the question is — What dynamic principle, true of the metamorphosis as a whole and in its details, expresses these ever-changing relations?

PRINTED BY NEILL AND CO., LTD., EDINBURGH.

Printed in the United States
54503LVS00001B/39